Fighter Aces!

Born of the sun they travelled a short while towards the sun,
And left the vivid air signed with their honour.

Stephen Spender

Fighter Aces!

The Constable Maxwell Brothers
Fighter Pilots in Two World Wars

ALEX REVELL

Foreword by
Air Chief Marshal
Sir Hugh Saunders
GCB, KBE, MC, DFC, MM

Pen & Sword
AVIATION

Published in Great Britain in 2010 by
Pen & Sword Aviation
an imprint of
Pen & Sword Books Ltd
47 Church Street
Barnsley
South Yorkshire S70 2AS

ISBN 978 1 84884 177 2

A CIP catalogue record for this book is
available from the British Library

First published in 1978 as *The Vivid Air* by
William Kimber & Co. Ltd, London

Printed and bound in England
by CPI Antony Rowe, Chippenham, Wiltshire

Pen & Sword Books Ltd incorporates the imprints of
Pen & Sword Aviation, Pen & Sword Maritime, Pen & Sword Military,
Wharncliffe Local History, Pen & Sword Select,
Pen & Sword Military Classics and Leo Cooper,
Remember When, Seaforth Publishing and Frontline Publishing

For a complete list of Pen & Sword titles please contact
PEN & SWORD BOOKS LIMITED
47 Church Street, Barnsley, South Yorkshire, S70 2AS, England
E-mail: enquiries@pen-and-sword.co.uk
Website: www.pen-and-sword.co.uk

CONTENTS

List of Illustrations

*Photographs are reproduced by courtesy of the
Constable Maxwell family unless otherwise indicated.*

* * *

Military Cross. 18/10/1917
Capt. Gerald Joseph Constable Maxwell, Yeo. and R.F.C.
For conspicuous gallantry and devotion to duty on many occasions. He has taken part in forty-three offensive patrols, in fourteen of which he acted as leader. He has destroyed at least three enemy aircraft, and driven down nine others completely out of control. He has consistently shown great skill in aerial combats, and his fearlessness and fine offensive spirit have been a splendid example to others.

Distinguished Flying Cross. 3/6/1918
Capt. Gerald Joseph Constable Maxwell, M.C.
This officer has at all times shown exceptional skill and gallantry, and on numerous occasions has fought against greatly superior numbers. During the last six weeks he has brought down five enemy aeroplanes. Recently, he approached unobserved to within ten yards of three Fokker triplanes, one of which he shot down. He was chased for about nine miles by the remaining two until he met a formation of six Camels; these he led to attack some enemy aircraft, although he had only twenty-five minutes' petrol left.

Gerald was also awarded an Air Force Cross on 3/2/19

Foreword

by
Air Chief Marshal
Sir Hugh Saunders
GCB KBE MC DFC MM

Writing this introduction to the biography of Gerald and Michael Constable Maxwell has revived many happy memories. I had the good fortune to serve with both in war, in conditions which reveal people in their true colours. Both the brothers were well endowed with considerable qualities of initiative, courage and determination, all of which are essential for success in war in the air.

Gerald served with distinction during World War I as a fighter pilot with 56 Squadron, one of the crack fighter squadrons in France and, on his return to Home Establishment, as Chief Flying Instructor at No. 1 Fighter and Gunnery School at Turnberry in Scotland. It was here that I first met Gerald and learnt something from him of the art of leadership and man management. In World War II Gerald served under my command for two years as the Station Commander at Ford, a night fighter station near Arundel in Sussex. His wide experience and high qualities of leadership were a major factor in making Ford one of the most efficient and happy stations in No. 11 Group. When Gerald retired the RAF lost an officer it could ill afford.

Michael was one of the many young officers who fought with great distinction in the Battle of Britain. He led a charmed life and had several miraculous escapes in crashes. Promotion came rapidly and led to the command of a night fighter squadron with a fine war record. The Battle of Britain was the beginning of the end of the defensive phase of the air war and Fighter Command and its squadrons gradually assumed an offensive role. The day and night fighter sweeps and intruder operations over enemy territory were developed to destroy enemy aircraft in the air and on their airfields. Road and rail communications and many other military targets, including the VI launching sites, came under continuous attack. Cover for the Normandy landings and support for the army in the break out and final operations leading to the defeat of Germany kept the RAF at full stretch.

Each new phase of the air war demanded new methods and tactics;

much was left to the initiative of the squadron commanders and group and sector commanders. In this field both Gerald and Michael made valuable contributions.

With the end of the war some younger officers with good war records found difficulty in settling down – in many cases with loss of acting rank. Michael applied for study leave with the possibility of becoming a priest. In the end he came back to the RAF but finally decided to retire. I was very sorry to hear of his decision for I was quite sure he had the qualities necessary for high command and would have contributed much to post war developments in the RAF.

Acknowledgements

This book could not have been written without the help and encouragement of many people. Firstly, of course, come the members of the Constable Maxwell family, who gave freely of their time and hospitality, and answered my innumerable questions with unfailing patience. My thanks to Mrs G. Constable Maxwell, the Duchess of Norfolk, Mrs D. Boyd Wilson, Countess de Salis, Mrs A. Chambers, Mr and Mrs P. Constable Maxwell, Miss B. Constable Mawell, Mrs C. Davidson, the Hon. Mrs H. Bridgeman, Mr D. Constable Maxwell, Miss J. Constable Maxwell, Mrs C. Costello.

My thanks also to Wing Commander and Mrs Michael Constable Maxwell, both for their hospitality and Michael's patient correction of my technical errors; any that remain are entirely my own.

I am also indebted to those who served with both Gerald and Michael Constable Maxwell: Air Commodore R. E. Chisholm CBE DSO DFC, Group Captain N. Ryder CBE DFC, Group Captain H. M. Pinfold, Group Captain F. B. Sutton DFC, Wing Commander I. B. Westmacott DFC, Wing Commander T. F. Neil DFC AFC, Wing Commander G. Smythe MBE DFM, J. Howard-Williams DFC, J. A. Nordberg, C. H. Jeffs, E. L. L. Turnbull, C. A. Lewis.

I would like to acknowledge the help given by the following, E. J. Baldwin, B. Honeywell, B. J. Gray, P. Jarrett, B. Philpott, J. Rawlings, E. H. Turner and Flying Officer G. M. Viney.

The lines from 'I Think Continually of Those' by Stephen Spender are published by kind permission of Faber and Faber Ltd.

My grateful thanks also to Air Chief Marshal Sir Hugh Saunders, who responded so generously to my request that he write a foreword to this book.

Finally, my thanks to Amy Howlett of Kimber, for her help and encouragement.

Alex Revell

To
Bernard and Alice Constable Maxwell
Carrie, Gerald, Billy and Michael

CHAPTER I

Early Years

The year 1890, the beginning of the last decade of the nineteenth century, a decade that was to see far reaching changes for the peoples of Europe, was relatively modest in its events. In Germany, Bismarck the Iron Chancellor finally fell from power – resigning in March – and the brash young Wilhelm II began his personal rule: a rule which was to bring tragedy to Europe. In August, Tsar Alexander III met Wilhelm at Narva, but failed to convince the German Emperor of the desirability of an entente between their two countries and another irrevocable step was taken towards the catastrophe of 1914.

In Great Britain, exactly halfway between the two Boer wars, events were of a more domestic nature. Free elementary education was introduced; the first electrical power station was inaugurated; the first 'tube' railway was opened, running under the Thames; the City was shaken by the failure of the Baring Bros. In the world of the arts the Pre-Raphaelites were still popular and few if any people noted the death by his own hand of an unsuccessful artist in Auvers-sur-Oise, France. William Morris founded the Kelmscott Press and, for more plebeian tastes, the *Daily Graphic*, the nation's first fully illustrated newspaper, commenced publication. A young musician, Edward Elgar, came to London to seek recognition as a composer.

In more material fields, the prices of commodities continued to fall while wages rose. Although the divisions between the social classes were clearly marked, and there was still widespread poverty, conditions were gradually improving for the majority. The staple commodities of meat, cheese, vegetables, tea, frozen meat and canned goods, were becoming plentiful and their distribution to the masses more efficient. Chain stores were beginning to make a national appearance – Thomas Lipton, a Glasgow grocer, had seventy shops in London alone – and the new department stores catered for a wider and less affluent clientele than the few exclusive stores in the capital.

But to the people of Scotland, and in particular those of Inverness-shire, a more parochial event took precedence in the spring of 1890. On the last day of April the Hon Alice Fraser, daughter of Simon, fifteenth Lord Lovat, married the Hon Bernard Constable Maxwell, fourth son of the tenth Lord Herries, in the family church at Eskadale, four miles from Beaufort Castle, the Lovat family home.

In the days preceding the wedding, tenants and farmers on the Lovat estates had been entertained to tea at Beaufort, and on the day itself, after a family and neighbours' lunch and house party, the rest of the day was taken up with sports, organized by the brothers of the bride. It was intended that there should be a firework display in the village and a toast drunk to the happy couple, but in the event only one solitary rocket exploded in the evening sky. The firework money, with a true Scottish sense of priorities, had been spent on whisky.

The wedding of Bernard Constable Maxwell and Alice Fraser saw the joining of two remarkable families. Their children – two of whom are the subjects of this book – have fourteen lines of direct descent from Edward III through their four grandparents: Fraser and Weld on their maternal side; Maxwell and Stourton on their paternal; and have family connections reaching back to the very beginning of recorded European, Scottish and English history.

Maxwells and Frasers sat in the Scottish parliaments and Grand Councils, and fought in the Scottish and English wars for over eight hundred years. Soldiers, statesmen, and confidants of kings, both of Scotland and England, their names run like a thread through centuries of Scottish and English history. From the twelfth century, to the European wars of the twentieth, Maxwells and Frasers have fought and died in the service of their King and country: from the Highlands of Scotland to the fields of Flanders; from the Borders to the hedgerows of Normandy; from the heights above Quebec to the Far East.[1]

The Constable Maxwells spent their honeymoon at Glencoe Lodge, 'surrounded by that wonderful view of mountains, with Loch Ness and Fort Augustus at our feet'. They then lived for a while at Everingham, the Maxwells' ancestral home, until taking a four year lease on Walworth Castle, near Darlington in Yorkshire. Bernard had been born at Everingham, but had spent much of his early life in lands his father owned in Dumfriesshire, from where the Maxwells had originated. Because of this connection, Bernard Constable Maxwell decided to live in Dumfriesshire, but his brother-in-law, Simon Lord

---

[1] For further reading on the history of the Constable Maxwell family, *Avenue of Ancestors* by Alice Constable Maxwell. Messrs Blacklock Farries, Dumfries, 1965, is highly recommended.

Lovat, persuaded him to settle in the Highlands, on the Lovat estates at Beauly, where he bought some land and had built Farlie House. The family lived in several houses on the Lovat estates while Farlie was being completed, and it was while staying with friends at Dores, on the Aldourie estate, that Alice Constable Maxwell gave birth to her third son, Gerald Joseph, on 8 September 1895.

Gerald was the fourth child, being preceded by two brothers: Ian (1891), Ronald (1892), and a sister, Mary (1893). Gerald was a quiet boy, a little shy, but at an early age he had already begun to show the essential gentle kindness of his nature which was such a facet of his character, remarked upon by all who knew him or came in contact with him throughout his life. Like his father and brothers he enjoyed the hunt, shooting and fishing – although he was never overkeen on horses – but in common with his brothers he was keenly interested in mechanical gadgets. His sister Joan remembers that, unlike their father, 'who wouldn't have known which way the wheels went round on a motorcar', all three boys were mechanically minded.

'Our uncle, Simon Lovat, had an old Panhard and all the boys could drive it perfectly. Uncle Simon used to say, "You can have it for the weekend" and they would drive it about the estate. His chauffeur, who was really more of a groom, used to say, "Well, you boys are born mechanics, but I'm only a made one".'

The brothers also had 'The Little House': a small wooden shed in the grounds of Farlie. 'They had two small engines there', Joan remembers. 'They put a telephone into The Little House – which was maybe less than a quarter of a mile from Farlie, but the telephone bell did ring in the house and we could answer it. They had all their tools there and used to work there for hours on end – no trouble at all to anybody.'

In later years, while at Cambridge, both Ian and Ronnie owned powerful motorcycles and competed in races and hill climbs against Oxford. Ian also raced at Brooklands, driving one of the two cars owned by his friend William McBain: either the huge 80hp De Dietrich, which McBain had bought after it had won the St Petersburg to Moscow race of 1910; or a racing Delage – 'much smaller, but very fast'.

The years before the First World War were ideally happy for the Constable Maxwell children. In his autobiography, Ian describes their childhood as 'the happiest period of childhood and youth anyone could expect'. All the children – there were eventually twelve – got on extraordinarily well together, being fundamentally devoted to each other, an aspect of her childhood Joan remembers well. 'The boys were really very good to us; always so kind and thoughtful'. The centre and spirit of this happy family life were their parents. Their father was a much travelled man who would enthrall the boys with tales of the American West in the early and middle eighties, while their mother was a remarkable woman who believed in giving young children their freedom. Her own mother had believed that 'after a child has reached the age of reason, usually about seven, the less they are interfered with the better, short of preventing serious sin', and Alice Constable Maxwell followed the same precept.

The children were never happier than when they were all together, especially in large family gatherings with their near relatives. Christmas was always spent at Beaufort Castle, the home of their maternal grandmother, and throughout the year they were constant guests at the homes of their many relatives and close friends, always staying at Everingham Park on their way back to school after the holidays.

Until the brothers were old enough to attend school they were taught by a succession of tutors and governesses. Joan remembers that Gerald was rather frightened of the dark, and early coaching by the village schoolmaster had to be discontinued because of the walk to and from the village in the dark winter months.

As they reached prep school age the boys were sent to Downside School in Somerset. Downside School had been founded in 1606 at Douai – a town Gerald was later to know well from the air – to provide the sons of English Catholics with the opportunities of education which was at that time denied to them in Reformation England. During the French Revolution the school was evacuated to England; first to Acton Burnell, near Shrewsbury, and later, in 1814, to its present location at Stratton on the Foss.

Gerald entered Downside in the September term of 1905. Although he seems to have made no great impact scholastically he was both happy and popular at Downside, quickly entering into the life of the school, no doubt helped over those first traumatic weeks as a new boy by his two brothers. Gerald was a good all round sportsman and won a place in the Junior Football XIs of 1907–8–9. In 1910 he won his colours in the First XI, quickly followed by those for the Rugby XV and Hockey XI. He was an original member of Barlow house, when it was formed in 1913, and was made House Prefect, representing the house in sports and athletics.

The quieter side of his nature is reflected in his having been a member of the school choir between 1907 and 1910, and he played the chapel organ at Downside many times. But he could also display a quiet determination. Angry at what he considered an excessive amount of discipline in the school OTC, he and his great friend Dick Stokes – later Minister of Works in the post-war Labour Government – organized a strike, everyone lying on their beds and refusing to move until the more unreasonable of the rules were rescinded. It was not that Gerald was a natural rebel against authority, but rather that he could not bear to see people treated with a lack of consideration, a trait which was to be so evident in later years.

Gerald finally left Downside in June 1913. In a little over thirteen months Europe was to be at war.

CHAPTER II

War

As with so many families, the outbreak of war in 1914 scattered the close knit Constable Maxwell family. Bernard and Alice Constable Maxwell were in London when war was declared, but left almost immediately for Edinburgh to see their eldest son Ian before he left for France with his regiment, the Queen's Own Cameron Highlanders. The regiment mustered at Edinburgh Castle and left for France on 6 August 1914. Few were to return; Ian was severely wounded at the battle of the Aisne and invalided back to England.

Ronnie had left Cambridge in 1912 and had gone out to the Sudan to work for the Sudan Plantation Syndicate, which had been founded by his uncle Simon, Lord Lovat. When war broke out Ronnie made every effort to return to England, 'to get into the fight', but he was persistently refused permission. He eventually managed to secure a commission in the Camel Corps, served with the Corps at El Obeid, and was mentioned in dispatches. While at El Obeid he caught black water fever and was given a year's sick leave in England to enable him to recover fully. Once back in England, his original goal, he immediately joined the Royal Naval Air Service, 'because they teach you to fly quicker'. Successfully passing his medical, although still suffering from bouts of fever, he soon gained his wings and was made an instructor.

Gerald joined the 1st Regiment of the Lovat Scouts on 4 August 1914, the day war was declared. During the early days of the Boer War his uncle Simon had taken a party of fifty Highland ghillies and stalkers out to South Africa. These had been attached to various bodies of troops in a scouting capacity, in an attempt to counter the guerrilla tactics being used by the highly mobile Boers. This met with such success that Lord Lovat was sent back to England to recruit a force of two hundred and fifty men to be known as 'Lovat's Scouts'. The response was immediate. Highlanders flocked from all over the world to join the Scouts, many paying their own passages from as far as Australia and Canada and bringing their own mounts with them. These men were all self-sufficient; reliant and extremely tough; used since early childhood to living in the Highlands, stalking and shooting the deer; skilled horsemen and excellent shots.

The Lovat Scouts served with distinction in South Africa, at one time narrowly missing capturing the Boer leader, Christian de Wit. After the conclusion of the war, Lord Lovat was given authorisation to raise two regiments of yeomanry, each five hundred strong, to be known as the 1st and 2nd Lovat Scouts. The training ground was Beaufort Castle, and on the first evening a thousand men rode into camp. At the outbreak of war in 1914 Lord Lovat was given command of the Highland Brigade and during the next few months the Lovat Scouts moved to various depots and camps throughout the country, until April 1915 found them at Hunstanton in Norfolk. The Scouts were dismounted in August, while still at Hunstanton, and on 7 September entrained for Devonport, sailing for Gallipoli the following day in the SS *Andania*. The *Andania* docked at Alexandria on the 18th and after a short stay ashore the Scouts embarked for Lemnos, the base of operations for the Gallipoli campaign.

The Lovat Scouts landed at Suvla Bay after dark on 28 September and moved up into trenches overlooking the Turkish positions on Sari Bair Heights on 8 October. The natural hazards of dysentery, enteric fever and frostbite added their toll to the casualties of war and the twenty-year-old Gerald soon found himself a temporary captain in command of a squadron, all his senior officers – including his uncles Simon and Alastair – having been killed, wounded or taken sick in the pestilent conditions.

The Lovat Scouts were evacuated from Suvla Bay in the middle of December 1915 and sent to Egypt, where they were attached to the Western Frontier Force in defence of the Suez Canal.

The situation in Egypt was relatively static after the unsuccessful campaign by the Turkish forces the previous year and Gerald quickly became 'fed up, with little to do'. He visited places of interest with Ronnie, who was still in Egypt at this time, and his interest in cars and motorcycles found expression when he put forward a plan to his squadron commander that the mounted patrols, sent out into the desert to report on any possible Turkish attack developing, could be more efficiently and easily carried out by motorcycle detachments. Gerald had found by personal reconnaissance that the desert sand was firm enough to support a motorcycle and his idea was adopted and later used throughout the Canal Zone.

His brothers had become interested in aviation while at Cambridge before the war and Ronnie had had his first flight – which ended in a crash – at Brooklands in 1912, but perhaps Gerald's first interest in the use of aeroplanes in war, and the germ of the idea that he should transfer to the Royal Flying Corps, was sown during the operations at Suvla Bay. During the evacuation period British aeroplanes were in constant patrol over the beaches, preventing enemy machines from flying over and discovering the withdrawal.

Restless at the lack of activity in Egypt, Gerald bombarded Ian, now at the War Office, with a constant stream of letters, asking Ian to pull all possible strings to get him seconded to the RFC. Ian eventually succeeded and Gerald returned to England in the middle of 1916. After a short leave he reported to the No 2 Military School of Aeronautics at Oxford on 20 September 1916 as a flying officer in the Royal Flying Corps.

The cadets at Oxford were housed in the various colleges of the University, instruction being given in wooden buildings on the perimeter of Port Meadow. The complete course lasted a month and Gerald successfully passed out on 20 October 1916. After a period of leave he received orders to report to Turnhouse, on the outskirts of Edinburgh, for his initial flying training and he arrived there on 14 November.

Gerald made his first flight in an aeroplane on 11 December 1916: twelve minutes' dual instruction from a Captain Hervey in Maurice Farman Longhorn No 6701, taking off at 8.00 am and landing at 8.12. An hour and a quarter later he was in the air again, having a further ten minutes of dual with Captain Hervey. When they landed from this second flight, Hervey climbed down and nonchalantly told Gerald to take the Longhorn up solo, to do a circuit and land.

After twenty-two minutes of dual instruction, with a total of three landings, Gerald flew solo: surely a record time for a pilot under instruction, even in the days of haphazard flying training in 1916. He flew again the next day, having an additional four minutes of dual with Captain Hervey before a longer solo flight of nine minutes. On 13 December Gerald made no less than five separate flights in the Longhorn, adding a total of eighty-one minutes to his solo time, and over the next two days he added a further fifty-six minutes, bringing his solo time for the four days to 152 minutes. On 15 December he was posted to No 18 Reserve Squadron at Montrose for further flying instruction on more advanced types of aeroplane.

Montrose aerodrome, on the east coast of Scotland, had been a service aerodrome since No 2 Squadron had arrived there from Farnborough in February 1913. In 1916 No 18 Reserve Squadron was equipped with BE2cs, Avro 504ks, some Curtiss JN3s, and a few Martinsyde Scouts, and was commanded by Major C. E. C. Rabagliati. Euan Rabagliati was a small, slim man, with a lively and likable character, and although he possessed a sharp mind and an even sharper tongue, he was affectionately known throughout the RFC as 'Ragbags'. As a second lieutenant, seconded from his regiment, The Yorkshire Light Infantry, he had flown to France with No 5 Squadron at the outbreak of war. The day after his arrival at Montrose, Gerald was taken up in a BE2c by a Lieutenant Sandys for a familiarisation flight of fifteen minutes; followed the next day by another, also of fifteen minutes, with Captain Sloan as instructor, Gerald this time taking the controls and making one landing. On 19 December Gerald made a longer flight of forty minutes with Lieutenant Hamilton, and two days before Christmas Captain Sloan gave him another twenty five minutes of dual. On Christmas Eve, with a fresh east wind blowing, Gerald set out with Sandys in a BE2c, but an engine failure forced them to land after only five minutes. There was a break from flying on Christmas Day, but Gerald was in the air early on Boxing Day, doing five landings under the instruction of Captain Sloan, with another two landings the next day. But although his training was progressing well, it was not until the New Year that he was to fly his first solo in a BE2c. Fate intervened in the shape of a poisoned foot and he was sent home to Farlie on leave on the first day of 1917.

Gerald returned to Montrose on 10 January, and after another two hours ten minutes of dual instruction he flew his first solo in a BE2c on 22 January, having made seventeen landings and flying four hours, forty minutes of dual instruction on the type. Gerald commented in his diary: 'Did my first solo on BE2c. Thirty Mins up. Good landing'. During the next two days he took up a BE whenever he could, weather permitting, and flew another one hour twenty five minutes in flights of thirty-five to fifty minutes duration, climbing to 3,000 feet.

On 25 January, Lieutenant Hamilton gave Gerald his first dual instruction in an Avro 504, introducing him to the vagaries of the rotary engine. After an hour and a half instruction on the Avro, including three landings, Gerald flew it solo on 29 January. His instruction on the Avro was interspersed with more ambitious solo flights in the BE, including several cross country flights and one successfully negotiated forced landing. On 30 January he passed his wireless test in the BE and on the last day of the month he crammed in nearly three hours of solo flying – a respectable amount of hours for a pilot under training at that period – finishing the first month of 1917 with a grand total of thirteen hours fifty seven minutes of solo flying time.

In the first two days of February, Gerald flew a further six hours ten minutes solo in both the BE2c and Avro 504, making triangular cross country flights between Montrose, Arbroath and Brechin – a distance of sixteen miles – and successfully making a forced landing, and two landings at night. On 2 February he entered in his diary: 'Finished my twenty hours flying before graduation', and the next day wrote to his father.

Darling Papa,
I have now passed all my tests and have qualified as a pilot. I am going today to Horncliffe until Monday, when I go to Cramlington, near Newcastle on Tyne. We have been having lovely weather here for some time and I have been flying 3 or 4 hours a day.

I have sent off today, to Farlie, 3 parcels (my guncase, suitcase, and 200 cartridges, which I have not used). Please ask them to unpack the suitcase and wash all dirty clothes, etc. Tell Oona there is a lot of music in the suitcase.

No more news just now. In my confidential report the C.O. said I was 'an exceptionally good pilot' (swank).

Love from Gerald.

On Sunday, 4 February, Gerald was given his graduation certificate and ordered to report to No 58 Reserve Squadron at Cramlington. On 6 February he took the final tests for his wings by flying a contact patrol in an Armstrong Whitworth FK3, and on Wednesday 7 February, he proudly entered into his diary: 'Flew BE12 for the first time (12 cylinder RAF 120 hp) Have now flown: Maurice Farman (Longhorn), Avro, AW, BE2c and BE2d, BE12, and BE12a.'

The following day the diary has a jubilant entry: 'In orders for pilots wings from today.'

On 21 February, Gerald received orders to report to the Central Flying School at Upavon, 'at once'. Despite the injunction, he arrived at Upavon after a weekend in London, where he saw *The Double Event*, *A Little Bit of Fluff* and *Three Cheers* ('Harry Lauder, very good', was the diary comment) theatre going while in London being an almost compulsory duty for serving officers of that period. He reported to Upavon on the Monday morning and was put into C Squadron. He took up a BE for fifteen minutes the next day and over the succeeding four days flew a Martinsyde G100 Scout for seven hours ten minutes. The Martinsyde, powered with a 120 HP Beardmore engine, was the most powerful aeroplane Gerald had yet flown, and the type was still on active service with No 27 Squadron in France. Gerald's superiors had evidently by now realised that this quiet, unassuming, almost shy Scotsman was a natural pilot and would make an ideal fighter pilot, and his logbook entries for the Martinsyde flights carry the comment: 'Fighting practice'.

Gerald left Upavon on 2 March to report to No 42 Reserve Squadron at Hounslow. He was not sorry to leave Upavon. His diary carries a succinct entry: 'CFS Upavon is the worst place I have ever been to'. Although Gerald was happy with his posting to Hounslow – 'very nice Squadron, Major Sandy is CO' – he was less keen on the aeroplanes the squadron flew. The squadron was equipped with the RE8 and Gerald commented: 'machines not very nice'. He was glad to finish his time on them after a fifty-five minute solo flight, and on Saturday, 10 March 1917 he received orders to report to No 56 Squadron, stationed at London Colney in Hertfordshire.

After a weekend in London, where he stayed with family friends at the South Kensington Hotel, he reported to London Colney aerodrome on the Monday morning. His diary entry reads:

Reported 56 Squadron, London Colney. Major Blomfield CO. Captain Albert Ball is my flight commander. Fly Sopwith two seaters, Bristol Scouts and BE12. SE5 coming soon.

It was the beginning of a life long association.

CHAPTER III

France

Fifty-six Squadron had been formed at Gosport on 23 June 1916, three air mechanics having previously been posted from Farnborough on 8 June 1916 to No 28 Reserve Squadron, Gosport, as a nucleus flight for the new squadron. On 14 July 56 Squadron, now grown to around twenty men under the command of Major E. L. Gossage, arrived at London Colney in Hertfordshire and began to build up strength. On 6 February 1917, Major Richard Graham Blomfield arrived to take command and the squadron entered the last stages of its training before leaving for France.

Major Blomfield, 'a prince of organizers', was determined to lead the finest fighting squadron in France and left no avenue unexplored to further his ambitions for the squadron. At this period of the war, new squadrons leaving for France had only a small proportion of pilots – if any – who had seen service with squadrons at the front, with the exceptions of the flight commanders, who were usually pilots who had seen active service. Blomfield knew that a great deal depended on the quality of these flight commanders and he picked his own carefully.

Blomfield's first acquisition was Captain Albert Ball. Ball had served in France from February 1916 until posted to Home Establishment in October. With thirty aerial victories, and a DSO with two bars and an MC, Ball was the Royal Flying Corps' first 'ace' and his capture gave 56 Squadron the standing of a potentially successful fighter squadron from the outset.

Ball's fellow flight commanders were also pilots of great experience. Captain Ian Henry David Henderson, son of the RFC's first GOC, Brigadier-General Sir David Henderson, had served with No 19 Squadron throughout the Somme battles of 1916 and had done particularly well.

The third flight commander was also a pilot of some ability and a much loved character in the RFC. Cyril Marconi Crowe – known to everyone as Billy – had learnt to fly before the war and had served in France since 1914 with Nos 4 and 8 Squadrons, flying Bristol Scouts with the latter squadron. For all his easy going ways and mercurial character, Billy Crowe was a careful tactician and 56 Squadron was later to owe a great deal to his example and expertise.

One of Major Blomfield's first ideas was to send Ball to the training schools to spot potential fighter pilot material. One of those picked by Ball was Gerald, most probably while Gerald was at Gosport, and Gerald's posting to 56 Squadron was a direct result of Ball's interest. The Maxwell family still remember, with some amusement, that Ball was much taken with Gerald's Lochaber bonnet which he still wore from his Lovat Scout days. 'I'll have that Scotsman,' Ball is reputed to have remarked after seeing Gerald fly, and he took Gerald into his flight.

Gerald made his first flight in 56 Squadron the day after his arrival, flying both the Bristol Scout and the Sopwith 1½ Strutter. On 13 March Ball collected the first of the squadron's SE5s from Farnborough, flying it back to London Colney. The pilots had heard glowing reports concerning the new fighter from the Royal Aircraft Factory at Farnborough, and a great deal was expected of it but their first view of the SE5 was far from encouraging. Ball circled London Colney 'very slowly' before landing. The radiator was boiling and the aeroplane seemed 'hopelessly slow'. The squadron engineering officer, H. N. Charles, and his mechanics, soon found that the SE5 had a number of 'rather obvious technical faults' and it was evident that a great deal of work would be needed to bring the aeroplanes and their armament to an operational state. Blomfield counselled patience over the various modifications and alterations needed, arguing that nothing should be allowed to impede the squadron leaving for France; that the aeroplanes could be modified once the squadron was safely at the front.

Gerald flew an SE5 for the first time on 16 March, making a short ten minute flight in the vicinity of the aerodrome at two thousand feet. Despite its poor performance the SE5 was a more powerful aeroplane than any Gerald had yet flown, including the Martinsyde, and the landing speed was high. The higher landing speed rather frightened Gerald: not for his own personal safety, but because he knew that Blomfield would drop from the squadron anyone who 'broke' an SE5. After his first flight he carefully avoided any further flights in the SE5 and to his relief, on 24 March, he was told to report to the No 2 Auxiliary School of Gunnery at Turnberry for a short course. During the day he had received a telegram from his brother Ronnie to say he had landed in England on a year's sick leave to recover from Black

Water fever, and Gerald travelled up to London in the evening and they saw the obligatory show together – this time *The Bing Boys are Here* at the Alhambra. Gerald left London Colney at noon the next day and took the night train for Scotland; but he was only at Turnberry for three days before receiving orders to return to London Colney at once as the squadron was leaving for France 'within the week'.

There are no diary entries for four days after 31 March, which simply states: 'getting ready to go to France'. Gerald was evidently ready by 5 April as he went up to London and spent a pleasant evening with Ronnie and Oona at the London Hippodrome, where *Zig Zag* was the latest hit. The next day Ronnie, Ian and Oona went out to London Colney and Gerald took up a Bristol Scout in the afternoon to show them his prowess with 'a few stunts'.

Fifty-six Squadron was now ready to leave for France. At 11.55 am on 7 April 1917, the thirteen SE5s were 'revving up and ready to go', and at Major Blomfield's signal, Cecil Lewis led the squadron out on to the field. One by one the SE5s turned into the wind and took off, Gerald flying SE5 A4863. The little khaki aeroplanes circled the field once, while they formed up, then disappeared, flying to the east on the first leg of their journey to France. It was twelve noon.

The squadron had an uneventful flight across the Channel – the lifebelts issued to the pilots were not needed – landing safely at St Omer for lunch. After the aeroplanes had been checked and refuelled the squadron flew on to its first base in France: Vert Galant aerodrome, thirteen miles north of Amiens.

Vert Galant Farm lies on the long straight road from Doullens to Amiens, straddling the crossroads to Naours to Beauquesne. In 1917, the aerodrome, situated on the southern side of the crossroads, with the farm itself on the north, was a pleasant spot and had not yet degenerated into the urban-like sprawl it was to become in 1918, choked with the detritus of four years of war. 56 Squadron shared the east field with 19 Squadron, equipped with Spads; the west field housed the Sopwith Pups of 66 Squadron. The three squadrons comprised the fighter strength of 9th Wing, whose headquarters was at Fienvillers aerodrome, six miles to the northwest.

Fifty-six Squadron quickly settled into its new quarters. The weather was extremely unpleasant: bitterly cold, with frequent flurries of snow and sleet. Major Blomfield, Marson the recording officer, and two or three of the more fortunate officers were billeted in the farmhouse itself, but the remainder of the officers and men were housed in tents at the northern end of the aerodrome. There were few grumbles about the weather or conditions, however. The squadron was where it had eagerly longed to be: in France and 'impatient to have a crack at the Hun'.

On Sunday morning all the pilots flew short flights in the vicinity of the aerodrome. Gerald took off at 11.25 and flew A4863 for three quarters of an hour, orientating himself with the surrounding countryside and picking out useful landmarks. His diary entry for the next day simply reads: 'Started altering machines, taking off windscreens etc', and the lack of entries for the following ten days gives mute evidence of the work involved in modifying the SE5s in readiness for war flying.

As Charles and his mechanics and fitters worked on the engines, rigging, fuel systems and guns of the SEs, the clumsy windscreens were removed and replaced by the much simpler 'Avro type'; the armoured seat was taken out to save weight and a plain board substituted, positioned lower than the original seat and placing the pilot lower in the cockpit.

While the squadron tackled these modifications, the battle of Arras began on 9 April in snow and sleet, and during the next three weeks 19 and 66 Squadrons were fully engaged in the fighting above the trenches. Some measure of the unsuitability of the SE5 for combat flying is evident in that, although the RFC squadrons were hard pressed and casualties were mounting daily, 56 Squadron, flying the Corp's latest fighter, could not be used to relieve the pressure on its sister squadrons of the 9th Wing. During the early months of 1917 the pendulum of technical superiority in the air had once again swung in favour of the *Luftstreitkrafte* (German airforce) and with the introduction of the Albatros DIII fighter in late March the scene was set for the heavy casualties of April and May 1917. Although the Sopwith Pup and Triplane, the Nieuport and Spad, were all more manoevrable than the German Albatros, they were armed with a single machine-gun against the twin Spandau carried by the German fighter, and the slightly higher top speed of the Albatros at operational height enabled the German fighter pilots to initiate or break off combat at will.

As the SE5s became ready they were test flown by their pilots. Gerald flew his first test in A4863 on 16 April – a short flight of twenty-five minutes – followed by a longer flight of an hour on 17 April. By the evening of 21 April all the squadron's aeroplanes had been tested and pronounced satisfactory and Blomfield informed Wing Headquarters that the squadron was ready to commence operations. Orders came through that a defensive patrol was to be flown the next morning, 22 April, and the honour of the squadron's first war patrol fell to A Flight, including Gerald. He had flown exactly four hours twenty minutes in SE5s.

For Gerald his first war flight was something of an anticlimax. Ball led the flight off the ground at 10.18 am with orders to patrol, but under no circumstances to cross, the front lines from Aix to St Leger. The six SEs climbed to 11,000 feet and patrolled from Lievin to Croisilles; but Gerald's engine began to run badly and he was forced to return to Vert Galant. He missed little action. Ball dived on an enemy two seater over Adinfer, closing to within a hundred and fifty yards, but the enemy pilot dived hard for the safety of his own lines and Ball, mindful of his orders, was forced to let him escape.

The following morning, A Flight not having a patrol, and eager to fly, Gerald elected to fly with B Flight. Captain Crowe led the flight across the lines on the squadron's first offensive patrol of the war. Yet again Gerald was plagued with mechanical troubles and after thirty-five minutes was forced to return with a faulty magneto. He was finding it difficult to take his part in the Great War. But the following day amply compensated for the frustrations of his first two days of active war flying.

April 24 was fine and clear. Ball led Gerald and Lieutenant Knight in the third patrol of the day, taking off at 1.00 pm. After an hour and a half, patrolling from Gravelle to Bullecourt, Ball returned with gun trouble, but Gerald and Clarence Knight carried on, flying towards Douai at 11,000 feet. Just south of the town they saw a lone Albatros single seater, a thousand feet below them, and the two SEs hurtled down at full throttle. Gerald continued his dive past the green coloured Albatros, zoomed up under its tail, closed to within ten yards and fired a whole drum of Lewis into the underbelly of the enemy machine, which turned over on to its back and went down. Gerald and Knight followed the stricken scout down to 1,500 feet, firing bursts of Vickers into it, but at this height they came under heavy and accurate anti-aircraft fire – jocularly known throughout the RFC as 'Archie' – and were forced to climb away to a safer height.

Gerald and Knight returned to Vert Galant, made out their combat reports, and were jointly credited with the Albatros as driven down out of control. Gerald, however, had no doubts as to the outcome of the fight, nor of his own part in it. He confided in his diary. ' . . . got my first Hun. Single seater Albatros scout. Came right up under his tail to about ten yards and loosed off. He dived to earth and crashed.'

This Albatros, the squadron's fourth victory, was quickly followed by another, shot down by Knaggs later in the day, and at dinner that night morale was high.[1] The squadron had fought six actions during the day, and although robbed of more victories by continual gun jams, they had found their SE5s more than a match for the enemy Albatros.

The next two days were frustrating, flying being curtailed by the inclement weather – although Ball, flying alone on the evening of 26 April, shot down two Albatros scouts for the squadron's seventh and eighth victories. The following evening, flying with Ball, Knight and Knaggs in the squadron's third patrol of the day, Gerald had more than his share of the action. The flight was heavily archied east of Albert and a close burst hit A4863 in the radiator and elevators. Gerald quickly turned for the British lines, water pouring from the punctured radiator. Luckily he had plenty of height in hand, having been hit while at 10,000 feet, and he throttled back, carefully nursing his engine. Despite this precaution the engine finally seized up over Combles and Gerald settled down to glide as far as possible. He eventually hit the ground at Station 126 on the Decauville railway, and some indication of the uncontrollability of the SE during the forced landing, due to the damaged elevators, is given in his diary: 'Engine fell out of machine and machine turned over. Me not hurt. Hit ground at about 140mph.' Although 'me not hurt' was factually correct, A4863 was a total wreck and Gerald was sufficiently shaken to record the incident in his diary on the wrong day.

Gerald had a period of enforced inactivity for the next two days, there being no spare aeroplane for him to fly, and he suffered the frustration of seeing his comrades taking off on daily patrols and listening to their stories of the actions which saw another four victories added to the squadron's score by the last day of the month. There was sadness too, when Maurice Kay failed to return from a morning patrol on 30 April, the squadron's first casualty.

A diary entry on 30 April, recording a joyride to St Omer in the squadron's BE2c, piloted by Ball, is followed by a jubilant entry on 1 May. 'Got my new machine, SE5 with clipped wings'. This was SE5 A8902, collected from Candas on 1 May by Arthur Rhys Davids, Ball collecting SE5 A8898 the same day.

A8898 and A8902 were the first SE5s of the second production batch to be issued to 56 Squadron, A8898 being the initial aeroplane of

1. The squadron's first victory had been scored by Albert Ball on 23 April.

the order. Martlesham Heath had criticised the aileron control on the first SE5s and those of the second production batch had a slightly different plantform at the wingtips, which shortened the wingspan by eighteen inches – hence Gerald's reference to 'clipped wings'.

In two days the new SE was rigged to Gerald's liking, his personal gear installed, and he was once again ready for the war.

May 4 – the last day of the battle of Arras – was fine and warm, with good visibility. Ball, Knaggs and Gerald took off at 5.15 am to patrol from Douai to Cambrai. They had several clashes with enemy scouts and two seaters, but gun jams and a reluctance to engage by the enemy pilots robbed them of any decisive results. They were to fare better during the evening patrol.

Ball, Knaggs and Gerald took off again at 5.30 pm. The three SEs flew first to view the German aerodrome near Cambrai, where they stayed long enough to note the number and disposition of the sheds, and to observe aeroplanes taking off, before flying northwestwards towards the front line. The SEs were at 11,000 feet, with the evening sun at their backs, and approaching the village of Riencourt when they sighted a formation of eight Albatros scouts, the sun catching their top wings in flashes of reflected sunlight. The enemy scouts were on roughly the same level and the SEs climbed to 12,000 feet for a little extra height, each picking an opponent. Gerald hurtled down, a red-coloured Albatros growing rapidly in his sights. He fastened on its tail, closed to fifty yards and fired a long burst from both guns, holding down his triggers until he was within twenty yards of the hostile scout. The enemy pilot slumped forward over his control column and the Albatros dived away to crash near Sauchy-Lestrée.

Ball had also shot down one of the Albatri[1] – although Knaggs had had no luck. The remaining enemy scouts having cleared towards Cambrai, the SEs reformed, and as both Gerald and Knaggs had bad gun jams, Ball led them to 23 Squadron's aerodrome at Baizieux. They landed and cleared their jams, but Knaggs' machine refused to restart and Ball and Gerald took off alone. They climbed to 12,000 feet and patrolled along the Arras to Douai road, where they sighted a pair of two seaters working at 8,000 feet. Ball and Gerald swept down on these from their 4,000 feet height advantage, but were attacked in turn

1. Arthur Rhys Davids, a classical scholar of some repute, insisted that the correct plural of Albatros was 'Albatri' and 56 Squadron always employed the term, preferring it to 'the verbal atrocity' of 'Albatrosses'. It was later widely used throughout the RFC.

by four red Albatri from Jasta II, the enemy scouts climbing to meet them. A furious fight developed, the SEs and Albatri manoeuvring for advantageous positions.

Suddenly, in that disconcerting manner known to all fighter pilots, the sky was clear, the Albatri diving away towards Douai. Ball looked round for Gerald and saw him below, pulling out of a dive, 'all OK'. Ball turned towards the front lines, but was immediately attacked by thirty enemy aeroplanes – both scouts and two seaters. From his position below, Gerald could see Ball's predicament, but was unable to go to his flight commander's assistance. He had lost pressure in his dive and his engine refused to restart. In the event Ball successfully evaded the attentions of the enemy aeroplanes and returned safely to Vert Galant; but by 8.30 pm, when the reports were made up, Gerald had failed to return. There was some anxiety at first, but he later telephoned from 40 Squadron's aerodrome at Bruay to say he had forced landed there and was staying the night.

Gerald returned to Vert Galant the next morning and he and Ball went up at 9.45 to look for an enemy two seater reported to be over Hesdin. They failed to spot the elusive two seater and returned. Ball led an evening patrol at 6.00, but Gerald and Captain Broadberry were forced to return with the ever present engine trouble and missed a great deal of action, in which Ball added two more Albatros scouts to his rapidly mounting score and both Lewis and Hoidge also scored.

Sunday, 6 May was fine, but the wind was very strong. Towards evening the wind dropped a little and Ball led a patrol off the ground at 7.00 pm. Flying his Nieuport, Ball led Gerald, Knaggs, Lewis, Crowe and Barlow to Arras, where he left them and banked away towards Douai – always his happy hunting ground.[1] Ball gained another victory – an enemy scout over Sancourt – but the SEs saw no action and returned, landing at 8.30.

The next day, although the spring weather continued and it was fine and warm, there was a hint of thunder in the air. At half past twelve, Gerald took off with Ball and Knaggs to escort the Sopwith 1½ Strutters of 70 Squadron on a photo-reconnaissance of the German aerodromes at Caudry and Neuvilly. The sky was quiet; they saw

1. When 56 Squadron first arrived in France, Ball had made no secret of his dislike of the SE5 and had personally requested of General Trenchard the use of a Nieuport, the type on which he had scored his earlier victories. Trenchard had agreed and Ball used his SE5 for his normal squadron work and a Nieuport 17 for his individual patrols. This evening patrol of 6 May was the last time he was to fly the Nieuport.

no hostile aeroplanes and the enemy aerodromes appeared deserted. Several enemy formations appeared as the British formation turned for home, and followed them to the lines, but only one aeroplane came near enough to be a threat and this was driven off by Ball. Keeping a thousand yards to the rear, the enemy force shadowed the SEs and Sopwiths, but sheered off each time the SEs made to attack them. They were obviously a lure to draw the SEs away from their charges and the bait was refused.

During the afternoon the weather gradually worsened and storm clouds began to gather. There seemed every prospect of patrols being cancelled for the remainder of the day and everyone relaxed, looking forward to a lazy afternoon and evening, but during the afternoon Wing Headquarters telephoned to order the usual patrol, and at half past five all three flights took off into the rapidly darkening sky.

The order for such an unusually large patrol seems to have been Major Blomfield's. He had been told that each evening a large number of enemy scouts were in the habit of patrolling in the Arras area; keeping to their own side of the lines, but curtailing the activities of the British Corps squadrons. Furthermore, it was believed that these scouts were elements of Manfred von Richthofen's Jasta II and Blomfield was keen to force a conclusion with the German Jasta, confident that the SE5 would be more than a match for the German Albatros. Whether he believed that the slight edge in performance enjoyed by the SE5 over the Albatros, would offset the inexperience of the majority of his pilots compared with those of Jasta II, or whether he simply forgot or ignored the fact, cannot now be known, but the decision – if it was his – was to cost 56 Squadron dear.

As the eleven SEs approached the front line the weather was deteriorating rapidly. Thick banks of cumulus cloud were vertically layered from 2,000 to 10,000 feet, and dark cumulonimbus was forming, its dark anvil shaped heads giving a threatening aspect to the evening sky.

Ball, Knaggs and Gerald crossed the trenches just south of the Cambrai road. Ball kept the flight at 7,000 feet, flying just under the cloud bank, and made towards the northern outskirts of Cambrai. The other two flights, stepped at 9,000 and 10,000 feet, also made for the general area of Cambrai, all the SEs flying northeastwards. The patrol line ordered was Cambrai, Arras, Douai, and it seems that the plan was to approach from the east any enemy scouts that were seen.

Soon after crossing the lines, Gerald lost Ball and Knaggs in the heavy cloud. He flew alone for an hour, but failing to find his companions, and in view of the bad weather, he returned to Vert Galant. An idea of conditions in the evening sky can be gained by the fact that, while Gerald was unsuccessfully searching for the other SEs, they were all fighting a series of actions between Lens, Arras and Douai. Whatever tactics had been decided before take-off – and they appear to have been sketchy – the SEs became separated and few flew to the prearranged rendezvous of east of Arras at 10,000 feet. As a consequence they fought a number of actions against red nosed Albatros scouts; were split up by these actions and the heavy cloud, then fought further actions: either alone or in twos and threes.

Back at Vert Galant, as the endurance time of the SEs was approached, then passed, there was first disbelief then shock. Of the eleven SEs which had taken off, only two had returned by half past seven: Knight, who had returned at twenty past six with a failing engine; and Gerald who had landed at twenty past seven. Some relief was felt at five to eight, when Knaggs, 'Georgie' Hoidge and Cecil Lewis appeared over the eastern edge of the aerodrome, staggering home on the last dregs of their petrol, but when anxiously questioned they could give little news of the other SEs. Knaggs had seen Rhys Davids down in a field near Belle Vue, 'apparently all right', but as the minutes passed it became obvious that they would be the only ones to return. Blomfield and Marson began telephoning along the front, asking for news of the missing pilots. Slowly it began to come in. There was some comfort in the news that Crowe was safe, having landed at Naval 8's aerodrome, and that Leach, although wounded, was down on the British side and in No 4 Canadian Hospital. But there was no news of Ball, Meintjes or Chaworth-Musters and it became evident that they were either dead or prisoners of war.

The mess was very quiet that night. The squadron had taken a severe mauling at the hands of the experienced German fighter pilots and morale was low. There was a tendency to blame the SE5, for its lack of manoeuvrability compared to that of the other Allied fighters, the Sopwiths and Nieuport, and Ball's dislike of it was remembered and discussed. Of the four casualties, two were experienced flight commanders, Ball and Meintjes, and the squadron could ill afford their loss. The loss of Ball, of course, was a blow to the entire RFC. As the top scoring 'ace' of the corps his death was keenly felt and as late as the summer of 1918 a new pilot – who was later to almost equal Ball's score – carried a card pinned to his dashboard: 'He must fall. Remember Ball'.

The weather clamped down next day. Low clouds and driving rain made flying impossible. During the morning the news came through that Meintjes, the solid South African, was in hospital near Gouy with a fractured forearm, but the mood was still black. Everyone waited in the mess or hung around the hangars, hoping for more news. The weather cleared a little towards evening and Crowe returned from Naval 8 to give the story of his last sight of Ball, flying into a dark thunderstorm over Loos. Major Blomfield left to visit Meintjes in hospital and take his report. There was no flying. The day dragged to a close.

The next morning the skies had cleared and the bright sun helped to lift the mood of depression a little. No flying was done, other than a few test flights, but the positive results of the previous evening were talked of and offset against the losses. Five enemy aeroplanes had been claimed – three having been seen to crash – and the squadron began to feel that it had perhaps given as good as it had got. Crowe argued vehemently in defence of the SE5. It was fast and strong, he said, and a good steady gun platform: it called for a different style of fighting than the highly manoeuvrable type of aeroplane, but it would prove its worth when these lessons had been learnt. With the loss of Ball and Meintjes the leadership and organisation of all three flights devolved on to Captain Crowe for several weeks – even when the replacement flight commanders arrived they were slightly out of touch with the fast developing art of airfighting – and it was mainly his leadership and example which restored the morale of the squadron.

The loss of Ball personally affected Gerald. His diary entry for 7 May reads: 'Very sad about Ball', and that of 8 May notes: 'Took over Ball's flight temporarily'. Despite his lack of experience, Gerald was the obvious choice to lead the flight until a new flight commander arrived. To offset the loss of the flight commanders the squadron now flew larger patrols, mounting six, seven, or on one occasion even eight SEs, instead of the three or four hitherto flown. The first of these patrols took place on the afternoon of 10 May, when Barlow led seven SEs, and on the following morning Crowe led another formation of six. Gerald flew in this patrol and scored his third victory.

The SEs patrolled ten miles east of the front line and attacked a group of Albatri near Lens. These avoided the British scouts by diving away, and soon afterwards Crowe returned with engine trouble. Lewis took over the leadership of the flight and led them northwards. Over Pont-à-Vendin they attacked four Albatros single seaters, but these also evaded the SEs, clearing to the east, and the flight flew on towards Vimy. After another unsuccessful attempt to bring a third group of Albatri to combat, the SEs finally caught four red Albatri attacking a British two seater. The SEs hurried to its assistance, Gerald and Cecil Lewis both selecting the same opponent. Gerald attacked from above, Lewis from below, each closing to within thirty yards. The Albatros turned over on its back and fell away out of control. Gerald followed it down to 7,000 feet, firing all the time, and the enemy machine was seen to crash by the British anti-aircraft batteries.

Gerald led a patrol for the first time on the morning of 12 May, taking off at 8.00 am. East of Lens he spotted a formation of green Albatros scouts, a thousand feet below the SEs. Gerald had learned his lessons well. He led the flight round until the sun was behind them, blinding the enemy pilots, then dived steeply to the attack. But one of the SE pilots opened fire too soon; the Albatri scattered in all directions, and only one was engaged at a worthwhile range. Gerald, Broadberry and Lloyd attacked this Albatros and it dived vertically down through the clouds. The visibility was now very poor, and Gerald's engine had begun to give trouble, so he returned, being escorted home by Broadberry. A telegram was received later from Third Army AA batteries confirming that the Albatros had crashed.

Gerald again led his flight in an evening patrol on 1 May. No enemy aeroplanes were seen, but the SEs were heavily archied and Gerald's machine was hit in the mainplanes.

The next day the weather was again very bad and the pilots had a welcome rest. Gerald, Arthur Rhys Davids and Kenneth Knaggs, went into Amiens to view the town and shop for personal needs. The following two days were also 'dud' and Gerald passed the time playing tennis and croquet. Next day, tiring of these activities, he went with Blomfield and Crowe to Amiens, taking the CO's car and picnicking by the roadside. On 19 May the day was again overcast. A number of tests were flown in the vicinity of the aerodrome, Gerald testing his guns and engine. In the afternoon he was told he was to go on leave the next day, and he and Knaggs left in the squadron tender for Boulogne, where they spent the night.

After visiting various friends and relatives in London, Gerald left for Scotland on Sunday evening. Arriving at Inverness he was met by Ronnie in the car and was at Farlie by the early evening.

On his return to the squadron, which had moved north to Estrée Blanche, Gerald found that Lieutenant Toogood had been shot down on 26 May, while flying his SE5 A8902, and he therefore had no personal aeroplane until a replacement arrived. The squadron had been extremely active during the period of his leave. Twenty-four victories had been claimed, but five pilots had been lost in action. Small wonder that Gerald's diary entry for 7 June reads: 'Of original lot only Major Blomfield, Marson, Adj. Lewis, Maxwell, Knaggs, Rhys Davids, Hoidge and Barlow left'. Although the same entry records: 'No machine, so did not do patrol', he did in fact fly in the last patrol of the afternoon, patrolling the Roulers-Menin road area with Rhys Davids, Turnbull, Muspratt and Rogerson, but they saw no action.

The battle of Messines, which had begun on the morning of 7 June, had opened with a tremendous artillery barrage, and the exploding of nearly a million pounds of explosive in mines under the German trenches. 56 Squadron opened its personal contribution to the battle with a solo mission by Leonard Barlow.

Barlow took off at ten past three, ten minutes after zero hour, and crossed the front lines at 1,500 feet. Once over the German back areas he dropped down to two hundred feet and flew to the German aerodrome at Bisseghem. After strafing the aerodrome from a height of only twenty feet, he attacked a train, his fire stopping it in a cloud of steam and smoke. He then flew on to Reckem aerodrome, shooting up the sheds and a machine gun nest – the SEs were not yet equipped to carry bombs. Only lack of ammunition made him finally return for home and he landed safely at 5.00 am. Barlow was later awarded a well-earned Military Cross for this action.

While Barlow was out, B Flight flew a patrol, the six SEs patrolling the Ypres-Menin area. Arthur Rhys Davids and Harry Rogerson each knocked down an Albatros scout, and A Flight later upheld these successes by shooting down a pair of two seaters, both falling under Edric Broadberry's guns. C Flight, in the third squadron patrol of the day, claimed another victory: an Albatros scout to Cecil Lewis.

The next morning, 8 June, Gerald collected a new SE5 from St Omer and flew it in the evening patrol, taking off at a quarter to seven under the leadership of his new flight commander, Captain Phillip Prothero. But visibility was extremely poor and the SEs returned without having crossed the front lines. Visibility remained doubtful the next day and Gerald flew no patrols. He flew several tests during the day, getting the new SE5, A8921, ready for the war, and in the evening he flew a height test, climbing to 18,200 feet in sixty-one minutes.

A Flight stood by all day on the 10th, hoping the weather would improve, but conditions deteriorated still further and the low clouds and mist persisted, with thunderstorms in the evening. Gerald noted: 'The others went up to the trenches to see the war', and the next day, the weather showing no signs of improvement, he joined another sightseeing party.

Went up to trenches with Prothero, Knaggs, Broadberry; had good fun. Went up between Wytschate and Messines to about half a mile from the front line. Heavy German shelling going on. Had tea with a battery of artillery. Got back about 8.00 pm.

Gerald flew no patrols on 12 June. He practised fighting with Edric Broadberry in the morning and in the afternoon tested SE5 A4563. A4563 was the third prototype SE5 which had now been re-engined with the 200hp geared Hispano Suiza engine to become the prototype SE5a. Gerald recorded: 'Pitot tube dud, so could not tell speed. Result, very dud landing.'

On 15 June the weather at last cleared, and although a little hazy the day was fine and warm. Prothero led the flight off the ground at midday and crossed the lines at 11,000 feet over Ypres. After an hour and a quarter the SEs caught a pair of enemy two seaters at 8,000 feet over Fort Carnot. Gerald, Prothero and Turnbull tackled one two seater, Knaggs the other. Gerald opened fire with both guns, but after thirty rounds the trigger bar of his Vickers gun snapped. Gerald zoomed away, then dived again, closing to within ten yards and firing his Lewis into the two seater, which began to spiral slowly down, the rear gunner either dead or wounded. Gerald and Prothero followed it down to 3,500 feet and Gerald saw it hit the ground near the Fort and smash to pieces.

Gerald flew another patrol the next day; he had no combats, but was heavily shelled – 'the worst archie I have ever had'. Gerald escaped serious damage, but Edric Broadberry had all his aileron controls shot away and only his superb piloting enabled him to return safely to Estrée Blanche. A Flight had no patrol the following day, but C Flight lost two pilots over Lille when they were jumped by eight Albatri from Jasta 6.

There was little activity for the next two days, the weather becoming stormy, with a severe thunderstorm on the 19th. On 20 June the squadron stood by all day, with orders to move out at a moment's notice, but the weather was too bad for any flying. At standdown excitement was intense: after a day of wild, impossible rumour and counter rumour, orders at last came through. The squadron was to fly to England in the morning.

On 13 June, German Gothas had bombed London for the first time, and it had been decided to bring an experienced fighter squadron back from France to defend the capital and give the next raiders 'one or two sharp lessons'. 56 Squadron had been the squadron chosen and on the morning of 21 June the SE5s, flown by sixteen jubilant pilots, left Estrée Blanche for England.

The squadron landed at Lympne, breakfasted, then flew on to Bekesbourne aerodrome near Canterbury. The next day Gerald and the rest of A Flight flew to Rochford in Essex, where they were to remain for the remainder of the squadron's stay in England.

Gerald was now a captain, his rank having been confirmed on 19 June, but his new rank did not sit heavily on his shoulders: on 23 June he went up to test his guns and engine and recorded in his diary. 'Fired both machine guns at about 15,000 feet over Southend to put wind up people, then looped etc.'

The Gothas declined to come and the days passed pleasantly enough. Gerald travelled up to London on Saturday 30 June and dined at Norfolk House with his parents and his sisters Oona and Mary. He now had a new brother, Michael, born on 3 June while he was travelling back to France from his last leave. Twenty-three years later, in another war, this new addition to the family would also be serving in 56 Squadron, flying over England to defend it from the same enemy.

On 4 July there was an air raid alarm – the Gothas had come at last, eighteen bombing the naval station and army camp at Felixstowe. A total of eighty-three British aeroplanes took off to intercept the raiders, including the ten SEs from Bekesbourne and the four from Rochford, but no interceptions were reported as the Gothas had dropped their bombs and quickly retreated out to sea, having hardly crossed the coast. That evening A Flight received orders to fly to Bekesbourne in the morning. The squadron was to return to France the next day.

CHAPTER IV

Flight Commander

Back in France and refreshed by their two weeks in England, the squadron was eager to re-enter the air war. After a day of an uneventful escort and patrol the victory list was opened again on 7 July with four victories. Gerald flew an offensive patrol in the evening, the flight attacking four black and white two seaters over Poelcapelle, but these escaped destruction by virtue of all six SEs suffering gun stoppages.

The weather was still generally bad, with high winds and stormy conditions, and there was no flying for the next three days. Bored with the inactivity, the squadron busied themselves by painting their aeroplanes in emulation of the colourful schemes adopted by the German fighter squadrons. A Spanish dancer and a fearsome looking crocodile were among the more bizarre of the designs, but Gerald contented himself with having the nose of A8921 painted a bright red: an echo of Albert Ball's personal marking. Wing, however, quickly learnt of these flamboyant floutings of official policy and orders were soon received to convert the aeroplanes back to their original drab colour.

July 11 was a fine warm day and five offensive patrols were flown. Gerald flew in two of these, the second of which saw a combat between the five SEs and a large formation of twenty enemy scouts and two seaters.

Prothero first spotted the hostile formation over Houthulst Forest, catching and attacking it over Staden. Prothero, Broadberry and Turnbull each claimed a victory, but Gerald was unlucky. He got on the tail of one enemy scout and fired a short burst, but before he could press home his advantage he was attacked from the rear by two others. He managed to shake these off his tail, but looking around for his companions he was startled to see an Albatros heading straight for him, firing both guns. Gerald turned to meet the attack, holding steady on a head on collision course and returning the enemy's fire as the two scouts converged at a closing speed of nearly two hundred miles per hour. At five yards both pilots broke away: Gerald zooming, the enemy pilot diving under him. Looking down Gerald saw Prothero under attack from another Albatros and he hastened to his flight commander's aid, driving the enemy scout down until a gun stoppage forced him to clear. Gerald recorded the fight in his diary. 'Met 23 Hun machines over Houthulst Forest and had a scrap. Only five of us. They were the Travelling Circus and very good pilots. We all got back all right.'

July 12 saw a great deal of action and some loss. B Flight scored four victories in the afternoon and A Flight took off at six o'clock, anxious to uphold the scoring rate. Gerald returned after three quarters of an hour with an overheating engine and missed the ensuing action in which three of the flight were shot down. The five SEs were jumped by fifteen Albatros V Strutters from Jasta 6. Edric Broadberry, John Turnbull and Ernest Messervy were all shot down in the first attack, both Broadberry and Turnbull being wounded in the legs.

Gerald took over a new SE5 on 13 July. This aeroplane, a 200 hp SE5a, B502, was to serve him well for the next three months. Gerald commented in his diary entry of 13 July:

Lovely day. Got my new 200 hp SE5. Fitting it out so no patrol. B Flight got three Huns in evening. Lewis left for England and Crowe for hospital in St Omer. Only four left in squadron now: Barlow, Rhys Davids, Hoidge and self.

This last reference was to the original pilots who had flown out on 7 April.

July 20 was to see a change in pace and luck. Although the morning was warm it was also hazy, and visibility was poor. Conditions improved, however, the day becoming fine and clear, and the squadron flew three patrols in the evening. B Flight, taking off at half past five, escorted three DH4s of 55 Squadron on a bombing mission and had no combats, but a combined patrol of A and C Flights had better luck.

The twelve SEs left the ground at ten minutes to seven and crossed the lines at 14,000 feet over Ypres. Both Prothero and Fisher signalled engine trouble and returned to base, and for some reason Gerald became separated from the remainder of the flight and joined up with C Flight, led by Geoffrey Bowman.

Bowman soon spotted three Albatros scouts over Westroosebeke and settled down to give chase; but the strong easterly wind defeated the SEs and Bowman, having no intention of leading the flight a long way behind the enemy lines, gave up the pursuit, returning to the front lines. Gerald, however, flying a speedier 200 hp SE5a, and being under no obligation to follow the orders of the C Flight Commander, continued the chase and finally caught the Albatri over Poelcapelle. He dived on the rearmost, got right on its tail and opened fire with both guns, watching his tracer pushing into the rounded fuselage. The Albatros stalled, sideslipped, and fell away out of control, the pilot either dead or wounded.

Gerald followed the stricken scout down to 5,000 feet, but was then attacked by three of its companions. The black and white Albatri fastened onto his tail, but he quickly reversed the positions, outmanoeuvring the German pilots and getting behind them. A burst from both guns sent one of the Albatri down in a slow spiral, which deteriorated into an out of control spin, and Gerald zoomed away. Flying towards Ypres in the hope of picking up the other SEs, he sighted an Albatros two seater and he dived to attack it, closing to very close range and firing a short burst from his Vickers gun. To Gerald's intense annoyance the trigger bar broke and he hurriedly switched to his overhead Lewis gun, anxious not to waste such a favourable attacking position. In his haste he pulled the wrong ring, releasing the Lewis gun from its front clip, and instead of firing the gun slid down the Foster mounting and hit Gerald a resounding blow on the head. Head spinning, he dived away, struggling to reposition the Lewis back on to the top wing, but when he finally succeeded the enemy two seater had disappeared.

With the trigger bar of his Vickers gun broken, and two magnetos missing badly, Gerald set course for Estrée Blanche. On his return he found that A and C Flights had both lost a pilot, Jardine and Messervy having been shot down and killed.

This patrol, in which he tackled the three Albatros scouts single-handed, clearly demonstrates that at this time, after three and a half months in France, Gerald had developed into a confident and skilled airfighter.

Owing to the dense mist there was no flying until the evening on 21 July. Prothero, Gerald, Arthur Rhys Davids and James McCudden took off at 6.35, all flying 200 hp SE5as. McCudden was a guest of the squadron on this patrol. He was flying a month's refresher course with 66 Squadron – also using the aerodrome at Estrée Blanche – and Blomfield had asked him if he would like to fly a patrol with the squadron. McCudden, who made no secret of his desire to eventually join 56 Squadron as a flight commander, was quick to take the opportunity to fly an SE5a in combat.

After patrolling unsuccessfully for sometime, Prothero led the SEs down to attack four Albatros V Strutters over Houthulst Forest. Gerald dived on one scout, firing both guns and forcing the Albatros down to 6,000 feet until it was lost from sight in the evening haze. Gerald then came under attack from two black and white Albatri. He zoomed above these, outclimbing them, but oil began to pour from his engine and his oil pressure dropped to zero. To his great relief the two enemy scouts had broken off their attack and he quickly throttled back and staggered home to Estrée Blanche. On landing it was found that an oil pipe had cracked, a common fault on the SE5a.

Prothero and Rhys Davids each shot down an enemy scout on this patrol, and Cronyn of B Flight – which was also out – shot down a two seater for the squadron's hundredth victory.

It was again very warm the next day. Gerald took off alone in the morning and flew to the lines to intercept a pair of enemy two seaters reported to be working over the British back areas. A two hour long search failed to flush out these two seaters and he returned.

Prothero took the whole flight out at seven that evening crossing the lines over Ypres. After patrolling for some time, a patrol of Albatri was seen, manoeuvring into a favourable position to attack three Nieuports. The SEs dived on the enemy formation, which scattered east after a short but sharp exchange of fire. Six additional enemy scouts then appeared, but these had the advantage of height, and Prothero withdrew the flight to the trenches, dropping down to 8,000 feet in the hope of surprising any enemy two seaters working over the front lines. They caught a two seater thus occupied and Gerald attacked it. Suddenly, 'out of the corner of my eye', he saw an enemy scout: 'above five yards from my tail and firing hard. I did a sharp climb and turn and saw the tracers just missing my head and top plane'. Eric Turnbull, seeing Gerald's predicament, swung towards the Albatros, forcing it to turn away and break off its attack.

Gerald flew his next patrol on the evening of 26 July: a patrol which was to have a tragic outcome. The morning and afternoon were cloudy and no patrols were flown, but at seven o'clock Prothero led six SEs to patrol the Roulers area. Gerald, Eric Turnbull, David Henderson (the B Flight Commander), Barlow of B Flight and Robert Sloley, a new pilot who had joined the squadron five days previously.

There was plenty of activity in the evening sky. No sooner had the SEs crossed the front lines then Prothero led them down to attack a formation of ten Albatros V Strutters over Gheluvelt. Turnbull and Sloley stayed up to deal with a single enemy scout at their level, and after driving it away dived to rejoin their companions. These were now in the middle of what was to prove to be the biggest dogfight of the war to that date. British Spads, Sopwith Camels, DH5s, Sopwith Triplanes and the SE5s, were all inextricably mixed with over fifty enemy fighters. Enemy two seaters were at 5,000 feet; three thousand feet above them their escort, twenty Albatri, were fighting to prevent the DH5s of 32 Squadron from attacking their charges. Between 12,000 and 14,000 feet another ten Albatri were fighting the SEs of 56 Squadron, the Spads of 19 Squadron, and 70 Squadron, flying its newly issued Sopwith Camels. Above this fight, at 17,000 feet, the Sopwith Triplanes of the RNAS squadrons were fighting with another formation of Albatri, preventing them from diving to the aid of their Jasta comrades below.

In the confusion of the general melée four German two seaters managed to cross the front lines, but Gerald forced one of these down out of control. There are no details of this combat, Gerald not having submitted a combat report, his diary merely recording: 'I got one Hun, also Barlow.'

During the fierce fighting Phillip Prothero had been shot down and killed. Gerald's diary carried an entry in the matter of fact tone of the era. 'Prothero killed. Seen going down from 12,000 feet with wings broken off. I take over Flight. Flight commander from today.' Even in the privacy of their diary entries the young pilots of the RFC rarely relaxed the air of seemingly casual acceptance of the loss of friends. It was essential for survival that such losses were not brooded upon.

July 27 continued fine and warm. There were no patrols in the morning and Gerald had the unhappy task of packing up Phillip Prothero's kit and personal belongings. In the evening a large, combined patrol of ten SEs, elements of all three flights, took off to take part in an attempt to trap the numerous formations of enemy fighters which were in the habit of patrolling the front lines each evening. Eight FE2ds were used as 'bait', with orders to patrol the main area until attacked. They were then to draw the enemy fighters towards Cambrai, where the British fighters would be laying in wait.

Gerald flew in this patrol, under the leadership of David Henderson, with Eric Turnbull and Robert Sloley making a total of four SEs. After patrolling the Roulers/Menin area, Henderson led them back to the lines. They joined forces with C Flight for a while, but the flights then split up: C Flight to attack nine enemy scouts to the east of the Menin to Roulers road; Henderson's force to tackle four Albatri over St Eloi-Winkle. Gerald dived with his leader, getting on the tail of one of the Albatri and opening fire with both guns. The enemy pilot dived away, with Gerald still on his tail, but at 9,000 feet the engine of the SE began to splutter badly – probably due to lack of pressure – and Gerald was forced to pull out of his dive and clear. Realising that he was close to Cambrai, and well east of the lines, Gerald turned west, climbing as hard as he could to regain his height. His engine then picked up and began to run smoothly again and he rejoined Turnbull and Sloley.

A little later six V Strutters approached the SEs and made a series of dive and zoom attacks, firing at each of the SEs in turn, but never coming closer than three hundred yards, despite their advantage in numbers and height. The three SEs turned for the lines, climbing hard to close the height advantage, but when they finally turned to engage the enemy scouts they saw them diving away beyond Iseghem. Gerald then turned his attentions to an enemy two seater. Although he got into a favourable position behind it, and fired a long burst from both guns, his engine again began to miss badly and he was forced to let the two seater go.

The evening of 27 July was a successful close to the day for the RFC. The Corps had scored eighteen victories during the day, four of these going to C Flight of 56 Squadron for the loss of one pilot. The following day was to equal this success – as far as 56 Squadron was concerned – with another four victories.

On 29 July the storm, which had been threatening the previous day, finally broke and no flying was possible. Gerald worked on the carburetters of B502 'all day', having been forced to return from a patrol the previous evening by engine trouble, and although Eric Turnbull and Richard Maybery both flew lone missions on the morning of 31 July – the opening day of the Third Battle of Ypres – it was raining hard by the afternoon, effectively stopping all flying.

Gerald ended July 1917 as one of the 'star turns' of 56 Squadron. He was now commanding A Flight and was developing into an aggressive and confident airfighter, with eight victories to his credit. He was to do even better in the coming months.

During the first days of August the weather deteriorated even further, heavy rain blotting out the landscape; the aerodrome rain-soaked and desolate. Gerald visited the trenches at St Jean, near Ypres, with Geoffrey Bowman, Marson and Blomfield. 'Saw the old front line. Lots of shelling going on'. During the period of inactivity people took the opportunity to visit other squadrons, catching up on the news of friends and acquaintances. Gerald's diary entry for 4 August conveys the general mood. 'No flying. Raining all day. Did nothing much. Hoidge went away on leave.'

There were bright intervals between the rain on 10 August and three patrols were flown by the squadron, Gerald leading the first off the ground at ten minutes to one.

Crossing the front lines at 9,000 feet over Ypres, the four SEs – Gerald, Sloley, Page and Fleming – patrolled between Roulers and Iseghem. An hour after take-off they attacked a group of six enemy fighters – described by Gerald as 'new type single seater Albatros scouts' – a mile east of the lines at Ypres. Gerald singled out his opponent and fired thirty rounds of Vickers and a full drum of Lewis into the Albatros, which spun away, flattening out lower down and making off east to the safety of its own back areas. Gerald then turned his attentions to the other Albatri, fighting with several of them until his Aldis sight blurred, forcing him to break off the action and climb west. As he climbed away he saw Fleming fighting with three Albatri and it was only too apparent that he was 'having rather a bad time'. Gerald dived the 3,000 feet separating him from the fight and attacked the Albatros on Fleming's tail.

This Albatros, described by Gerald as 'very good', and flying a long red streamer from its tail, was firing long bursts into Fleming's SE from fifteen yards' range. It broke away under Gerald's attack and together with its companions made off east. Gerald joined up with Fleming, the two SEs flying west, but they became separated in a thick cloud and Gerald did not see Fleming again, meeting Sloley and returning with him to Estrée Blanche. The Albatros pilot had either wounded Fleming, or badly damaged his aeroplane, for it was later learnt that he had fatally crashed at Ledeghem. Gerald's diary: 'Fleming missing, was scrapping very well.'

Gerald flew his next patrol on 12 August. With two new pilots in the flight, Young and Rushworth, he led the SEs over the lines to escort a formation of DH4s from 55 Squadron, whose orders were to bomb the enemy aerodrome at Inglemunster. Although the SEs patrolled the area for sometime they failed to make contact with the DH4s and they returned after an hour and a half. The engine of B502 was running badly, due to water in the petrol, and both Young and Rushworth crashed on landing, badly damaging their machines, but with no harm to themselves. Gerald was forced to return to St Omer in the evening to collect another SE.

Gerald had better luck the next day, shooting down a two seater in

the afternoon patrol. Taking off at five o'clock, Gerald led Coote
(normally of B Flight) Sloley, Page, Young and Rushworth across the
lines over Ypres at 15,000 feet, patrolling towards Moorslede. East of
the town they suddenly saw an enemy two seater, flying straight
towards them. Gerald opened fire at twenty yards, before stall turning
on to the two seater's tail. Sloley also shot at it as it passed over him
and, together with Gerald, chased it east, killing or wounding the
enemy observer before the pilot succeeded in losing them in the cloud
cover. The SEs reformed and a quarter of an hour later attacked a
formation of enemy two seaters over Iseghem. Gerald had at first
mistaken these for the DH4s of 55 Squadron, which had been bombing the enemy aerodrome at Abeelhoek, but realising his mistake he
led the SEs down on them.

Gerald singled out 'one big EA, painted green' and fired a whole
drum of Lewis and 'a lot of Vickers' into it from a range of twenty
yards. The two seater spun away and went down out of control west of
Roulers. By this time the two seaters' escort had arrived, in the shape
of nine Albatri. Seeing these beginning to dive on the SEs, Gerald
reformed the flight and led it towards Ypres, but the enemy scouts
overtook them and one dived on the rearmost SE, flown by Young.
Gerald turned back and attacked the Albatros, which made off,
leaving Young spiralling down. Gerald watched Young flatten out
over Houthulst Forest and fly westwards. Satisfied that Young was
unhurt, and seeing no other enemy aeroplanes near him, Gerald
joined up with Robert Sloley and they 'patrolled about', finally attacking another group of enemy two seaters. They gained no decisive
result over these, and as their petrol was now running low they
returned.

On landing they found that both Young and Page were missing.
Page had landed behind the German lines, mortally wounded, but
Young had survived to be taken prisoner of war.

Gerald and Sloley were jointly credited with the green two seater,
bringing the total bag for the day to five. In accordance with tradition,
the loss of Young and Page was not allowed to dampen spirits at
dinner that evening, and toasts were drunk to a new flight commander: James Thomas Byford McCudden, who had taken over command of B Flight from Ian Henderson, who had left for England, to
take up 'a staff job', five days before.

A Flight flew no patrols the next day, but on 16 August, the opening
day of the offensive at Langemarck, all the flights were up, the fighter
squadrons of 9th Wing fighting over the battlefield from dawn to dusk.

Gerald led 56 Squadron's first offensive patrol of the day, taking off at ten past six. The four SEs flew first to Ypres to escort home a formation of DH4s, but once again they failed to make contact with the bombers, and Sloley returned with a badly running engine, landing at 100 Squadron's aerodrome. Rushworth had also returned, having lost the others in the clouds, but Gerald and Eric Turnbull carried on, patrolling together until 7.15 when they attacked a formation of eight Albatros scouts east of Houthulst Forest. As the SEs dived to attack them the Albatros leader fired a white light and he and one other climbed to meet the two SEs, the other Albatri circling below 'presumably to wait until we had been driven down by the top two EA'. Gerald and Turnbull fought these Albatri for sometime – Gerald noting that both had fuselages circled with alternate bands of green and white – until the enemy pilots, deciding that the two SEs were far from easy meat, and would not be driven down into the clutches of their *Jasta* comrades waiting below, broke off the action and dived east.

Gerald flew his next patrol on 18 August. Things had not gone well for the squadron the previous day: although three victories had been claimed, C Flight had lost two pilots, both prisoners of war. The bad luck was to continue with A Flight, which lost Rushworth in a fight with enemy two seaters.

The flight took off at six o'clock and made for their patrol area of Staden to Menin. The SEs first attacked a formation of two seaters and Gerald killed or wounded the observer of one before the entire formation dived away east. Looking up, Gerald saw a group of eight black and white Albatros single seaters, five thousand feet above the SEs, and he led the flight up to attack them. The enemy scouts accepted the challenge, diving to meet the British scouts, and a general dogfight began. Gerald picked out one black and white Albatros, securing a favourable position on its tail and firing a hundred rounds of Vickers and a whole drum of Lewis into it. The Albatros went down: first in a slow spiral, 'without making any effort to get me off his tail', then stalling and sideslipping to the right before finally turning upside down and falling away out of control. Gerald watched it fall to within 5,000 feet of the ground, but his engine then cut out, forcing him to turn for home. With one magneto completely dead and several plugs missing, Gerald succeeded in staggering back to Estrée Blanche.

The remainder of the flight had had no luck in the fight and were split up by the action. Sloley joined up with Johnston, who was out with B Flight, and they attacked a two seater over Polygon Wood. Although they silenced the enemy gunner, the pilot made good his escape by diving steeply east.

Eric Turnbull joined up with Potts and Rushworth, and it was during an indecisive attack on three two seaters that Rushworth was wounded in the foot, shot down and taken prisoner.

Gerald was credited with two Albatri from the fight. Although his combat report and logbook mention only one decisive engagement – with the black and white Albatri – his diary entry reads: 'I got two Huns. Plenty of Huns about.'

Gerald flew again the following evening, joining a patrol led by McCudden. He had a sharp engagement with an enemy scout which attacked him at 14,000 feet over Houthulst Forest. Gerald quickly reversed the positions, getting on to the enemy's tail and firing both guns from close range. Although the Albatros dived steeply for 6,000 feet, finally disappearing into the clouds, Gerald was of the opinion that: 'He was probably OK' and made no claim for a victory.

Monday, 20 August, was a dry, fine day but Gerald did not fly in the scheduled evening patrol. The carburetters of B502 had been giving trouble and it was not yet ready to fly, but Robert Sloley knocked down an Albatros for the flight. Flying in a large patrol of eleven SEs, led by McCudden, he 'avoided' an Albatros which attacked him over Moorslede and shot it down out of control.

Gerald added another enemy scout to his rapidly mounting victory score during an evening patrol the next day. The flight hurried to the assistance of some Bristol Fighters, scrapping with six enemy scouts east of Dixmude, and during the fighting Gerald saw Wilkinson in trouble.

I noticed an SE5 (Lt Wilkinson) a long way below over Thourout with two EA on his tail and going down rapidly. I therefore dived from 14,000 to 5,000 feet and got on to one of the EA's tail. He was painted black and white, with curious 'V' markings round the fuselage. I fired a drum of Lewis and about 100 Vickers into him, and he stalled, and sideslipped, and crashed north of Thourout.

The following day was one of great success – both personally for Gerald and for A Flight as a whole. The flight took off at half past five in the morning, crossing the lines just north of Houthulst Forest. The sky seemed alive with enemy machines of all descriptions, and picking out a formation of six Albatri, Gerald led the flight down into them. He quickly got on the tail of one Albatros and gave it a burst from both guns. The enemy scout stalled, sideslipped, then went down, smoke pouring from its fuselage.

Another large formation of enemy aeroplanes – 'about twenty-five' – then came up to join the dogfight, and Gerald dived at seven in turn, firing bursts into each. 'I got one directly out of control and he turned upside down and went down in a series of stalls and sideslips.' Jeffs, Sloley and Potts, all claimed victories from this patrol, making a total of five for the flight, two of which were Gerald's. His diary entry reflected the successes of the day. 'Splendid scrap, about forty Huns over Ypres.'

The weather deteriorated the following day and there was little flying over the next few days. On Friday, 24 August, Gerald lunched with Lieutenant-Colonel C. L. N. Newall, commenting in his diary: 'He is the best wing commander in France.' On Sunday Gerald flew a morning patrol, but the weather was 'dud', the visibility being very poor, and the SEs returned after fifty minutes. The squadron flew no patrols for the next four days, the weather becoming stormy, with intermittent rain and gales. Gerald's diary entries for the 27th and 28th record: 'Very dud and windy. Did nothing all day. Played Ping Pong. Gale all night, very windy and wet all day. Did nothing.' Gerald was one of the squadron's ping-pong experts, being surpassed only by Richard Maybery. Ping-pong was a favourite game in 56 Squadron; indeed McCudden once commented: 'I believe that there was keener competition in the squadron to be ping-pong champion than to be the star turn Hun-strafer.'

On Thursday evening, the penultimate day of the month, 56 Squadron played rugby against a team drawn from 70 and 66 Squadrons. 56 Squadron both fought and played hard, and excelled on the ground, as well as in the sky above France. They decisively beat the combined team of 70 and 66 by thirteen points to five, with Richard Maybery scoring one try and Gerald two.

August was to end with a successful patrol for A Flight. The day opened with the usual low cloud, wind and rain of the last few days, but began to clear during the afternoon, and by evening conditions were good enough for a combined patrol of A and B Flights to take off at 6.00 pm. Both flights made for the patrol area of Houthulst Forest to Gheluvelt. At 13,000 feet over Moorslede, Gerald saw a formation of eight Albatri circling lazily: 1,000 feet below the SEs and in an ideal position for an attack. Too ideal. Looking up, Gerald saw another formation of enemy scouts, 5,000 feet above the SEs and flying west, with the clear intention of attacking the SEs from the glare of the sun when they dived to attack the lower formation. It was a transparently obvious trap, but Gerald was unworried. He knew that McCudden and B Flight were in the vicinity and could more than adequately deal with the top Albatri while A Flight tackled the lower. Letting the Albatri get a little further north he led the flight down on to them. The first Albatros Gerald attacked went down in the usual evasive spin before flattening out and diving east. Gerald then flew 'straight for another EA and fired end on at him'. The Albatros pilot returned Gerald's fire, hitting the SE in the tail. Gerald's guns then jammed and he turned away, being chased to Ypres by the persistent red nosed Albatros which kept on his tail, firing all the time.

Gerald dived to 5,000 feet, under the cover of the friendly AA batteries round the town, but Wilkinson then appeared and, returning the compliment of ten days before, shot the Albatros off his flight commander's tail, the red nosed Albatros going down out of control. Gerald's machine had been hit in the mainplanes and tail and he returned to Estrée Blanche. Wilkinson was credited with the Albatros and Coote of B Flight was credited with another, so August ended well for 56 Squadron.

Gerald now had fourteen victories – fifteen by his own personal tally – and his logbook carried a summation of 176 hours 15 minutes of total flying time; a total of fifty eight hours over the lines, with fifteen hours flown as a flight commander.

September saw a great deal of fighting in the air, resulting in a victory score for 56 Squadron of 53 enemy aeroplanes – the largest monthly total since the squadron had commenced operations. Gerald started the month slowly, being plagued with engine and gun troubles. He fought several indecisive actions, but it was not until the 11th of the month that he was able to celebrate both his Military Cross – awarded on 6 September – and his twenty-second birthday on the 8th, by shooting down a two seater out of control during the morning patrol.

A and B Flights were out together and attacked a formation of Albatros V Strutters over Houthulst Forest. Gun trouble robbed both Gerald and McCudden of any decisive results over these and Gerald climbed away from the scene of the action to clear his guns. Having done this he saw a pair of two seaters over the forest and he dived to attack one of them. The enemy observer put up a spirited resistance, but Gerald silenced him with a series of long bursts before closing in on the two seater's tail and firing a complete drum of Lewis and sixty rounds of Vickers into it. The enemy machine went down in a slow spiral and Gerald estimated that it would crash east of the forest. He was unable to watch the end of the two seater as two green and black Albatros scouts dived on to his tail and he was forced to zoom away to avoid their attack. The enemy scouts chased him some distance west, but seeing two other SEs in the vicinity – McCudden and Johnston – they gave up the chase and flew east. Joining up with McCudden and Johnston, Gerald attacked another hostile machine over the forest, but the green and black Albatri appeared again, diving on his tail, and as his Vickers had stopped with a hopeless jam he returned to the front lines with McCudden and Johnston.

Gerald saw no further action until an evening patrol on 14 September. He led the patrol across the lines at 12,000 feet and at 6.00 pm saw B Flight fighting with seven Albatros V Strutters from Jasta 10. Gerald hurried A Flight to the scene of the action, but before they could join the fight the German scouts made off east, having lost two of their number to McCudden's flight. The SEs joined forces and continued their patrol until 6.40 when they encountered another twelve to fourteen Albatros scouts over the trenches to the east of Ypres. One of the hostile scouts, with a red nose and green tail, flown by Leutnant Karl Menckhoff of Jasta 3, attacked Rhys Davids of B Flight and Gerald saw Rhys Davids' SE go down with clouds of smoke coming from its engine. After a little indecisive skirmishing for position the Albatri made off east and the SEs returned to Estrée Blanche. Rhys Davids had survived the attack by Menckhoff and had managed to land his damaged SE at Bailleul.

The next day Gerald and Robert Sloley fought an indecisive action with a pair of Albatros V Strutters over Ypres. These had detached themselves from a main body of eight, had come west, and were attacked by Gerald and Sloley. Although the SEs fired 'a large number of rounds' into one of the enemy machines, which was painted a bright yellow, the results were inconclusive. The German pilot shut off his engine, going down through the clouds in a steep dive, and Gerald was uncertain whether he was out of control or merely taking evasive action.

The next day, Sunday, was hardly a day of rest, with the squadron flying three patrols. Barlow of B Flight, Gerald and Sloley all claimed victories during the day.

Gerald led A Flight off the ground at half past three, crossed the lines south of Dixmude and rendezvoused with a formation of Martinsydes of 27 Squadron. With the Bristol Fighters of 22 Squadron, the SEs formed an escort for the Martinsydes on a bombing mission to the fortified village of Hooglede. Over the target the bombers were attacked by a pair of enemy two seaters and Gerald hurried to their assistance, diving on to the tail of the nearest attacker, which was already firing at one of the Martinsydes. He silenced the enemy observer with his first burst and the two seater went down in a spin.

The weather had improved by morning, 19 September. McCudden took off alone at 10.30 am, followed, thirty-five minutes later, by Gerald and Robert Sloley. Forty minutes after take-off the SEs sighted an enemy two seater, 'just over the lines, east of Ypres'. Gerald affected not to have seen it and turned west, hoping to encourage the enemy pilot to cross to the British side of the lines. The enemy pilot, perhaps thinking by their obvious lack of interest in him that the SEs were friendly scouts, turned west and flew directly towards them. Gerald pulled up in a steep climbing turn, coming out behind the two seater, while Sloley, also turning, but in a tighter radius, attacked from the front. The German pilot held to his course, replying to Sloley's fire with his front gun, breaking away when only fifty yards separated him from the SE. Gerald, attacking from the rear, had silenced the enemy gunner with his first burst and the enemy pilot continued his turn, diving steeply east.

The two SEs now made to return to base, but British AA fire pointed out another two seater to them, the white bursts ringing the enemy machine over Armentières. Gerald and Sloley turned back and began to climb, 'fast'. The enemy pilot spotted Sloley first and turned east, nose down to recross the lines. He ran smack into Gerald, who had dived from the north. Gerald opened fire at a hundred yards, using the remainder of his Lewis gun ammunition. After fifty rounds from the Vickers, the gun jammed and Gerald was forced to let the two seater go, having to be content with having killed or wounded the observer in his first attack.

September 20 saw the opening of the battle of the Menin Road Ridge. Weather conditions were far from ideal, but Gerald and Sloley took off at ten to eleven and flew at 9,000 feet above the thick clouds to Armentières. Over Wervicq they attacked a two seater, escorted by a scout. Ignoring the scout, the SEs concentrated on the two seater, which went down in a vertical dive with 'a tremendous lot of smoke coming out of the engine'. Gerald followed it down and estimated that it would crash just east of Ypres. Separated from Sloley, he climbed back through the clouds and joined a number of Spads, a lone Camel and an SE5 from another squadron, all of which were fighting a formation of seven black and white Albatros scouts. Gerald succeeded in driving one of the enemy scouts down through the thick cloud before the remainder broke off the action and cleared east. Gerald then returned, the weather becoming 'very dud'.

The next day saw more positive results. Gerald led A Flight off the ground at 8.00 am and made for the scene of the previous day's actions. Close by Armentières he spotted a formation of four enemy two seaters, escorted by six Albatri, all flying west. The SEs first chased the enemy fighters east, then turned back to tackle the two seaters. Gerald dived underneath one and fired a complete drum of Lewis and a hundred rounds of Vickers into it from fifteen yards range. The enemy machine made no attempt to take any evasive action. Its nose dropped and it burst into flames. As it fell away into the depths a wing broke off and the remainder of the wreckage smashed into a small wood near Verlingham. As Gerald zoomed away he saw Lieutenant Potts' SE, its wings 'folded up', crash near the remains of the two seater. Another member of the flight, Lieutenant G. M. Wilkinson, had also shot down one of the two seaters, but it was poor compensation for the loss of Potts.

There was no flying the next day, weather conditions being too bad. Gerald played rugby in the evening and was able to relax the following day, having no patrol to fly. His diary entry for the day, 23 September, briefly recounts one of the classic airfights of the war, when elements of B and C Flights fought with the German ace Werner Voss, who was finally shot down and killed by Arthur Rhys Davids. 'B Flight got two Huns crashed. Rhys Davids got a very good Hun triplane this side.'

The next week started quietly, Gerald's entry for the Monday stating: 'No show in morning as misty. Show in the afternoon, got nothing', and the next day: 'Show in morning. Saw large numbers of Huns, but got nothing. Went up to lines in the evening to test machine.' His combat report, which recounts the indecisive jockeying for favourable positions which took place during this patrol, has a codicil. 'EA were very cautious and took care to give no favourable opportunity for attack.'

The morning of 26 September saw an unusual combat. A Flight took off at twenty past ten, flying to their patrol area of Courtmarck to Menin. Gerald saw several large formations of enemy machines over the Menin/Roulers road, but he did not attack these as a formation of eight enemy scouts was above the SE5s, obviously waiting for a favourable opportunity to attack. After a while the eight scouts flew east and a formation of eleven large aeroplanes came across the lines. Gerald was puzzled by the size, type and colouring of these machines, some of which had twin engines. He could see no national markings and they were painted a uniform 'green khaki colour'. The SE formation shadowed these aeroplanes, keeping a hundred yards apart, but the large machines completely ignored them. Gerald turned east and dived underneath the nearest. From this vantage point he could just make out 'a very small black cross' so he attacked, firing a full drum of Lewis and a hundred rounds of Vickers into the leader of the enemy formation. The enemy aeroplane turned east, its nose well down. Gerald immediately attacked another, which ignoring its leader had continued to fly west. After firing another drum of Lewis and a hundred rounds from his Vickers, Gerald stalled, fell away and lost a great deal of height. Regaining control, he chased the enemy machines east of the Menin/Roulers road, firing the remainder of his Lewis gun ammunition, 'but I did not seem to make much impression on them'.

Gerald concluded that the twin engined machines were Gothas, counting 'at least seven', with about five more 'ordinary, very large two seaters'. These aeroplanes were probably from a Staffel of Kagohl IV, which was equipped with a mixed complement of AEG GIVs and DFW CVs. Gerald's diary entry, relating the fight, has a succinct entry: 'Saw and attacked seven Gothas over lines east of Ypres. Got underneath one and fired a lot of rounds, but the Gothas did not notice at all. Played soccer in the evening with men. Draw.'

Gerald was next in action the following evening when the flight caught a formation of enemy scouts over Houthulst Forest. He got on the tail of one and gave it a full drum of Lewis and a hundred and fifty rounds of Vickers from 'very close range', but his shooting was faulty and the enemy machine 'spiralled down, apparently OK'.

Although Gerald flew a patrol with Sloley on the morning of 28 September, and another the same evening, there were very few enemy aeroplanes about and they fought no actions. It was not until the evening patrol the following day that Gerald scored his next conclusive victory: an Albatros over Staden.

The SEs attacked the enemy formation of twenty enemy machines at 6 o'clock, 13,000 feet over Houthulst Forest. Gerald dived on his selected opponent, closed to within ten yards and fired his customary complete drum of Lewis and a hundred and fifty rounds into it. The enemy scout dived vertically away, Gerald losing sight of it under the wing of his SE, but Lieutenant Young saw it break up in midair and go down in pieces. Gerald zoomed out of the action to change his Lewis gun drum, then dived back into the fight, fastening on to the tail of another Albatros and firing 'about two hundred rounds of Vickers and some Lewis'. The Albatros spun away and Gerald lost sight of it in the general melée. Looking round, Gerald saw that all the SEs were fully engaged and two more of the Albatri were going down out of control. He chased two of the remaining enemy scouts east, but was forced to break off the pursuit as his petrol was running low.

A Flight claimed three victories from this fight: one to Gerald, a second to Johnston, and another was credited to the flight as a whole, although Jeffs' combat report makes it quite clear that it was he who had shot it down. Gerald's diary entry for the day reads: 'No Huns until 6 pm. Then had great fun as there were about thirty Huns below us. I got one, which broke to pieces in air.'

The last day of September saw a certain amount of friendly competition for the honour of bringing down the squadron's 200th victory. By the morning of 30 September the squadron total stood at 198. A patrol in the morning by B Flight failed to bring any victories, and C and A Flights took off in the afternoon, keen to score the next two victories.

Richard Maybery of C Flight was the first to score, shooting down a Pfalz D III west of Roulers. Half an hour later Gerald shot down an Albatros over Comines for the squadron's 200th victory.

A Flight had patrolled the area for half an hour, without seeing any hostile aeroplanes, when friendly AA fire pointed out eight enemy scouts to them, south-east of Ypres. Gerald wasted no time. He dived at one scout, and fired a whole drum of Lewis and a hundred rounds of Vickers into it from point blank range. The enemy machine turned over onto its back and spun down to crash near Comines.

That evening the squadron celebrated. It was justifiably proud of its record. Gerald had played no small part in its successes. He had flown seventy-six offensive patrols and had shot down a total of twenty enemy aeroplanes – twenty-two by his own, personal account. He had another three weeks to serve in France before he was due to be posted to Home Establishment, but he had no doubts of his ability to survive those three weeks. He was now the third highest scorer in the squadron, being beaten only by Rhys Davids and Hoidge, with twenty-two and twenty-four victories respectively.

October was to prove a bad month for 56 Squadron. With eight casualties suffered during the month – despite twelve days of inactivity, when bad weather made flying impossible – several of the original members of the squadron were coming to the end of their tours and would be posted to Home Establishment before the end of the month. In addition to Major Blomfield, who was to relinquish command on 29 October, Leonard Barlow and Gerald were both to leave during October; closely followed in November by Hoidge, the last of the originals to be posted home.

The first casualty was a personal blow to Gerald. It fell during A Flight's first patrol of the month. Gerald had flown an uneventful mission on the morning of 1 October, taking off alone at 12.30 to search for an enemy two seater, reported to be working over the British positions. He saw nothing and returned at 2.35. An hour and a half later he led A Flight off the ground in a combined patrol with B Flight, led by McCudden.

The ten SEs crossed the front lines at 12,000 feet, B Flight flying to Becelaere and attacking a pair of enemy two seaters working in the area. Gerald, leading Lieutenants Johnston and Jeffs, attacked another pair of enemy observation machines at 4,000 feet, south east of Ypres, driving them east without obtaining a decisive result. Gerald's small force then joined B Flight – McCudden, Rhys Davids and Coote – which had been attacked by seven Albatri, led by a black and white Pfalz D III. The SEs were reinforced by a formation of Bristol Fighters; the enemy scouts by more Albatri, bringing their number to around twenty, and a furious dogfight developed: SEs, Bristols, Pfalz and Albatri inextricably mixed; all fighting hard to gain an advantage.

During the fierce fighting, Robert Sloley, who had fought with Gerald in many successful actions during his ten weeks with A Flight, and who was a particular friend, was shot down and killed. McCudden saw Sloley circling inside four of the black and white Albatri, 'as usual, where the Huns were thickest', and as he watched, one of the Albatri, flown by Leutnant Danhuber of Jasta 26, got on Sloley's tail and shot the wings off the SE5 from twenty-five yards range. Sick at heart, Gerald also witnessed Sloley's death. 'Saw Sloley going down with a Hun on his tail. He was absolutely in bits.'[1]

Rhys Davids was also in trouble, fighting in the middle of another group of the black and white Albatri. McCudden and Gerald dived to Rhys Davids' aid, and for the next few minutes, in McCudden's own words, 'fought like anything, but the Huns were all very good and had

---

1. Robert Sloley was the only son of Sir Herbert Cecil and Lady Charlotte Sloley.

not Maxwell and I gone to Rhys Davids' assistance when we did I think the boy would have had rather a thin time.'[1]

Having extricated themselves from the Albatri with no further losses, the SEs returned to Estrée Blanche. Rhys Davids was awarded an Albatros from the fight, with another credited to B Flight as a whole. But the squadron could ill afford the loss of Robert Sloley. He had joined the squadron on 21 July, had scored six personal victories and had shared in two others, both while flying with Gerald.

Gerald took the flight out again the next day, taking off at 10.00 am with Lieutenants Johnston, Young, Preston Cobb and Coote to patrol the same area as the previous day. Soon after crossing the lines at 12,000 feet over Armentières, Gerald saw a force of enemy two seaters, flying very low over Ploegsteert Wood, and he led the SEs down to attack them.

Gerald quickly gained a favourable position, closed to within twenty yards and fired a short burst at one of the two seaters, but the enemy machine dived steeply away, clearing to the east. Climbing back to his original height, Gerald saw another two seater: this one over Comines, a little further east. The two seater crew failed to spot the SE and Gerald successfully stalked them, coming up underneath the two seater's fuselage and closing to within ten yards before opening fire. To his intense annoyance his Lewis gun refused to fire at all, but his Vickers functioned well and he fired a large number of rounds into the belly of the enemy machine.

'EA turned and I saw observer leaning over the side of the cockpit with his arms hanging down, obviously dead.' The enemy pilot switched off his engine, glided down to the east, and Gerald lost sight of him, commenting: 'EA may have been under control, but was absolutely riddled with shots.'

After attacking another formation of two seaters, five miles east of the front lines, but failing to gain any decisive results, Gerald returned to Estrée Blanche. He later commented in his diary: 'Plenty of scrapping. Large numbers of Hun two seaters about.'

October 5 was dry but very cold. Gerald flew the first offensive patrol of the day, leading Johnston, Young, Muspratt, Preston Cobb and Jeffs off the ground at seven in the morning. The day was crisp and clear, the air paralysingly cold as the SEs climbed to their operational height of 13,000 feet and crossed the front lines.

Gerald soon sighted a formation of hostile aeroplanes at 16,000 feet

1. *Five Years in the Royal Flying Corps.* J. T. B. McCudden.

to the south east of Ypres and he turned the flight south, climbing hard to close the height advantage held by the enemy aeroplanes. Having gained enough height he led the flight north and dived on the eight enemy scouts over the little hamlet of America. The SEs drove the Albatri east, Gerald firing a large number of rounds into one enemy scout from directly astern. He then noticed some additional enemy scouts hurrying to the scene of the fight and as the SEs were a long way east of the lines he reformed the flight and led them westwards. Arriving at the Menin to Roulers road the SEs surprised a large number of Albatros scouts flying to the east of road and immediately attacked them.

Gerald was virtually unarmed at the beginning of this fight, both his guns refusing to fire owing to the intense cold, but after a while he managed to induce his Vickers gun to fire single shots and he dived on several of the Albatri, causing one to spin away from his fire. A formation of Bristol Fighters kept above the fight, preventing several other enemy scouts from diving into the fight, but there were so many hostile aeroplanes in the vicinity that Gerald found it impossible to follow or concentrate on any single adversary for any conclusive time.

A Flight lost Jeffs during this fight. He was shot down and taken prisoner of war by Hauptmann Bruno Loerzer, Staffel Führer of Jasta 26. Forty years later Gerald and Jeffs were near neighbours in Hampshire, neither aware of the other's proximity, a cause of great regret to Jeffs when he finally learnt of it only after Gerald's death. Jeffs held Gerald in particular respect.

> Your flight commander was your best friend, guide, mentor – and everything else. If you had any troubles or difficulties you always went to him. I had a particularly nice flight commander, Gerald Maxwell – a complete gentleman.

Gerald felt very ill the next morning, suffering from a heavy cold, and he stayed in bed all day. He missed no action. The day was both wet and very cold and there was no flying.

The bad weather continued for the next few days and there was no war flying until 12 October, Gerald leading the fourth patrol of the day, leaving the ground at ten to four in the afternoon. He led Johnston, Wilkinson, Harmon and Preston Cobb across the front lines at 14,000 feet and patrolled from Cortemarck to Menin. At five o'clock the SEs attacked a formation of twelve enemy scouts east of Ypres. Gerald took snap shots at several before gaining a good position on the tail of one and firing a drum of Lewis and a hundred rounds of Vickers into it from very close range. 'EA went down very steeply and I lost sight of him.' Ten minutes later Gerald saw Wilkinson going down with an enemy scout on his tail. Powerless to help he saw the SE5 break into pieces and crash near Gheluvelt.

Gerald flew no more patrols for five days, a combination of bad weather and the flight schedule keeping him on the ground until the morning of the 17th when he flew in a patrol led by Geoffrey Bowman, the C Flight Commander. Gerald got 'very close' to an enemy two seater during this patrol. It was a frustrating combat. 'Guns would not fire. Had a shot with Very pistol but that also would not fire'.

A strong force of SE5s took off from Estrée Blanche at ten minutes past eight on the morning of 18 October. The seven SEs saw a great deal of action over the Houthulst Forest area, but Gerald had already returned to base with a broken connecting rod. After diving on a trio of two seaters over Armentières, and driving them east, Gerald's engine had begun to vibrate badly and he fired a red light and returned.

This patrol was the last time Gerald was to lead his flight into action – a sadly undramatic end to his period as a flight commander. He next flew on 20 October, giving practice fights over the aerodrome to several new pilots and at 11.30 he took off alone for a last look at the front line. He saw no enemy aeroplanes and he returned after an hour and ten minutes.

Gerald was now at the end of his tour with 56 Squadron, having served nearly seven months in France with the squadron. Leaving was a sad occasion for him. He was intensely proud of the squadron; of the fact that he was an original member, and a part of its successes, won at such great cost. He had taken part in 84 patrols while with the squadron, had flown 212 hours in France and was credited in the squadron score book with 20 victories – 22 by his own, personal tally which like all fighter pilots he privately kept. He had led A Flight since the death of Prothero in July and the flight had accounted for 34 enemy aeroplanes under his capable leadership. The tyro of April 1917 had matured in seven short but crowded months into a superbly aggressive and confident airfighter. But if Gerald's leave-taking was an unhappy moment it was no doubt tempered by a determination to return. He would be back.

Gerald left 56 Squadron on the morning of 21 October, travelling home with Leonard Barlow, who had also come to the end of his tour. They arrived in London at 8.30 that evening and Gerald stayed with his cousin Ela Drummond. The next day he relaxed in London, going to see *Round the Map* at the Alhambra in the evening. The next morning he reported to the Air Board and was given two weeks' leave. In the afternoon a happy family party went to see *Zig Zag* and Gerald, his brother Ronnie and sister Mary all caught the night train to Scotland, arriving home at Farlie the next morning.

CHAPTER V

Fighting Instructor

Gerald stayed at Farlie until the beginning of November, relaxing in the calm unhurried atmosphere of the Beauly estate. On the afternoon of 5 November he travelled down to London and reported to the Air Board, where he was told to report to the School of Special Flying at Gosport on 12 November for an instructor's course.

The Gosport School of Special Flying was the conception of one remarkable man, a much loved eccentric in the RFC: Robert Smith-Barry, whom Trenchard was later to refer to as 'the man who taught the airforces of the world to fly'.

While commanding 60 Squadron in 1916, Smith-Barry had been appalled by the heavy casualties the squadron had suffered during the fighting over the Somme battlefield, and horrified by the inadequate flying training his replacement pilots had received in England. To his mind they were little better than 'Fokker fodder' and he said so in no uncertain terms to higher authority. Trenchard, under severe criticism for the heavy casualties being sustained by the RFC, received a paper from Smith-Barry, setting out his ideas for the training of pilots, and on Christmas Eve 1916 Smith-Barry was sent to England, given command of No. 1 Reserve Squadron at Gosport and immediately began to put his theories into practice.

By the end of 1917 all pilots earmarked to be instructors, however experienced, were required to take the instructor's course at the school and many such pilots, returning from active service in France, some with high scores of enemy aeroplanes shot down, first realized at Gosport that they knew very little about the real art of flying; that in fact they could not really fly at all. By the end of 1918 over 1,200 instructors had taken the two weeks course at Gosport and the average hours of a new pilot, arriving in France for the first time, had risen from 17½ hours in 1917 to 50 in 1918.

When Gerald arrived at Gosport he was delighted to find Leonard Barlow already there and they swopped 56 Squadron news and gossip. Gerald found that the equipment of the school had just been

standardised from a rather oddly mixed conglomeration of aeroplanes to a single type: the Avro 504J, powered with either the 100 hp
Monosoupape or 110 hp Le Rhone engine. Flying a rotary engined
aeroplane again, after nearly nine months of flying the stationary
engined SE5, must have called for considerable adjustment on
Gerald's part, but his diary entry on 19 November, only a week after
starting the course, carries the crisp entry: 'Gosport. Passed out Test
A1 Class.' The next morning he attended a courtmartial, travelling up
to London in the afternoon. Reporting to the Air Board the following
morning he was told that he had been appointed as a fighting instructor at the No 1 School of Aerial Fighting at Ayr, on the west coast of
Scotland, and he caught the night train, arriving at Ayr on the
morning of 22 November. Ayr was a fortunate posting for Gerald,
being only 150 miles from Farlie, and he immediately obtained a
weekend leave, arriving at Farlie the next day.

The No 1 School of Aerial Fighting was situated on the peacetime
racecourse at Ayr, and was commanded by Lieutenant Colonel L. W.
B. Rees, who had won a well-earned Victoria Cross while commanding 32 Squadron in France.

The course of instruction at Ayr was, in the word of a famous fighter
pilot, 'simple'. The instructor, an experienced fighter pilot, showed
the pupil just what to do and, more important, what not to do in aerial
combat. Pupils were encouraged to throw their aeroplanes – always
the same type they were to fly in action – about with abandon, thereby
gaining absolute and complete confidence in their machines.

Gerald's first flight at Ayr was in an Avro 504k, with Leonard
Barlow, who had followed him to Ayr, as a passenger. During the next
month Gerald flew Avros and SE5s, passing on his hard won expertise
in aerial fighting to his pupils, and his logbook carries the constant
entry of 'Fighting. Scrapping and stunting' in the remarks column.
On the last day of 1917 he made his first flight in a Sopwith Camel, a
short, thirty minute flight which brought his flying hours to 290 hours
35 minutes and added another type to the rapidly growing list in his
logbook.

The first months of 1918 seem to have been a busy time for the pilots at
Ayr – both for flying and socialising. Gerald attending many dinner
parties, dances and shows. He was an excellent pianist – 'incapable of
passing a piano without playing it' – and he enjoyed a musical show,
although his diary entry for 19 January records: 'Went to opera in
evening. *Bohemian Girl*. Very dud show'. The weather continued very

cold throughout January, with people skating on the frozen river, Gerald even playing ice hockey on one occasion.

On 3 February, despite the wet and windy conditions, Gerald and Captain C. E. Foggin – known throughout the RFC as 'Foggy' – flew twenty miles down the coast from Ayr to the No 2 School of Aerial Gunnery at Turnberry, to fly the captured Albatros scout which was there. This Albatros DI 391/16 had been flown by Leutnant Büttner of Jasta 2. Büttner had been shot down on 16 November 1916 by Captains Parker and Harvey of 8 Squadron and his personal marking, 'Bü', was still clearly visible on the fuselage of the Albatros, only partially obscured by a new fuselage band carrying a British roundel. Gerald flew the Albatros again the following afternoon, before returning to Ayr. The next day, 5 February, was a fine day and a great deal of flying was done at Ayr. A pupil named Baker had a very bad crash on an SE5 while practising fighting with Gerald. Gerald landed immediately and pulled Baker from the wreckage of his aeroplane. His leg was badly broken and his head extensively cut.

There was no flying the next day and Gerald had bad news in the afternoon when he was told that Leonard Barlow had been killed in a flying accident the previous day. Barlow had left Ayr on 23 January to report to the aeroplane testing station at Martlesham Heath and on Tuesday, 5 February, he had taken off in a Sopwith Dolphin, C3779, to test a new type of propeller that had been fitted. At 150 feet the entire wing structure was seen to collapse and the Dolphin crashed, bursting into flames on impact. Barlow had left 56 Squadron with 18 victories to his credit, having served with the squadron since its earliest days in France. It was a tragic end for one of 56 Squadron's finest pilots.

The days settled down at Ayr into a routine of flying, instructing, and what appears to have been a busy social life. Gerald had many friends and acquaintances in the area; his fellow instructors were a cheery, likable crowd and the months passed pleasantly enough, with only the occasional diary entry recording an unusual or first time event. Friday 1 March is an example, when Gerald flew a Spad for the first time, remarking: 'Did not like it much'. On 6 March he flew an SE5 to Edinburgh, landing at Turnhouse aerodrome, where he had learnt to fly only two short but crowded years before. The journey of eighty miles took exactly fifty five minutes against a fresh headwind, a far cry from the Maurice Farman Longhorn of 1916. After an enjoyable two days in Edinburgh with some of the family, Gerald flew back to Ayr on 8 March, the return journey taking only forty-five minutes.

A new batch of twenty-five pupils arrived on 9 March. Gerald now had a flight of seven SE5s, three Avros and a Spad. Training casualties in the SE5 flight were rare at Ayr, but those pupils flying Camels in C Flight found that the fiery little Sopwith fighter, with its fierce torque, needed careful handling. Two pupils were killed on 7 March, and another the next day. Two American pilots were also killed flying Camels, one of them an instructor with over 300 hours of flying time, and to raise morale and renew confidence in the Sopwith Camel, Rees gave an exhibition of startling brilliance. Never going above 500 feet, he 'fought the treetops', spinning the Camel repeatedly and never recovering above fifty feet. After he had landed, Rees made all the instructors repeat his performance. He then made a short speech to the assembled pupils, assuring them that there was nothing to worry about in flying Camels, and 'to go to it'. Elliott White Springs, then at Ayr, succinctly remarked: 'Only one was killed.' Gerald lost one of his American pupils, 'Cush' Nathan, when the top wing of his SE5 broke off at 5,000 feet. The SE crashed into the roof of a three storied house and Nathan was found in the basement.

Gerald was now living in a house in Ayr with Captains Henderson, Zink and Latta. He was very fit, playing a great deal of lacrosse, walking alone the shore daily and even having ju-jitsu lessons. When weather permitted a great deal of flying was done each day. On 11 March, a typical diary entry records: 'Lot of flying. My flight did 26 hours. The Group did 42 hours.'

On Saturday, 30 March, Gerald's mother, his sister Joan and brothers Ronnie and Ian arrived for a weekend visit. Gerald refused absolutely to take up his mother for a flight, saying 'it wouldn't feel right', but was happy to entrust her to Foggin. He had no inhibitions, however, over taking up his sister Joan, then seventeen years old. Joan remembers the flight well and enjoyed it immensely, despite the fact that it was fully aerobatic. Ian had a flying lesson, Gerald pronouncing him 'very good', and it was planned to stage a mock family combat the next day, with Gerald and Ronnie flying Avros with Joan and Ian as passengers, but the necessary aeroplanes were not obtainable and the idea was regretfully abandoned. Ian was the last to leave Ayr and Gerald took him up for 'a good long time' on 2 April, flying along the coast to Turnberry.

There were a number of Bristol MC1 monoplanes at Ayr. This excellent little fighter had been designed by Frank Barnwell in the early summer of 1916, the prototype first flying in July of that year. Its speed for the time was amazing – a phenomenal 132 mph. At a time when the little Bristol could have gained supremacy of the air for the RFC, long before the appearance of the Camel or SE5, stupidity and prejudice in high quarters condemned it. Rumours of its performance had penetrated into the RFC messes in 1916 and it was eagerly awaited by pilots who were fighting and dying in inferior aeroplanes; but it was never put into full squadron service, only a few examples going to Palestine in 1917 and others to Macedonia and Mesopotamia.

At Ayr the Bristols were the personal mounts of some of the instructors and Gerald first flew one on 3 April, judging it 'very nice'. The following day he flew it again in a mock combat with an SE5 and a Camel. He was more enthusiastic about this second flight: 'Monoplane is the nicest machine I have ever flown', and on 5 April he fought another mock combat, this time against his fellow instructor, Foggin. 'Self on SE and he (Foggin) on monoplane. I could not do anything against him as the mono outzooms an SE everytime.'

The implications of this casual statement are staggering. An aeroplane which could have been in front line service in the autumn of 1916, in the era of the DH2 and FE8, was still, over eighteen months later, outflying the latest equipment of the fighter squadrons in France.

A quick trip to London and a flight in a Sopwith Dolphin at Hendon – 'very nice' – were followed by a period of bad weather at Ayr, with very little flying, and Gerald returned to London on 12 April. On 14 April he lunched at Claridges with Ian, Marjorie and Ronnie. It was a sad occasion, Ronnie had lost his long fight to stay in the RNAS and had been ordered back to the Sudan. His year of sick leave being up, he had received a cable ordering him back to Khartoum. He replied, regretting that this was impossible as he was now a pilot in the RNAS, and there then followed some 'caustic cabling' between the Lords of the Admiralty and HQ Cairo; but in the end Cairo won and Ronnie reluctantly left England on 14 April, Gerald, Ian and Marjorie seeing him off from Waterloo.

Gerald returned to Ayr by the night train on 15 April, and on his arrival found that an old friend had reported to the school in his absence. Captain James McCudden had left 56 Squadron in March, with fifty seven victories, his reputation as the RFC's most outstanding fighter pilot firmly established. On the morning of 16 April Gerald flew a lighthearted combat against McCudden: Gerald in an SE5, McCudden in a Bristol Fighter. It must have been well worth seeing. On 11 May the No 1 School of Aerial Fighting moved to Turnberry, the school expanding to include courses for two seater fighter pilots and gunners, and bomber crews. The pupils and instructors were housed in the Turnberry Hotel on the fringe of the golf course, a large and luxurious hotel, still standing today. The aerodrome extended to the edge of the cliffs at Turnberry and the windy, turbulent conditions at times made landing extremely difficult.

Gerald had visited Turnberry on 7 May, giving a lecture on aerial fighting in the evening, which he illustrated with slides. The lecture was a 'great success' and Gerald's pleasure was compounded by the news that he was to take over the SE5 group at Turnberry, the other groups being Camels, Bristol Fighters and DH9s. The new course started at Turnberry on 14 May, but three days later four machines were crashed – three SEs and an Avro – and Gerald commented: 'Washed out flying in afternoon because very few machines.' For the next few days he divided his time between Turnberry and Culzean Castle, but by the end of the month things were back to normal, with forty-three hours of flying by the group on 29 May. On 2 June, Gerald flew the 'Hun V Strutter for the first time'. He made no comment on the flying characteristics of the Albatros, so presumably he was unimpressed.

On 8 June, Gerald was told he was to return to France for a refresher course. He left Ayr by the night train, reported to the Air Board the next morning and left London on the 7.50 am leave train on the morning of 10 June, arriving in France at 3.00 pm. He was met in Boulogne by 'Billy' Crowe in the squadron car. They had dinner in the town, talking over old times, and left for 56 Squadron in the late evening, arriving at Valheureux aerodrome at 2.00 am. It was good to be back.

CHAPTER VI

France Again

Gerald found the squadron much changed in the nine months he had been away. There were now more Canadians in the squadron, the first of the American pilots had arrived and others were to be posted in during Gerald's tour. Gerald's old flight, A, was now led by Cyril Parry, a quietly serious Welshman.

The B Flight Commander was the indestructible 'Billy' Crowe, and C Flight was led by Captain Walter Copeland. The composition of the three flights was not as constant as in 1917, and pilots often flew with other than their officially designated flight. Gerald, being on attachment, had a roving commission, flying when he wished.

Despite the changes there were several familiar faces in the squadron mess. 56 Squadron was now commanded by Major Euan Gilchrist, whom Gerald had last met at Gosport in 1917; and Cyril Crowe was an old friend, being one of the London Colney originals. He had originally left the squadron in July 1917, but had rejoined in March 1918 as a flight commander, voluntarily relinquishing his majority to be able to do so. Apart from six weeks in hospital in April and May, Crowe had flown continually with the squadron, leading B Flight. Yet another old friend arrived on Gerald's first evening back with the squadron: Jimmy McCudden had flown a Sopwith Snipe to France for an inspection and acceptance of the production type by the RAF Headquarters staff and he took the opportunity to visit his old squadron.

Gerald wasted no time in getting back into action. On the afternoon of his return he took off with Crowe at ten past five on a patrol described rather primly in the Squadron Record Book as: 'Showing Captain Maxwell the lines' against Crowe's name; and 'seeing the lines with Captain Crowe' against Gerald's. Gerald's logbook entry carries a more accurate description of the purpose of the patrol. 'OP (offensive patrol) with Captain Crowe.' However, although the two SEs patrolled from Arras to Albert, they saw no enemy aeroplanes and returned after two and a half hours. Gerald flew Major Gilchrist's SE5a B8402 on this patrol, but he flew another SE, B8425, on a patrol the next morning, when he left the ground with McCudden, the latter flying a borrowed SE and also eager to get some action during his brief stay in France.

The two SEs climbed to 18,500 feet and patrolled the front from Arras to Montdidier, a considerable distance. But although they saw four Fokker triplanes near Villers Bretonneux, these dived away before the SEs could come within range, and they had no combats. Gerald recorded in his diary: 'Went up to 18,500 feet for two hours. Feeling very ill in consequence.'

The next day Gerald flew another patrol with McCudden, taking off at five past six in the morning, McCudden flying Lieutenant Irwin's machine. They crossed the lines over Miraumont and again patrolled south as far as Montdidier. At 6.45, two miles east of the lines, near Montdidier, Gerald attacked a Halberstadt C type, getting under its tail and firing 'a large number of rounds'. The enemy pilot put his aeroplane into a steep dive and escaped, flying east. Gerald then turned north and attacked a pair of enemy two seaters near Croisilles, but with 'no apparent result'.

Disappointed with this lack of positive results, Gerald next attacked a Hannover over Arras. The Hannover was escorting an LVG engaged on an artillery shoot, but Gerald decided to tackle the Hannover first, hoping to deal with the LVG after he had disposed of its escort. He came up under the enemy machine, closing to very close range, but although he fired the remainder of his ammunition the Hannover merely 'seemed to wobble a bit as though the pilot was hit' and carried on flying east, 'apparently OK'.

McCudden had also tackled several two seaters, four in all, but had also failed to gain a decisive result. Knowing from recent results with a camera gun at Ayr that his marksmanship was as accurate as ever, McCudden suspected that the guns of Irwin's SE were hopelessly out of alignment, a fact which he verified at the butts after he had landed. This earned Irwin a dressing down from a furious and disappointed McCudden – disappointed both because of the missed opportunity to add to his score and the fact that his teachings while with the squadron had been forgotten in three short months.

Although perhaps not in McCudden's class as a marksman – whom Bowman once described as a 'shooting genius' – Gerald was nevertheless an excellent shot and it is possible that his lack of success was also due to badly aligned guns, in this case on Captain Burden's SE. Gerald's diary records his delight in being back in France, despite the disappointments of the morning. 'Did a topping show in morning. Self and McCudden. Attacked four different two seaters which we filled with lead but did not get down.' His combat report also shows his respect for the enemy gunners. 'The observers' fire in the two seaters was extremely good.'

The next morning the cloud base was still low and extremely thick. Both Gerald and Cyril Parry flew solo patrols in the morning, but they saw no activity; and a later patrol at 5.00 pm, with Gerald teamed with Captain Boger as a fighting partner, also failed to find any action. 56 Squadron was a little disorganised at this time, having a number of pilots in hospital with the Spanish 'flu, an unpleasant illness with aches, pains, and a 'sort of grippe'.

The weather on 16 June was hardly an improvement on that of the previous day. It was still cloudy and the rain was intermittent but heavy. In spite of the conditions a patrol left Valheureux at 3.45 am followed, an hour later, by another: Fraser Tarbutt leading Eugene MacDonald, Bill Boger, Mulroy and Gerald. Why Fraser Tarbutt, a lieutenant, was leading this patrol, which included two captains, is not clear, but he led the SEs across the lines above Arras at 11,000 feet at ten minutes past five. Sometime later Tarbutt fired a green Very light and turned away, diving westwards. As he did so his SE broke up in mid-air, both wings folding up and falling clear of the fuselage.

Gerald attacked a trio of two seaters flying at 5,000 feet over Bapaume. but was forced to break off his attack and zoom away as a large piece of his engine cowling blew off. He returned to the lines, but was attacked over Hamelincourt by an enemy two seater which had evidently seen the SE was in trouble. Gerald and the two seater 'fought for sometime' but Gerald finally got into a good position under the tail of the enemy machine and fired a good burst from both guns. The two seater dived steeply east and Gerald lost sight of it. He crossed the lines and landed at 84 Squadron's aerodrome at Bertangles to replace the cowling. This accomplished he took off again, regained his height and circled over Arras.

At 7.30 he saw an enemy two seater at 8,000 feet over the trenches to the south-east of him. Gerald quickly dived and attacked this two seater from close range, firing a burst of thirty rounds from both guns. Smoke came out of the enemy machine and it suddenly burst into flames, the wreckage, blazing furiously, finally crashing near Wancourt. Climbing back to the lines, Gerald patrolled for some time, chasing away several enemy aeroplanes that were attempting to work over the British trenches. He failed to bring any of these to combat and finally returned to the Amiens area where he saw an enemy two seater being archied. The two seater, probably a Rumpler, was at 18,500 feet, but Gerald succeeded in climbing up under its tail, only to find that both his guns had jammed badly and that neither would fire a shot. He turned away, and finding the jams were incurable in the air, returned to Valheureux. On landing he found that the first two seater which had attacked him over Hamelincourt had been seen to crash by British anti-aircraft batteries and was confirmed by them as a positive victory.

Gerald and Euan Gilchrist took off together at 6.20 pm. Gerald's flight is openly referred to in the Squadron Record Book as a special mission, but Gilchrist's is listed as an 'engine test': a necessary stratagem as squadron commanders were forbidden to fly on patrols. Gerald and Gilchrist saw nothing of interest, but Crowe, who had taken off five minutes before them, stalked a two seater for twenty minutes before attacking it over Miraumont and forcing it to dive steeply east.

The next morning Gerald and Gilchrist again took off together: on a special mission and an 'engine test' respectively. An hour after take-off they attacked two DFWs which were approaching the front lines near Achiet-le-Petit. Accompanied by two Camels the SEs dived on the two seaters. Gerald got under the tail of one and fired fifty rounds from both guns, but the enemy machines both dived away to the safety of their own back areas. Twenty minutes later Gerald spotted a 'Roland two seater' – most probably a Rumpler – at 20,000 feet, going west near Arras. He unsuccessfully attempted to climb up to the Rumpler's height, finally being forced to break off the futile pursuit by lack of petrol. He failed to get higher than 18,500 feet, and although he tried a long range shot at this range, the Rumpler sailed contemptuously on and photographed the British back areas around Arras for the next hour.

Later in the day Gerald flew over to Lealvillers to lunch with Geoffrey Bowman, who was now commanding 41 Squadron. Taking off after lunch, the left hand V strut of the SE's undercarriage broke in half and the SE 'struck the ground violently'. Although the SE5a B4802 was extensively damaged and had to be returned to the depot for repair, Gerald was unhurt and he returned to Valheureux by road.

The weather on the morning of 18 June was bad, with low clouds, wind and rain, but Gerald took off alone at five minutes to seven. He patrolled between Arras and Albert at 12,000 feet and eventually sighted a DFW over Gommecourt. He successfully stalked this DFW, coming up unseen under its tail, but after only one shot his Lewis gun jammed and the Vickers stopped after firing only four or five times. Gerald's annoyance can be imagined, and by the time he had corrected the jams the DFW had dived away. Although he fired several long range shots after it the DFW cleared east, 'apparently OK', and Gerald's exasperation is echoed in his diary entry. 'Got to within about 20 yards' range without him seeing me but both guns jammed and he got away.'

The weather was again inclement the next day. There was no war flying in the morning, but Gerald fought a successful combat in the evening. He had taken off with a patrol led by Captain Copeland, the SEs leaving Valheureux at 6.30 pm, but Gerald left the other SEs and flew south along the railway line to Bapaume. At 7.10 he saw a number of enemy scouts, low down and to the east, and ten minutes later six more – one with a brilliant red tail – at 5,000 feet over Vitry. Gerald played with the idea of a quick attack on these four scouts, but a careful scrutiny of the sky revealed four additional enemy aeroplanes above them and he turned away to seek less heavy odds. Arriving over Arras, Gerald climbed to 14,000 feet and flew towards Douai, where he had noticed two Pfalz DIII. He attacked these Pfalz at 7.40, coming at them from out of the evening sun. One of the Pfalz was 'stunting' and Gerald got on its tail as it completed a roll. The enemy pilot was completely unaware of Gerald's presence until a full drum of Lewis and a hundred and fifty rounds of Vickers smashed into his aeroplane. Gerald could see his tracers reaching into the cockpit of the Pfalz and it spun away out of control. Gerald watched the stricken Pfalz fall for 5,000 feet before he was forced to turn his attentions to its companion, which had begun to attack him from the rear. Gerald turned to meet this threat, but the Pfalz pilot lost his nerve and dived steeply away, making for his aerodrome. Gerald began to give chase, but he noticed that his oil pressure gauge was showing zero, and he let the Pfalz go and returned to Valheureux. Although Gilchrist considered the first Pfalz as having been definitely out of control, he was forced to classify it as indecisive for lack of confirmation. Gerald was in no doubt: 'Had a scrap with two Pfalz. Got one.'

Weather conditions were bad for the next three days and Gerald flew no patrols. He rode every day in the vicinity of the aerodrome, usually with Cyril Parry, and on the morning of 28 June he rode over to the old aerodrome at Vert Galant. It must have been a nostalgic visit. So much had happened since he had last been there; so many friends killed or wounded. As Gerald looked at the remains of Ball's garden, so hopefully cultivated, it must have seemed to him that more than just a year had passed: Ball, Prothero, Kay, Sloley, Rhys Davids, Barlow, Muspratt, Henderson – all were dead.

Gerald did no flying the next day, relaxing at Le Touquet, and his next war flight was a special mission on the morning of 25 June. He found a lone Rumpler north west of Arras at 11.00 am but on spotting the SE the German pilot climbed to 19,000 feet and kept above Gerald, who could coax the SE no higher than 17,500 feet. On completion of his duties the Rumpler pilot turned for home, completely ignoring the SE.

The weather had improved on the morning of 27 June and Gerald and Boger accompanied a morning patrol led by Captain Crowe. Leaving the other SEs after crossing the lines, Gerald and Boger patrolled towards Beaumont, where they spotted a DFW at 5,000 feet. Gerald led Boger round to the east, putting the morning sun at their backs before diving on the DFW. Both Gerald and Boger fired long bursts at the two seater, but the German crew were old hands at the game and fought well, refusing to be panicked by the SEs' attacks. The pilot manoeuvred the DFW 'very well' and the observer got in some accurate shooting at both Gerald and Boger. The DFW finally made its escape by diving away towards Douai, 'with a lot of smoke coming out', and was chased further east by Crowe's flight.

In the evening Gerald asked Parry and Irwin if they would care to fly an extra patrol with him. As an original member of the squadron and an experienced flight commander, Gerald was regarded with no little respect by the later members of the squadron and many pilots were keen to be led by a patrol leader of his calibre. Both Parry and Irwin eagerly agreed to fly an extra patrol with Gerald, although Parry had some misgivings at Gerald's observation that: 'We'll only tackle up to fifteen Huns – more than that and we'll run.'

The three SEs took off at 6.20 and crossed the lines fifteen minutes later at 15,000 feet. After patrolling for an hour they sighted three Fokker DVIIs to the east of Bray. They attacked these Fokkers and Gerald got in a good burst at one which 'wobbled a bit' before diving away, pursued by Parry and Irwin. Gerald zoomed away to change his Lewis gun drum. Seeing that the other Fokkers had broken off the combat, leaving their Jasta comrade to the tender mercies of Parry and Irwin, Gerald climbed away and flew towards Peronne, where he had seen three Fokker triplanes preparing to attack Parry and Irwin. Climbing into the eye of the sun he got east of the Triplanes before attacking them with the sun at his back. Intent on their stalk of Parry and Irwin the Triplanes failed to see Gerald and he got on the tail of the nearest enemy pilot, closing to ten yards: 'so close that I could see his face and goggles'. A burst from both guns sent the Triplane down in a sideslip before it turned over onto its back and spun slowly down inverted. The remaining Triplanes turned on Gerald, forcing him back to the British lines before leaving him over Bray. The Triplane Gerald had shot down was his third officially confirmed victory since rejoining the squadron and it sported a black and white check around its fuselage.

Regaining his height over Albert, Gerald saw a formation of six Camels and he signalled for them to follow him. He led them back towards the Triplanes and some Albatros V Strutters which were now attacking Parry and Irwin, but over Bapaume the Camel leader mistook some SEs below them for hostile scouts and he dived to attack them. Gerald, with very little petrol left and, by the tone of the codicil on his combat report which recounts the incident, not a little disgusted with the Camels' leader, returned to Valheureux. Parry and Irwin managed to evade the attentions of the Albatri and Triplanes, but had been forced to contour chase back across the front line trenches at 2,000 feet, running the gauntlet of enemy groundfire.

Gerald led a patrol the next morning, taking off at ten to five; but the SEs saw no action and returned. In the evening Gerald and Cyril Crowe jointly led the last patrol of the day, taking off at 7.00 pm. An hour after take-off the SEs attacked a large enemy formation of Fokker DVIIs Albatri and Pfalz DIIIs over Dompierre, sparking off the largest dogfight the squadron had fought for sometime. The fight took place at 12,000 and Holleran, an American pilot with the squadron, gives a vivid picture in his diary of the start of the action.

Maxwell made war signals and dove under a bank of clouds. We came out all scattered among thirty or forty Huns. Pfalz, Fokker DVIIs and Albatri. As we fell out of the clouds we went for the Huns and I suppose they must have thought it was raining British machines.

Gerald later estimated that the fight lasted for forty minutes – 'spent about forty minutes dogfighting' – a long time by airfighting standards. He fired about two hundred rounds at various enemy machines until he got a double feed in his Vickers. An enemy scout then got on to his tail, but was shot off by Captain Copeland. Gerald tackled several more of the enemy before finally getting into a good position on the tail of a Fokker DVII and firing a long burst from his Lewis gun. The Fokker went down in a steep dive, smoke pouring from its fuselage, its right hand wings breaking off before it eventually crashed near Dompierre. Gerald 'went on scrapping with my Lewis gun until my petrol was finished and then returned'.

In addition to Gerald's Fokker the squadron had also shot down another three of the enemy scouts for the loss of only one SE. Holleran and Crowe had each shot down a Pfalz, and Irwin had shot down one of the Albatri. The missing SE was flown by Lieutenant Harry Austin who was shot down and taken prisoner. Hazen was forced to land at Harponville, shot through the radiator and petrol tank, and Holleran had been slightly wounded in the leg.

The weather was bad the next day. Gerald's diary reads: 'Very dud in morning and no flying. In the afternoon went over to see Hugh Kennedy and Jack Encombe. Watched the boxing for some time. Great fun. Also went for a ride in a tank'.

July started well for Gerald with a victory shared with Captain Crowe. Cyril Crowe led the patrol of three SEs across the lines at 14,000 feet over Albert and patrolled the Suzanne to Bapaume area. Seeing Archie bursting over Aveluy Wood, Crowe flew to investigate, followed by Gerald and Copeland. The object of Archie's hate was an enemy two seater and all three SEs attacked in turn. Copeland's guns jammed badly in his first attack and as he turned away to clear them he was attacked by a bright red Fokker Triplane. He dived steeply to shake the Triplane off his tail and Gerald, who was below the Fokker, 'stalled up' and fired a short burst from both guns. The Triplane promptly spun down at him, firing as it came, and Gerald was forced to take violent evasive action to avoid it.

As he reached Gerald's level the enemy pilot recovered from his spin and dived away for his own lines, with Gerald in close pursuit. No Fokker Triplane could outdive an SE5a and Gerald soon got into a favourable position on the Triplane's tail and fired a long burst from Vickers and Lewis. The Triplane immediately went into a spin and Gerald zoomed away to witness the crash, confident that he had either killed the pilot or seriously damaged his aeroplane. Further down, however, the Triplane recovered from its spin and began to dive in a straight line. Crowe then appeared just above it, and literally shot the unfortunate German pilot's aeroplane to pieces around him. 'I dived after him and at point blank range fired both guns. The Triplane fell to pieces in my Aldis sight. I was then about 3,000 feet over Thiepval.' Although the Triplane pilot had fought well, it was an unhappy chain of circumstances which had matched him against two such redoubtable fighter pilots as Gerald and Crowe.

Gerald was again in action the following day. He took off alone on a special mission and climbed towards the front lines. Conditions were cloudy, but he saw a Fokker DVII over Bapaume and he chased after it. But the lone Fokker was bait. Diving after it, some sixth sense warned Gerald to glance back over his shoulder. Nine Fokker DVIIs were chasing him, rapidly closing on to his tail. Gerald stayed only long enough to note that several of the Fokkers had sky blue tails before diving hard for the British lines and safety. Even Gerald drew the line at tackling nine Fokker DVIIs singlehanded. He regained his height, and after a careful scrutiny of the sky, found and attacked a Fokker DVII over Albert. After a short burst the Fokker went down in a steep dive to the east, in Gerald's opinion 'out of control as he kept on diving very low'. Gerald lost sight of the falling Fokker as it merged with the kaleidoscopic background of the fields around Albert and he climbed again to regain his height.

A little later he attacked another hostile machine – of unspecified type – but his Vickers gun jammed badly and he used up the remainder of his Lewis gun ammunition without gaining a decisive result. During this attack Gerald's Lewis gun fell down its slide, hitting him on the head and smashing his windscreen.

Gilchrist did not allow the Fokker DVII as a definite victory. He added a codicil on the bottom of Gerald's combat report arguing that if the Fokker had crashed it would have been reported to have done so by the anti-aircraft batteries in the area, but conceding that 'telephonic communication very bad here at present'.

There was no flying on the morning of 3 July, the day being very windy. Gerald and Crowe flew a patrol in the afternoon but saw no enemy activity. Two flights of eight SEs took off the following evening with Gerald leading the top four and Crowe the lower. Gerald's force saw no action, but Crowe was firmly seen off by an enemy two seater which he attacked north east of Albert. The enemy observer made good shooting at the SE, hitting it in the main spar. In Crowe's words, 'Tracer was flying all round.' His Aldis sight having fogged up, making accurate shooting almost impossible, and his Vickers being hopelessly jammed, Crowe returned, having lost sight of the two seater while changing a drum on his Lewis.

The next day saw another victory for Gerald. He led a patrol across the lines at 12,000 feet over Aveluy Wood, patrolling for an hour and fifty minutes before sighting a Fokker DVII at ten minutes to nine.

The DVII was over Dompierre at 13,000 feet and the enemy pilot had come out of the clouds without having seen the SEs above him. Gerald quickly got behind the Fokker and fired seventy rounds of Vickers and a complete drum of Lewis into it from close range. The Fokker went down in an uneven, flicking spin and Gerald watched it fall for 10,000 feet before losing sight of it under his wingtip. There were SEs from other squadrons in the vicinity and Gilchrist commented on Gerald's combat report: 'One lot of five or six SEs must have seen this combat. Should like to have their confirmation as to what happened to the EA below 3,000 feet.' A handwritten comment was later added. 'This is confirmed by 41 Squadron as having burst into flames and crashed.'

Sunday, 7 July was a day of low cloud and mist. Gerald took a new pilot, Lieutenant Herbert, to the lines to show him the disposition of the front line trenches, but they saw no action. Tommy Herbert had joined the squadron a week before, arriving with his great friend and fellow American, Paul Winslow. Paul Winslow recorded their arrival in his diary:

At last, after three weeks here (Rang du Flers No. 2 Pool, France) Tommy and I were posted to 60 Squadron. At eleven o'clock 60's tender came and picked us up, bag and baggage. We stopped at Abbeville and then carried on to 60, arriving at 2.30., and were told that we did not belong there, but at 56, and were shipped off without any lunch. Poor Frank Read nearly cried when we left and our impression of 60 was very poor. Arriving here (56) the change of atmosphere was very apparent. Captain Maxwell, the CO, Major Gilchrist, and everybody turned out to meet us. It seems they had us transferred when we were on route. I think we landed on both feet, as this is the top squadron in the RAF.

The next morning Gerald learnt that he had been awarded the DFC. He went up to see Crowe, who was on attachment to an anti-aircraft battery in Aveluy Wood, and took off in the afternoon on a special mission. He had a lucky escape during this patrol. The connecting rod of his engine broke, smashing several cylinders, and the engine seized solid. Despite this Gerald made a 'good landing' near Sarton. Harold Molyneux's diary entry, relating the subsequent search, has a slightly disgruntled note: 'Monday. Maxwell had a forced landing. Spent half the night finding him.'

The morning of 9 July was fine but extremely windy. Gerald flew a special mission but saw nothing of interest, and in the afternoon he went out with the tender to salvage his SE from Sarton. On his return to Valheureux he was stunned – as were all the squadron – to learn that McCudden had been killed that afternoon in a flying accident. McCudden had flown out from England during the day to take command of 60 Squadron. He landed at Auxi-le-Chateau aerodrome to ascertain his position and in taking off again he crashed in a small wood on the edge of the aerodrome, in circumstances which have never been fully explained.

Gerald flew a patrol on the morning of 10 July, but he saw no action; although several other pilots fought combats with enemy two seaters. During the afternoon all the pilots, with the exception of Molyneux, who was 'orderly dog', went to Wavans, near Auxi-le-Chateau, to attend McCudden's funeral. The conduct of the funeral angered many of those present, who considered that McCudden deserved more than the hurried ceremony he was given. Winslow recorded:

The whole of 60 were there, together with General Salmond and some members of other squadrons. The ceremony made my blood boil – all in Latin, mumbled, so that even if one knew the language he couldn't have heard it. Nothing human in it at all, and far from impressive. Richthofen – an enemy – had a far better funeral and if anyone deserved a real memorial it was McCudden.

Gerald flew several patrols during the next two days, but saw no action until the morning of 13 July, when he had a long fight with an LVG over Albert. He fought this aeroplane for over an hour, but the German crew fought well and Gerald could not obtain a decisive result. His petrol finally running low, he left the LVG being chased back across the lines by two Camels.

Gerald led a patrol in the evening, the four SEs crossing the lines over Albert at 8.00 pm. Ten minutes later Gerald saw three Fokker DVIIs over Combles. There were several other Fokkers in the distance, but Gerald rapidly summed up the situation and decided to attack the three over Combles. He led the flight round into the evening sun, rapidly overhauling the Fokkers. Lacking the time to climb up to the enemy's height before the other Fokkers arrived to interfere, Gerald dived and zoomed, firing on the top of his zoom. A burst of a hundred rounds of Vickers and a full drum of Lewis at a hundred yards range from the nearest Fokker failed to score any crippling hits and the German pilot dived away east. Gerald's Vickers had stopped with a double feed, but he reformed the flight and led them back towards the front lines. Although he tried a farewell burst at the leader of the Fokkers, 'who hadn't seen us', it had no effect and firing a green Very light he led the SEs back to base.

Gerald – rather reluctantly by the tone of his diary – got up early for the first patrol the next day, but a heavy mist covered the aerodrome. It turned out to be a 'very dud morning' and Gerald 'did nothing all day'.

On the afternoon of 16 July Gerald took off alone, leaving the ground at ten past three. Twenty minutes after take-off he sighted a Hannover CLIII at 15,000 feet over Forceville. Gerald was 1,000 feet below the enemy two seater and could not close the range. He opened fire from some distance away, firing a hundred rounds, but the Hannover pilot dived quickly away and escaped, easily outpacing the SE5. Ten minutes later Gerald saw a Rumpler; but this was even higher than the Hannover and he could not climb to its height to initiate an attack. The Rumpler had evidently completed its mission as it was flying east, back to its base, and it sailed easily over the SE. Gerald's attack on the Hannover was the last time he was to fire his guns in anger.

The next morning was also frustrating, with a lone morning patrol bringing no result. After a swim in the Somme after lunch, Gerald took out a large patrol in the evening. There was little enemy activity near the lines and a massive thunderstorm was building up in the east. Gerald hurriedly brought the flight home, landing just before the storm broke 'with hailstones as big as ordinary eggs'.

Gerald took Herbert and Winslow to the lines next day and the three SEs were archied very badly. The day was cloudy and very windy. Gerald felt 'rather ill' during this patrol and as a consequence he did not fly in the usual evening patrol.

Evidently feeling better the next day, Gerald took out a large patrol in the morning. The ten SEs were split into two flights, with Boger leading the top flight and Gerald the lower, in overall command. Gerald's force lost a two seater, which escaped them by diving into the ground mist, and the SEs were again heavily archied east of Albert.

Gerald was now coming to the end of his refresher course. He took off alone in the evening in an attempt to add to his score but although he patrolled for a considerable time he saw nothing. Another patrol the next morning, the 20th, brought no combats. Although the flight saw a pair of enemy two seaters over the lines, Gerald considered that they were too low to engage with any safety and he resisted the temptation to attack them.

That evening the squadron held a special dinner in Gerald's honour. His stay had earned him many new friends in the squadron and many old ones attended: Crowe, Bowman from 41 Squadron, and others being among the guests. The squadron band came out in full force and there were many speeches. Gerald was not due to leave the squadron until the Monday morning and he spent Sunday playing baseball and dining at Brigade Headquarters in the evening.

Gerald took his farewell from 56 Squadron on the morning of 22 July, travelling to Le Touquet with Billy Crowe. It was his final break with 56 Squadron. Winslow's diary entry illustrates well the affection and respect which all members of the squadron felt for him.

Saw Captain Maxwell and Majority Crowe off in a blaze of glory. The former was one of the nicest men I have ever met – cleancut, upright and white. He did not want to leave at all, but he is too valuable as an instructor to lose, so they sent him back to England.

CHAPTER VII

Flying Circus

Gerald stayed in London for a few days before returning to Farlie, where he spent the next three weeks in a welcome leave, relaxing in the familiar and well-loved surroundings. He travelled back to Turnberry on 17 August and took over the post of Chief Fighting Instructor from Major Gordon. The first day of his new duties was far from pleasant. A pupil dived a Camel into the sea and despite an exhaustive search neither aeroplane nor body could be found and recovered.

The diary entry relating this is almost the last in Gerald's diary for 1918: presumably his new command kept him extremely busy and he had no time for writing up the day's events, not even recording the Armistice. Apart from detailing a flight with Taylor in a Clerget Avro, when he flew to Kinharvie, the next entry is for Christmas Day 1918. 'Mary's birthday. Farlie. Papa, Mother, self, Oona and Joan and kids. Midnight Mass at Beaufort.' If 'kids' refers to all the younger members of the family, only Ian and Ronnie, the latter still in the Sudan, were missing from this family reunion for the first Christmas of peace in four years.

In the strange hiatus after the war, Gerald stayed on at Turnberry until early March 1919, when he was selected to go to America in connection with the Victory Loan Bond drive. The idea was that a 'flying circus' should barnstorm throughout America, giving flying displays and mock aerial combats in order to encourage the population to buy Victory or Liberty bonds. The Air Ministry picked a distinguished group of airfighters to undertake the tour. In loose overall command was Major S. E. Parker, the other pilots being Gerald, with 27 victories; Major P. F. Fullard, with 46 victories; Captain H. W. Woollett, 35 victories; Captain A.W. Beauchamp-Proctor, 54 victories; and Major P. Holliday, 8 victories. Apart from their impressive list of victories – 170 enemy aeroplanes between them – the contingent held one Victoria Cross; four DSOs; five MCs with three bars; two DFCs; a Croix de Chevalier and a Legion d'Honneur.

The six pilots embarked for America on 27 March 1919, sailing in the *Northland*, a Canadian troop transport taking Canadian troops back to their homeland. The *Northland* docked first at Halifax, where the Canadians were disembarked, then sailed on to Philadelphia, arriving on 8 April 1919. Here the pilots were met by the British Air Attaché, Colonel L. E. O. Charlton, and their duties specifically explained to them for the first time. They were to tour the country in special trains, stopping at selected towns and cities and giving displays of flying and aerial fighting. There were three such trains: one touring the Eastern Seaboard States, another the Middlewest and a third the far West and Pacific States. The trains were elaborate affairs, with sleeping accommodation for thirty officers and eighty other ranks, two restaurant cars, and additional trucks carrying eighteen aeroplanes, spares and workshops. It was intended that every important town in the United States should be visited, and that besides their flying duties the pilots would give talks relating their war experiences, attend at the booths where the Victory Bonds would be sold and give speeches at various dinners held in their honour.

With Gerald's shyness, and reticence to talk of his wartime exploits, he must have viewed this part of the itinerary with horror; his companions no doubt shared his feelings when they had their first experience of the full glare of American style publicity. Their initial shock occurred on their first evening in Philadelphia when they attended a talk given by the American ace, Captain Eddie Rickenbacker at the Academy of Music. During his talk Rickenbacker pointed them out to the assembly and the entire audience turned, stood, and cheered them. The next day, when they were interviewed on the roof of their hotel, the Adelphi, they were still a little peeved with Rickenbacker. The tone of their reception is well illustrated by the story of this interview, quoted here in full to give the full flavour of their impact on the American press.

MODEST ACES CAMERA SHY, BUT GLAD A YANK TO PACIFY
'Camera man, the Rotter, Zooms to Roof, Starts 'em Sidestepping and gets a Blighty Himself.

'It is hard to tell whether the photographer or the six British aviation heroes got the most complete shock when he photographed them on the roof of the Adelphi Hotel this morning. Out of the smoke of bloomin' badinage came these developments. A British air 'ace' insisted on photographing the photographer while the photographer was photographing the 'aces'. The photographer's opinion as to the height of the Adelphi Hotel was requested by these men who have been trained to guess distances in the air. The photographer issued commands and the British officers, with a slightly stunned air, obeyed him, though he is a man of peace and they all wear medals for their heroic deeds in war planes.

'The attacking party approached the Britons after they had concluded an insular breakfast of eggs and bacon, sausages, buttered toast and other incidentals, set off with the English national breakfast food, which is marmalade.

'Once cornered the warriors had recourse to considerable side-slipping. Major S. E. Parker, in command of the party, was only too willing, but feared that Captain Beauchamp-Proctor, wearer of the Victoria Cross, might object, since Captain Proctor's heroism is only equalled by his modesty. No, Captain Proctor did not object, but the whole thing seemed so bally silly to him – standing around and posing – what! But if Major Phillip F. Fullard and Captain N. W. Woollett and Major F. B. Holliday did not object –

'In the end the photographer pointed out the virtue of their pictures to the Liberty Loan and with sighs they consented. Shock number one ensued.

' "Move over a little there," snapped the photographer briskly.

' "Are you speaking to me?" enquired Captain Proctor in that tone of frigid politeness that the Briton uses to indicate a *faux pas* on the part of the incomprehensible American.

' "Yep," snapped the untitled pressman, clicking the machine.

'Captain Proctor drew a camera from his own pocket and revenged himself by taking the photographer's picture.

'Meanwhile, Major Fullard, peering over the wall hedging the roof, wondered how far it was to earth, and the photographer told him it was about two hundred feet. The Major agreed that he might be quite right.

Major Maxwell disclosed the fact that the Britons were fearfully shocked when the American ace, Eddie Rickenbacker, pointed them out to the audience during his talk to the Academy of Music last night.

' "He should know what's what", said Major Maxwell in a slightly peeved tone. "We had him in England long enough, you know".

' "Ah", rejoined Captain Proctor, "but he is simply topping you know – simply topping!"

'And the other air heroes agreed that Eddie Rickenbacker is topping. Then the young soldiers discussed the weather.

' "This job has added ten years to my life", said the photographer, as he went away after completing his work. Then the aces did a dignified vrille toward a better 'ole.'

Gerald and Woollett elected to undertake the tour with the east coast contingent. An American major, H. J. P. Miller, was in command of their detachment, and in addition to Gerald and Woollett there were seven American service pilots in the personnel: Captains H. M. Smith, A. E. Simonin, L. H. Harris, and F. B. Wieners; Lieutenants J. O. Donaldson, J. O. Creech, and J. G. Hall. Italy was represented by Lieutenant Alberto Cantoni, and several 'aerobatic and specialist pilots' were also in the party. Captain J. O. Donaldson had served in the RAF with 32 Squadron and had scored eight victories, winning a DSC and a DFC and bar. Jessie Creech had flown Camels with No 148 Aero Squadron, had also scored eight victories and held a DSC. The aeroplanes used during the tour were a pair of Fokker DVIIs, still carrying their national markings; a Nieuport 27; several 'Curtiss' SE5as; a 'Curtiss' SVA5, and a number of Curtiss Jennies, one of which, flown by Major Miller, was painted all red and named 'Ming Toy'.

The display team gave their first exhibition over Philadelphia and during the following weeks visited Baltimore, Detroit, Cincinatti, Portland, Boston, Cleveland, Nashville, Birmingham, Louisville, Concorde, Atlanta and many other American cities and towns of varying sizes.

The tour was not without its 'spills and thrills'. In Portland the wind was extremely strong and Gerald overturned one of the SE5s in landing.

AIRSHIP DAMAGED IN LANDING. 'CARRY ON' SHOUTS AIRMAN.

'Carry on' shouted Major Maxwell, the aviator of the flying circus who performed practically all the acrobatics (sic) during the flying exhibition over this City this afternoon, when the British Scout plane was badly damaged at the landing field at Scarboro.

With a strong westerly wind blowing, Major Maxwell attempted to make a 'cross end' landing after performing many stunts over the City. His machine was going about sixty miles an hour along the field when suddenly it turned on its nose, breaking the right wing, propeller and radiator.

Spectators rushed to the scene, expecting to find Major Maxwell had been injured, but he jumped from the machine with a smile and greeted the crowd with the 'carry on' exclamation.

Gerald also impressed the reporters at another venue.

There was a roar and a tempest of dust and a Sopworth (sic) Experimental No 5, a British plane, with some American modifications, was in the air. The mechanics know it as a 'fairly wild plane', but Major G. C. Maxwell, British Ace, who has all the British military decorations that can be had, without even donning helmet or goggles, threw a leg inside, settled down negligently, and took the air to do a few loops, barrel rolls, falling leaves and other curlicues, just to see, if you please, whether anything was wrong with a new rudder recently affixed to the machine. He came down to report that something was wrong, got his stick and strolled over for a talk with some Red Cross messengers.

By the time the tour had reached Nashville, eight or nine of the aeroplanes had been damaged or destroyed. Although nine aeroplanes staged a mock airbattle during the afternoon – with two Fokkers attacking a formation of seven 'Allied' machines – on the previous day, at Chattanooga, only two Curtiss Jennies and one Fokker DVII had been servicable.

The pilots were billeted in the lush Nashville Golf and Country Club and during the morning were able to relax playing golf and tennis. Woollett impressed a local reporter to write.

'While many suspect that the only thing they do in England is dress fancy and drink tea, Captain Woolet (sic) British Ace, thinks different. To prove it the Captain grabbed a tennis racket and vanquished two American opponents'.

Despite the loss of aeroplanes, the sometimes roughly prepared landing grounds and the misgivings of some reporters over the whole 'crazy business of flying machines', the tour was an unqualified success. It introduced a great number of Americans to their first experience of flying – many prominent citizens were taken up for joyrides – and still more to their first sight of an aeroplane. Gerald took up passengers in the Jennies, and in addition to his flying duties he made a number of speeches and gave talks and lectures to various social and religious organizations.

After visiting fifty-five cities in fifty-five days, Gerald and Woollett were badly in need of a rest, and Gerald was attached to the British Embassy in Washington. While in Washington he stayed at the home of an American family, who wrote to a friend, lawyer and stockbroker George Carden, to say they had staying with them just the young man for his daughter Carolyn. Carolyn – Carrie – an attractive, vivacious girl, still in her teens, with a great sparkle and sense of fun, was promptly dispatched to Washington, and she and Gerald, despite the rather unromantic circumstances of their meeting, were immediately attracted to each other.

Carrie was rather amused by the older people's efforts at match-making, and when Gerald returned to England in late June 1919, thought it was probably the end of the matter. Her father and eldest sister, Isobel, however, had further plans. In common with all their friends they were very much taken with Gerald, finding him extremely likeable. Carrie's father decided it was time she made a trip to Europe, impossible during the war years; her elder sister was delighted to accompany her and they arrived in London in the November of 1919. They stayed for ten days and when they returned to New York Carrie and Gerald were officially engaged.

Gerald was now with the Air Ministry Directorate of Organisation No 1 and early in 1920 he obtained leave and sailed for America. Gerald and Carrie were married on Monday, 8 March 1920 in the chapel of St Ignatius Loyola School, Park Avenue. The wedding was a small, intimate affair, owing to a recent death in Carrie's family, and only the immediate family and a few close friends were present. On 20 March Gerald and Carrie sailed for England in the *Mauretania*.

CHAPTER VIII

Between the Wars

Gerald resigned his commission in the RAF in 1921, retaining the rank of squadron leader, and in 1922 went back to America to look into the viability of various business ventures. While in the States for the Victory Bond tour, Gerald had met an American businessman, James Brady, son of the famous 'Diamond Jim', one of the richest men in the United States. Brady took an interest in Gerald, regarding him somewhat in the light as his protégé. One of Brady's business ventures was the Maxwell Motor Corporation of Detroit (no connection with the Constable Maxwell family) and in the spring of 1919 an English company, Maxwell Motors Ltd, had been formed to market the cars in Europe and England, Mr Arnold de la Poer being appointed Managing Director.

Under the able management of de la Poer the English company flourished, and helped by a boom in car sales made a profit of £180,000 in only ten months from de la Poer's appointment as Managing Director. But the boom year was followed by a slump in sales and de la Poer advised the American parent company that he did not expect to sell as many cars in the coming financial period, warning them not to supply the cars in such large quantities as before. Although de la Poer was complimented on his past record, and his salary raised, the American company ignored his advice, supplying cars as before, and the English company became heavily in debt to the parent company as a result.

Gerald had been introduced to the British company by Brady, and he and de la Poer were now interested in buying enough shares to gain control of Maxwell Motors, knowing that by careful and astute management they could make it a viable business proposition. The American company had now become Chrysler Motors and the English company changed its name to Maxwell Chrysler Motors Ltd, Gerald and de la Poer being the principal shareholders. They had taken a gamble on a new and untried motor car, but by hard work and enthusiasm they made a great success of the company, making profits of £100,000 in 1925, £37,000 in 1926 and £90,000 in 1927. These profits aroused the jealousy of the American company and threats were made to curtail the number of cars they would supply to Maxwell Chrysler Motors Ltd. Gerald went to America to discuss the affair and was told that if he and de la Poer did not agree to dispose of Maxwell Chrysler Motors Ltd cheaply to the American company they would flood the English market with cars, undersell the English company, and bankrupt Gerald and de la Poer. Gerald refused to agree to this proposal, but Hutchinson, the chief spokesman for the American company, pointed out that he had a corps of salesmen ready to come to England and sell the Chrysler car against the English company. Under these threats, Gerald and de la Poer had no choice but to agree and they sold their shares in Maxwell Chrysler Motors Ltd to the Suffolk Investment Company, who in turn sold them to the Chrysler Export Corporation.

Gerald then joined the New York Stock Exchange, working for G. M. P. Murphy and Company. He opened an office in London for the company, plus another in Paris, and was resident manager in charge of all Murphy's European business, which, from the start of business in 1929, grew to a turnover of twenty million pounds in 1934.

But Gerald had not yet finished with the Chrysler Motors affair. In 1935 Arnold de la Poer brought an action against the Chrysler Corporation, alleging that he and Gerald had been forced to sell their interest in Maxwell Chrysler Motors Ltd by threats and misrepresentations.

The case opened before Mr Justice Atkinson on Tuesday, 30 April, 1935, Gilbert Beyfus appearing for the plaintiffs, the chief defendants being the Chrysler Company of America, the President of the company, Walter P. Chrysler, with various subsidiary companies and their officers.

In the words of Beyfus, it was a 'case of very great complexity'. It ran for sixty-two days, nearly three million words were spoken, and the judge was forced to adjourn the case in July to undergo an operation for appendicitis.

It was an extremely worrying year for Gerald, now a family man with three young children, William, Anne and Diana, and Carrie's diary for 1935 reflects the anxieties of the year. With costs estimated at £600 a day, Gerald faced ruin if the case were lost. Carrie wrote in her diary on 28 June:

Case is most frightening. Our share in the costs will be at least £20,000 when finished. The Chrysler Co are dragging out as long as possible. Money means nothing to them and if they win they want us to have costs that will break us. I feel that all the worries of yesterday are like grains of sand beside this monument of anxiety.

Gerald gave evidence on 14 May and was in the witness box the entire afternoon. Carrie again:

He gave a flawless testimony. He was superb and in his quiet way he gave a stirring account of his negotiations with the Chrysler Corp. There was not a sound in court while he was speaking. He gave a vivid account of how the Chrysler representative had repudiated three contracts and forced him to sell out at £60,000 less than the assets were reckoned at. If he refused the American company would have a separate organisation in England and would flood the market with their cars. All the while Arnold (de la Poer) was so ill that he was being kept alive by oxygen, Gerald was trying to allay his fears and negotiate as best he could.

The case ended on 12 November. The judgement lasted eight hours, Justice Atkinson speaking for five hours on 11 November, adjourning in the afternoon and continuing the next day, when he pronounced judgement in favour of the plaintiffs: finding the defendants guilty of fraud, conspiracy and breach of warranty. He awarded damages of £39,500 with five per cent interest for seven years, dated from 1928. The case made headlines in the national press and the verdict was broadcast in the evening news bulletins.

With the successful conclusion of the Chrysler case, Gerald and Carrie were able to relax for the first time in nearly a year, and in December they sailed to America to spend Christmas and New Year with Carrie's family. During the year of litigation, economising because of the possible outcome of the case, the family had moved from their house in Eaton Square to 'The House on the Hill' in Arundel, owned by Gerald's cousin, the Duke of Norfolk. Although she dreaded being away from London, with its theatres, museums and galleries – all of which she loved – Carrie also loved the peace and quiet of the countryside, and she and Gerald looked at various country houses while living at Arundel, but found nothing they both liked. When they returned from America, Gerald continued to look for a suitable country house. Like many others of his generation he could see that another war in Europe was almost inevitable, and his knowledge of military aviation convinced him that in any future war cities would be bombed and civilians killed and maimed on a much more extensive scale than in 1917 and 1918. With this in mind he decided to move Carrie and the family to the country.

Gerald and Carrie viewed many houses, all unsuitable, and they had almost given up hope of finding one they liked, but early in 1939 they settled on Old Alresford house in Hampshire, built in 1750–52 with prize monies won by Admiral Rodney as a victorious young sea captain in the 1740s. Sir Malcom Campbell, the famous racing motorist, was also viewing the house, but Gerald sped back to London, barely beating Sir Malcom's bid, and he and the family moved to Alresford in July 1939. Two months later Britain and Germany were again at war.

CHAPTER IX

Michael

During the first quarter of the twentieth century there were always Constable Maxwell children growing up at Farlie, the closeness of their ages making them natural companions and playfellows – boys and girls alike. When the youngest son of Bernard and Alice Constable Maxwell, Michael Hugh, was born on 3 June 1917, several years separated him from his nearest sister and eleven from his brother Andrew, but he had no lack of boyhood companions. His sister Ursula more than made up for the lack of brothers of his own age, teaching him to climb trees and other skills of boyhood, and he was blessed with a number of cousins of his own age. Hugh and Veronica Fraser, the younger son and daughter of his uncle, Simon Lord Lovat, and Fanny and Sandy Fraser of Moniack Castle, the children of another uncle, Alastair Fraser – known and loved by his many nieces and nephews as 'Uncle Alligator'. These were all constant companions in roaming the 300,000 acre estate at Beauly, at that time the third largest in Great Britain, a glorious playground for adventurous children.

In those early days, Hugh Fraser was the budding aviator, calculating that the lift from a large umbrella would enable it to be used as a parachute, and he was discovered in the act of launching himself from one of the towers of Beaufort Castle. An old, disused drain on the estate also held a fearful fascination for the children. Caught as they were about to begin its exploration, Michael and Hugh were asked why they had allowed Veronica, a girl, to go first. They replied, quite seriously, that being smaller they thought she would be easier to rescue.

Michael was a well-built boy, with an engaging grin, and he had many friends among the estate workers, ghillies, stalkers and keepers of the Beauly estate. He learned from them all, not only the lore of the countryside, its pursuits and activities, but a philosophy of life and understanding of people that was later to stand him in good stead when in command of men, and his admiration and respect for his boyhood friends and teachers grew throughout his life.

Michael was devoted to the staff at Farlie, but above all to his nanny, Lily Dickinson. 'Nana' Dickinson, as she was known to the family, had been nanny to all the Constable Maxwell children, first arriving at Farlie in 1905, just before completion of the house, and in later years, when the children of her charges came to Farlie, all with nannies of their own, she held sway as Grandnana. Her devotion was reciprocated by that of the children. In the words of Michael's mother, 'she was one of the high aristocracy of nannies'.

Lily McFearn had come to the family earlier even than Nana Dickinson, first as a ladies' maid and then a parlour maid, a position she held for the remainder of her working life. In this exalted position she wielded considerable power, ruling her staff with a strictness which belied her heart of gold. She was devoted to the family, but woe betide any member, returning from Farlie after an absence, who had failed to visit Lily McFearn within half an hour of arriving home – they had no fire in their room that evening! She was certainly temperamental, Michael's eldest brother Ian once dryly observing that she was one of the few people he knew who could rattle a *single* plate.

Tom Donnelly was another old and valued friend. Originally a coachman, he had later learned to drive, and in addition to his duties as chauffeur was a talented carpenter and handyman. Michael spent many hours with Tom Donnelly, who taught him the appreciation and care of good tools.

Beaufort Castle always had a number of fascinating and often long-staying guests. Ronnie Knox – later Monseigneur – the great Catholic philosopher and writer, seemed to be almost constantly at Beaufort. The young Michael had no conception of his intellectual brilliance, respecting him for his great expertise in handling Hornby trains, which Michael took to be his main interest in life.

Another guest, and one with RFC connections, was Maurice Baring: man of letters, English eccentric and undoubted genius. Baring had joined the RFC at the outbreak of war in 1914, and after serving on Sir David Henderson's staff, had become General Trenchard's aide. He was 'Uncle Mumble' to the Constable Maxwell and Fraser children, and Michael remembered that he was always generous with a donation of half a guinea at the start of school term.

Compton MacKenzie – later Sir Compton MacKenzie – a life long friend of Alice Constable Maxwell, was also frequently at Beaufort. He was very fond of her youngest son and in later years would recount with delight how Michael, at the age of nine, had confided to him, with great solemnity, that 'as you get older the time goes quicker'.

The children of the old Scottish families, however exalted, were brought up to treat everyone with the utmost respect, whatever their station in life. Everyone, they were taught, was a unique person in their own right. Michael recalls that when older he was often amused to discover that many of his aunt's guests, to whom he had shown no more or no less respect than any other grown up, were in fact famous and rather exalted people.

Like his brothers before him, Michael was fascinated by his father's tales of the American West in the early 1880s, but he had an additional fund of stories. His three eldest brothers had fought in the greatest European war then known, and Gerald had been a famous airfighter, flying with Ball and McCudden in the renowned 56 Squadron. Heady stuff for a young boy, and although Gerald was reticent in talking of his flying experiences, enough filtered through to sow the seed of an idea that one day he, Michael, would also be a fighter pilot.

Although their three eldest sons had been educated at Downside, Bernard and Alice Constable Maxwell sent their fourth son, David, to Ampleforth College in Yorkshire, and Andrew followed two years later. Michael's primary schooling was by a governess, Miss Smythe, whom he shared with Ursula, but at the age of nine, at the start of the summer term of 1927, he too entered Ampleforth.

Michael disliked being at school, but was quite philosophical about it, considering Ampleforth the finest school in the world and the best place for him to be; a necessary evil, essential for his future. But he hated leaving his beloved Farlie, and an entry in his school notebook, 'Odds and Ends of Summer Term', has an anguished ring as he contemplated the long days ahead before he could return. '4 May, 1927. My first term. Summer. 3 Months, 12 weeks, 84 days, 1,008 hours, 60,480 minutes, 3,628,800 seconds'. Apparently Michael's day had only twelve hours. Perhaps like most boys he only counted those hours of the day when he was up and active.

Despite these misgivings, Michael led a full and varied school life. He had many relations at Ampleforth, including his cousin and best friend there, Hugh Stirling, and half holidays passed pleasantly enough, playing golf or out with the beagles on the surrounding Yorkshire moors. For a month or so in his last year, Michael had a small car, which he had bought for six pounds. This was absolutely forbidden, but he kept it in the main car park behind the monastery and no one suspected. Another pupil considered it foolhardy to keep a car so near school, keeping his own in a lonely spot some miles away, but to his chagrin it was he who was discovered and beaten, Michael still being undetected.

Michael left Ampleforth in July 1936. He felt sad as he bicycled the twenty one miles to York, for his appreciation of Ampleforth had increased with every year and he had many friends among the boys and monks, but paradoxically he knew that it was the happiest day of his life, the thought of the new challenges ahead exhilarating.

Michael went up to Oxford for the Michaelmas term of 1936, entering Hertford College to read history. His first act on reaching Oxford, 'before I had even spent one night in the establishment', was to apply to join the Oxford University Air Squadron, and he sat down that night to write to his mother: six impassioned pages of reasons why he should be allowed to fly with the OUAS. With her usual tact and understanding, his mother simply replied, 'Yes, why not?' a response which completely flabbergasted yet delighted Michael, who for no firm reason had expected parental opposition – and parental permission was a prerequisite for joining the OUAS.

Flying instruction with the OUAS in the 1930s was a leisured, not to say gentlemanly affair, carried out with style and panache. Instruction was given at the RAF station at Abingdon, just over six miles from Oxford, and pupils were conveyed there, eight at a time, in a large, opulent Rolls Royce. Leaving the first eight undergraduates to make their flights, the Rolls returned to Oxford for the second group. On delivering these at the aerodrome it would return the first group to Oxford, this procedure being followed throughout the afternoon. Each pupil made one flight of forty-five minutes each week, although an extra flight was sometimes possible if another pupil was ill or absent.

Michael made his first flight on 28 October 1936, Flight Lieutenant Addenbroke taking him up for thirty-five minutes' dual instruction in a Avro Tutor (K4819) and by the end of the Michaelmas term of 1936 he had flown 4 hours 40 minutes of dual. The schedule of flying only once a week made instruction a lengthy affair and it was not until the Hilary term of 1937, having completed another four hours of dual, that Michael went solo. On 17 March 1937, Flight-Lieutenant Addenbroke, who had given Michael most of his instruction, checked him out in Avro Tutor K3232 for forty minutes and on landing sent him off alone.

Michael made a good take-off, feeling 'extremely clever and capable', until the realisation dawned that he had to get down again – a different matter entirely! However, he successfully negotiated his first landing and logged his first five minutes of solo flight.

Once an undergraduate had soloed he was allowed an additional flight each week, and Michael rapidly added to his hours. By the end of Trinity term, 1937, he had flown 4 hours 15 minutes solo and 12 hours 45 minutes of dual. At Ford summer camp that year he flew solo for longer periods, making cross country flights to Lee on Solent, Rochester, Cranwell and Hendon, and at the end of the detachment period of ten days he had added 24 hours to his solo time and logged 20 minutes of dual in a Scarpa Flying Boat.

Summer was an extremely busy time for Michael. In the winter of 1935, during his last year at Ampleforth, Alasdair Maclean, adjutant of the Queen's Own Cameron Highlanders (TA) had approached Michael's mother on the question of Michael joining the regiment. The 4th Camerons were anxious to recruit in the Beauly area – at that time exclusively Lovat Scout territory – and Maclean considered that Michael's family name would be a great help in attracting recruits. Alasdair Maclean – later known throughout the Highlands as Mr Tattoo in recognition of his successful managing of the Edinburgh Tattoo over many years – was anxious to win Alice Constable Maxwell's permission to ask her son, but he was only too aware that her brother had raised the Lovat Scouts. Michael's mother had no objections, pointing out that while it was true her brother had raised the Lovat Scouts, her father had for many years commanded the Inverness Militia, which had later become the 4th Camerons, and she would be happy for Michael to join either regiment. When asked, Michael was equally unbiased, only pointing out that in the event of a war he wished to join the RAF. On Alasdair Maclean assuring him that joining the 4th Camerons would in no way prevent him from serving in the RAF at a later date, Michael agreed and, a fully fledged corporal in the OTC at Ampleforth, he was commissioned as a second lieutenant in the 4th Camerons. On his joining the OUAS the following year, Michael was therefore committed to four weeks of annual summer camp: two weeks with the OUAS and two with the Camerons, in addition to the tiring but enjoyable work of recruiting for the regiment.

Returning to Oxford for the Michaelmas term of 1937, Michael found a new group of flying instructors. During the last period of Trinity, Michael had flown three times with Sergeant Jenner – 'a super pilot' – and during Michaelmas he flew almost exclusively with Jenner, who initiated him in the art of spinning the Avro Tutor.

When Michael returned to Oxford for the Hilary term of 1938 his sadness at leaving Farlie was assuaged by flying the day of his return.

'Do slow rolls. They remind me of my first, which I did after only an hour's solo, when I lost 3,000 feet. Luckily I had started at 6,000.' On 4 February he recorded in his diary.

I do two slow rolls above the clouds – a great thrill. Cloud flying not allowed. One wing right down, but I get through. For a second I don't know which way to flatten out on upper or lower clouds!

During the term he logged another 9 hours 35 minutes' solo time.

Life was very pleasant at Oxford in the immediate pre-war years. Lunching and dining at the Grid, an undergraduate club – 'you were proposed by a member by his entering your name in a book; anyone who objected simply ripped out the page' – bridge parties; drinking parties; dances; a little serious drinking; slightly less serious gambling; trips to London, flirting with girls, travelling back on the 9.40 train, 'The Flying Fornicator'. The companionship; the talk, and of course the flying. All gave relaxation from study and work.

In 1938, considering how to spend the remainder of the summer after his two camps, Michael thought that he would like to spend some time in Europe, and he approached the Students Union on the possibility of a working holiday. Thinking it would be a little further afield and more interesting than the usual run of European countries, he expressed a preference for a Slav country, and in early May 1938 was given an appointment for an interview with a Polish lady. Michael expected a *Grande Dame*, but found instead 'a lovely girl, a year younger than me. We agreed it would be nice to spend the summer together, and then said, almost together, "Do I pay you or do you pay me?" ' The head of the establishment told them that the usual arrangement was for the visitor to have half his fare paid and the equivalent of a pound a month pocket money, and it was agreed that Michael would stay with the girl's family for two months, starting in July. His duties would be merely to speak English to the family and coach them in the customs and manners of English life. Michael was delighted with the arrangement and hated having to ask for any money at all as it seemed so much like an ordinary social visit. After the interview he called on Gerald and Carrie at Eaton Square and in the evening went with Gerald and Andrew to see *Hell's Angels*, the Howard Hughes' classic film of first world war airfighting. 'It was fun sitting next to Gerald and hearing lowdown. He was quite excited by it.'

Michael came of age on 3 June 1938 and gave a small lunch party, the guests including his brother David and his wife Alethea, Michael's sister Oona, his cousin Hugh Fraser and six close friends. Five days later he was packing to leave Oxford. Despite lunching at the Grid and dining in Hall he was profoundly depressed. He had had such a wonderful time at Oxford and was loath to leave, but family finances were strained and it seemed unlikely that he would be able to return to take his degree. Michael had always had at the back of his mind that he would eventually go into the priesthood, a vocation which he knew would please his mother, and he talked over this possibility with his brother Andrew, whose opinions he greatly valued. Andrew was full of encouragement, but thought it a sound idea to first gain some experience of life, advising the RAF for a spell; on leaving Oxford in early June, Michael had an interview at the Air Ministry with a view to obtaining a short term commission. The terms were far from attractive, but with Oxford uncertain it seemed a solution to the problem of what to do after he had returned from Poland.

After the yearly camp with the 4th Camerons, Michael attended the OUAS camp, that year held at Ford in Sussex. He arrived at Ford on the evening of 3 July and was thrilled to find that he would be flying service machines whilst at camp: Hawker Hinds, Harts and Audax. 'As I go to bed I look out with joy at the Hart I am to fly in the morning.'

He was up and ready punctually at 6.00 am the next morning and Flight Lieutenant Jimmy Kirkpatrick took him up in Hawker Hind L7202 for a thirty minutes' familiarisation flight, Michael feeling a 'real he-man' as he climbed into the Hind's cockpit. He was thrilled by the power of the Hind, but found the controls, although precise, a little heavy and easy to overcorrect. He and Kirkpatrick landed the Hind 'together' and Michael noted with some trepidation that it landed at 80 mph.

After breakfast he flew with Kirkpatrick for forty minutes in an Audax (K7387) and after three landings, 'which I think are appalling', was asked if he felt up to going solo.

'I taxi out inch by inch. The engine is so big it pulls quickly and is a terror for swinging. The breaks in the rudder are strange. I turn into wind. I am more frightened than for my first solo. Here goes. The speed gets up, full throttle, both hands on the steering wheel. She swings, I give her half rudder. More or less straight, we get off. Oh Joy! I do a double circuit so as to get the full thrill out of it. We hurtle round at 140. In we come, too fast, too slow. Will we? Won't we? We touch. We are a little fast so bounce, not much, then we begin to turn. I use full left rudder and brake and stick. It still seems to sway the wrong way. We turn slowly, we lose speed. Some time later we stop, 45 degrees off course. Gosh!'

Two hours later he flew K7382 again, still feeling that it was 'the most dangerous thing I have ever done or would do'. The take-off was good, but on landing he dropped one wing. He corrected quickly, and after three bounces, during which he felt he had lost control completely, he was safely down. The next day he flew a Hind solo for an hour and a half – 'much the same, but supercharged'. He still felt barely fifty percent in control and as a precaution made the sign of the Cross before each landing, a habit continued throughout his flying career. The following day he flew the Hind for two hours and felt much more confident – 'I am now well over the fifty percent, but still keep up the Cross habit' – and executed a few mild aerobatics.

During the last week of camp, Michael flew an Audax to North Weald, and while there sat in a Hurricane of 56 Squadron – a portent of things to come. Michael met several officers serving with the squadron, who were interested to learn he was Gerald's brother, and over anxious to impress them he made a 'damnable' take-off. 'I am not good enough to show off.'

On the penultimate day of camp, Michael made a long cross country flight in a Tutor, and while trying out some loops suddenly saw three black shapes rapidly approaching. 'I do some heroic aerobatics to get clear, but it is like a hen avoiding a kestrel. They are past before I start! Three Hurricanes! I wonder if they saw me!

At the end of the attachment at Ford, Michael had flown the Hawker Hind for two hours, the Hart for an hour and a half and the Audax for over four hours. He was now feeling thoroughly at home in the air and had done 'dozens' of rolls, one day 'rolling' all the way to Dover!

The last day of camp was hectic. After flying in the morning, the afternoon was spent in packing for the Polish trip. Arriving in London, Michael got his visa and ticket, then visited Eaton Square, talking over his plans with Gerald. He put forward his various ideas for his future – the priesthood, going to South America or joining the RAF – but Gerald strongly advised going back to Oxford and taking his degree, assuring him he would help in any way he could. Michael stayed the night at the Oxford and Cambridge Club, spoke to his mother on the telephone – who gave him last minute advice for the journey – and finally went to bed thrilled with the knowledge that the next two months would bring new friends and experiences.

CHAPTER X

The Coming of War

It was a long and tiring journey to Poland, enlivened somewhat by a pretty Swiss girl on the boat to Ostend and an even prettier one on the Berlin train. After a day of sightseeing in the German capital, and getting to bed rather later, Michael overslept the next morning and caught the train to Lwow by the narrowest of margins – 'oh relief'. From Lwow it was a short train journey of an hour and a half to Ozydow, the station for Konty, the home of his hosts. On arrival at Ozydow he was met by a servant. 'Where is the car? Then I see it. A beautiful Victorian four wheeled buggy with two horses. With the grandeur of a duke getting into his Phantom III I am helped in and given a cloth for my knees. In the meantime a crowd of peasants stand nearby watching. I have never wanted to laugh so much. Everything is so solemn and done so carefully. Then at last, my case strapped on, the coachman and flunky up in front, off we go.'

The Gniewosz family, Michael's hosts, he found charming, and over the next two months he became very fond of them all. The father had died, but the remainder of the family consisted of Madame Gniewosz, who was Hungarian by birth; the eldest daughter Norah, whom Michael had met in London; a daughter of seventeen, Anelia (Nella); Josef, a son of sixteen, and an older brother, Wadich, who was away serving with his regiment.

Michael's duties were far from onerous. He had simply to live with the family, speak English to them – not teach in the strict sense of the term – and answer questions about life in England.

Michael's two months in Poland were extremely enjoyable. He found the Poles loved life, enjoyed themselves enormously, never letting details spoil their pleasure, and were generally a gay, lovable people. They were immensely patriotic, with a deep love of their country, and fiercely proud of their army, which they literally worshipped.

So proud were the Poles of their army that they had no fear of aggression from Germany, considering that if war was to come with

Germany it would be over the question of the Danzig Corridor. The real enemy, they considered, was Russia. Michael discussed the political situation, and the feelings of the Poles, in his letters home to his mother: intensely interested as always in the experiences of her youngest son.

There was a great deal of social life to enjoy in Poland: dances at Konty and other country houses; swimming and canoeing in the lakes; bridge evenings; tennis; hunting pig; riding; alfresco meals in the woods, 'huge dish of fried onions and potatoes, which we ate out of a frying pan with our fingers, lying full length on the ground. Our fingers were dirty before, but clear after. A delicious meal'.

Michael left Poland at the end of September. He had £3.00, quite enough for the journey home. 'The train comes – it goes, I watch all the places I know slowly departing and feel most dejected. It really was fun being there. They are so gay and full of life. Many English friends will seem most dull and dowdy. They (the Poles) get the best out of life and do enjoy things a lot.'

Neither Michael nor his new found friends realized that it had been the last year of peace; the last perfect summer before war destroyed for ever the idyllic existence at Konty. Michael never saw any of the Gniewosz family again and bitterly regretted that he did not make more extensive enquiries in 1940, when he heard a rumour that they had fled to England. As he wryly commented. 'It was rather a busy time.' He remembered them all with affection and the happy time he spent at Konty.

Michael arrived in Berlin the next morning, travelling on to Cologne that evening. After finding an hotel he wandered around the city, going to Benediction at the cathedral – 'most impressive' – and buying beer and sausages – 'very cheap and very good'. His mother had offered to buy him a camera for his twenty first birthday, leaving the choice to him, and he had decided to buy one in Germany on the way home. After a little bargaining he chose a camera and made friends with the salesman in the shop, who invited Michael to join him and some friends at a revue that evening.

Continuing to wander round the city and trying out his present, Michael noticed a large crowd in front of the cathedral. Investigating, he found that Hitler was to broadcast at 8 o'clock. 'Barely a person moves. Every house seems to have a radio. Any car is surrounded.' Michael went to the revue, to join his friend of the morning. 'All are listening. There is little clapping, and the most is for Chamberlain. It was interesting hearing so momentous a speech.'

Michael's new friends welcomed him warmly and the party was excellent.

They produce a sort of spirit with a slice of sausage and mustard over the glass. 'Bet you can't drink the Führer's health with your mouth full,' says one to me. The whole spirit is so friendly and cheerful. No one thinks war is likely – save a little one in Czechoslovakia. I am treated royally.

A pretty girl, who spoke no English, joined the party. Coached by the English speaking members of the gathering she said 'wonderful things' to Michael, such as 'Darling, I love you', and Michael was prompted to reply in German, again coached by his hosts. 'By the laughter and the girl's embarrassment, the remarks must have been good to say the least'. None of the happy little group of young people foresaw that in little under a year they would be enemies.

Despite the good time he had had and the hospitality of his hosts, Michael was relieved, as always, to leave Germany. 'I did not feel war was likely, but Belgium feels a lot nearer (to home) than Cologne. It is a joy to see England again.'

Arriving in London, Michael took a taxi to Eaton Square, where he found a dinner party in progress. He was astonished to find everyone in a frenzy.

All expect war. It is a shock to find such agitation. At Dover the guns were manned. I will always remember this evening. War appeared certain.

War was not to come for another year. If the German Luftwaffe had made use of that year to speed up its tardy production of fighter aeroplanes, and to set up new bases in Czechoslovakia, the RAF also gained a valuable respite. At the time of the Munich crisis the majority of the RAF squadrons were still equipped with obsolescent biplanes, only two squadrons having the new, eight gun monoplane fighter, the Hawker Hurricane. But directly after Munich the re-equipment of the RAF fighter squadrons became top priority. By July 1939 the RAF had twelve Hurricane squadrons, and throughout the year other squadrons began to re-equip with the Supermarine Spitfire in increasing numbers.

There were also changes in the higher command of the RAF; changes which were to have far reaching effects. The Commander in Chief of Fighter Command, Air Marshal Hugh Dowding, had been informed in August 1938 that the Air Ministry would be unable to offer him any 'further employment' after June 1939, but in February the Chief of Air Staff, Newall, telephoned Dowding to tell him that no changes were contemplated during 1939. Dowding, the architect of Fighter Command, had been cavalierly treated by the Air Ministry, despite his efforts to remedy the years of neglect in the vital matters of air defence. Newall's telephone call was the first indication that the Air Ministry had changed its mind over his retirement and, smarting from this new discourtesy, Dowding wrote to the Air Ministry advising them of his intention to still retire in June. If it was desired that he carry on at Fighter Command, he felt – rightly – that he should be officially informed and given the full support of the Air Council. On 20 March 1939, Dowding received a letter from Newall asking him to defer his retirement until after March 1940. By then circumstances would be very different.

Financial difficulties having been resolved, by the generosity of his mother and sisters Mary and Joan, Michael returned to Oxford for the Michaelmas term of 1938, his happiness during the term only marred by the death of his father in late October at the age of ninety. Michael continued his flying with the OUAS. He still flew the Avro Tutor, but in April 1939 he flew an hour and forty five minutes in a Hawker Audax (K7429) and at summer camp, that year held at Lympne, he flew Hinds and Audax exclusively.

In July 1939 Michael went to France on a bicycling tour. Travelling via Rouen, Evreux, Dreux and Chartres, he arrived in Orleans on 22 June. From Orleans he travelled across France to Macon; then southwards to Lyons and Nimes, which he reached on 31 July. While staying at the Hotel Menant in Nimes he received a telegram from his mother with the news that he had graduated with an Honours Degree in history. Staying at youth hostel and estaminet, he made his way – sometimes by train, sometimes by bicycle – to Montpellier, Narbonne, La Rochelle, Nantes, and finally to Dieppe. It was the last view of a Europe that was soon to be engulfed in the catastrophe of war. When Michael next saw France it would be from a very different standpoint. He landed back in England on 12 August. In three weeks Europe was at war.

In the spring of 1939 Michael had applied for a permanent commission in the RAF, and on 28 August, while staying at Kinharvie in the south of Scotland, he heard he had been accepted. He was warmly congratulated by his godfather, Major General Sir Maxwell Scott of Abbotsford, also at Kinharvie, and the next day Michael and his mother returned to Farlie. On 3 September war was declared.

Michael was still a commissioned officer in the Camerons, and he spent the first month of the war as a soldier, but on 10 October 1939, having resigned his army commission, he was instructed to report to No 9 Flying Training School at Hullavington in Wiltshire. It was the beginning of his career in the RAF, a career which, save for one short break, would span nearly twenty-four years.

The whole intake of the course at Hullavington was composed of University Air Squadron pupils, undergraduates and graduates, and this called for some adjustment on the part of the flying instructors. They were accustomed to dealing with very new acting pilot officers, straight from Elementary Flying School, which the University Air Squadron people were excused, and some of the instructors had very few more flying hours than their pupils. At the University Air Squadrons the pupils had had the cream of instructors, most of whom had over 2,000 hours of *instructing*, quite apart from their normal hours.

Michael's instructor at Hullavington was Pilot Officer Page, who had only twenty hours' experience of instructing. With his – as he admitted – slightly malicious sense of humour, Michael would ask Page, tongue in cheek as always, 'Please Sir, could you give me a demonstration of stopping the engine in the air.' As a very young, inexperienced pilot officer, Page still had his hands full simply flying an aeroplane and was certainly not going to do anything 'as stupid' as stopping an engine in flight.

Michael enjoyed his time at Hullavington, flying Hawker Hinds – 'the instructors soon adjusted to us, we were all absolutely dead keen' – and he was awarded his Wings on 15 December 1939 with an assessment of average proficiency, Group Captain Elliott Smith adding a recommendation that he 'must not allow his keenness to lead to overconfidence'. Michael had flown 138 hrs 15 mins solo, with 69 hrs 15 mins of dual instruction, and an additional twenty-five minutes of solo at night.

In March 1940, Michael was posted to No 7 Bombing and Gunnery School at Stormy Down, Porthcawl, for a course in gunnery. The school was commanded by Wing Commander J. I. T. 'Taffy' Jones DSO MC DFC MM, a renowned fighter pilot of the first war with forty victories. A squadron compatriot, admirer, and biographer of Major

Edward 'Mick' Mannock VC, the top scoring British fighter pilot of the 1914–1918 war, 'Taffy' Jones was a great patriot. He had left the RAF in June 1936 after twenty-one years of service, and was recalled on 25 August 1939 by a thunderous knocking on his door at five o'clock in the morning. Jumping out of bed and opening the window, Taffy saw below the village policeman and postman. In response to his demanding what the devil they wanted at that hour, the policeman, who knew him well, asked pompously: 'Are you Squadron Leader J. I. T. Jones DSO MC DFC MC. On the exasperated Taffy replying that of course he was, he was requested to take delivery of an important letter. It was his recall papers.

Under the easy going command of Taffy Jones, the station at Porthcawl was a happy one and Michael had a 'relaxed' time there, doing little work other than salvaging cases of Guinness from a wrecked ship, sunk off the coast. The cases of precious liquid were washed ashore and Taffy Jones, having had them loaded on to RAF trucks, appropriated the Guinness for the station.

With his training finally at an end, and having been selected as a fighter pilot, Michael was posted to an operational squadron. With his family connections with the RAF there was really only one squadron he could have joined: 56 Squadron. Gerald, now back in the RAF and serving at the Air Ministry, was extremely anxious that his young brother should carry on the family tradition in his old squadron and, as Ian had for him in 1916, pulled all the strings he could think of to arrange Michael's posting. Many of Gerald's contemporaries in the first war now held high rank in the RAF and he wrote to Air Vice Marshal E. L. Gossage to ask if anything could be done. Gossage had himself briefly commanded 56 Squadron in 1916 and he viewed Gerald's request with sympathy. Gerald's fraternal feelings, however, did not override his pride in his old squadron, or his realization of the high standard it demanded of its pilots – standards he himself had done so much to formulate. He qualified his request to Gossage with the proviso that it only be granted if Michael was 'good enough' for 56 Squadron.

CHAPTER XI

56 Squadron

Michael arrived at North Weald, 56 Squadron's base, on 20 April 1940. He went into the mess, made himself known, and was introduced to those of his new squadron who were present, plus several members of 151 Squadron, which shared the aerodrome with 56. One of the first people Michael met was his future flight commander, Flight Lieutenant Ian Soden, an ex-Cranwell cadet and a first class pilot. Soden immediately impressed Michael with his cheerfulness and charm, and when he later suggested that they all retired to a pub down the road, to celebrate Michael's arrival with 'a little pissy', Soden's pet term for a party, Michael was pleased and not a little flattered. Even more so by the many congratulations he received on having done so well at FTS. Michael had not been aware that he had, but he was assured that only people who had distinguished themselves in their initial training could get into a crack squadron like 56. In the coming months Michael was himself to welcome newcomers with this harmless but morale boosting deception; one of the many small ploys to instil into the new boys a confidence in themselves and a pride in their squadron.

In April 1940, 56 Squadron was commanded by Squadron Leader E. V. Knowles: 'Teddy' to his contemporaries, 'The Führer' to his pilots, and he allocated Michael to 'B' Flight, commanded by Ian Soden. Michael found his fellow members of the flight as likable as their commander. Pilot Officer Tommy Rose immediately took to Michael – as soon as he learnt that Michael was the proud possessor of a motor car. 'Betty, my sister, had given me a lovely little Ford 10. It had a new engine and she had paid £50 for it.' Tommy Rose, being recently married and in the habit of going home to his wife every night, magnanimously offered to help Michael run in his new engine by borrowing the Ford for his journey each evening, promising he would drive slowly. 'I'm quite sure he didn't. He'd get in and drive absolutely flat out,' Michael recalled. 'But I didn't really mind. Tommy was very much a hero-boy of mine. Rough as anything, with a thick woolly mass of black hair, and an absolutely delightful chap.'

Rose introduced Michael to F. W. Higginson, who on being told that Michael would be joining them in 'B' Flight solemnly pronounced, 'Oh, very definitely the better flight'. Higginson, 'Taffy' to all, was one of the several sergeant pilots in 56 Squadron, including George Smythe, Cliff Whitehead, Peter Hillwood and C. J. Cooney – 'a most marvellous lot'.

Michael's fellow pilot officers were a mixed bunch in temperament and background, linked by their keenness and pride in their squadron. Barry Sutton, born in Oxfordshire, but a much travelled young man; 'Fish' Fisher, a New Zealander; 'Klon' Coe, a Canadian with a passion for all things mechanical; 'Boy' Brooker, a schoolmaster pre-war until he had decided to take a short term commission; Peter Davies, a pilot of some experience, with over 600 hours on different types of aeroplanes; Peter Down, who had recently been reduced from flight lieutenant for flying into the wireless masts at North Weald; Brian Wicks; 'Slim' Coghlan, and several others.

But the two key people in the squadron were undoubtedly Ian Soden and the 'A' Flight Commander, Flight Lieutenant J. D. C. Joslin, a large, ginger-haired and ginger-tempered individual who could consume vast quantities of beer without apparent effect. Barry Sutton wrote, 'He had a huge laugh, a charming wife, a spaniel, but never any cigarettes'.[1] Michael recalled seeing Ian Soden and Joslin just before Joslin departed to take command of 79 Squadron and Soden left for France. They were standing by a Hurricane one evening, deep in conversation, and Michael regretted that he did not photograph them at that moment – a moment indelibly impressed on his memory.[2]

On his part, Michael also made an impression on his squadron contemporaries. George Smythe remembers him as a 'tall, rather gawky PO, with a charming, friendly smile and manner', while another recalls, 'He was an extremely courteous and pleasant boy, tall and rather angular, who always looked as if he had slept in his clothes. His hair always stood up at the back, rather in the manner of Richmal Crompton's William. With his Oxford accent, his general manner and background, the squadron soon came to regard him as their "tame aristocrat".'

Michael had been given a great build up on the merits of 56

---

1. *The Way of a Pilot*, Barry Sullon, Macmillan 1942.
2. Joslin was killed on 7 July 1940, when his Hurricane crashed at Chilberton Elms, near Folkestone. The cause of the crash was never discovered.

Squadron from Gerald, and when he had landed at North Weald while with the OUAS in 1938 he had been greatly impressed. The first time he saw the squadron fly at North Weald in 1940 only confirmed his conviction that he was now a member of the finest fighter squadron in the RAF. 'It really was so super. I saw them going off in a close formation. Twelve Hurricanes in a tight formation take-off over grass. It was staggering, the perfection of their flying. Ian Soden was a marvellous leader.'

Walking down to the hangars the morning after his arrival, Michael was accosted by a tall, ramrod figure whom he realized must be the AOC, Air Vice Marshal Sir Keith Park, commanding 11 Group.

'What squadron are you with?' enquired Park.

'56, sir', brightly, from Michael.

'Where's your CO?'

'I don't know, sir.'

'Well, where's his office?'

'I don't know that either, sir.'

'How long have you been in 56?'

'I'm just on my way there, sir.'

'Oh well', laughed Park. 'Then you'd better come with me and we'll find them together.'

On 23 April Ian Soden took Michael up in the squadron Magister, to check out his flying and show him the local landmarks. He had shown Michael the 'taps' on the Hurricane the previous day, counter-signing Michael's statement in his logbook that he fully understood the 'fuel, cooling, ignition, undercarriage and flap systems of the Hurricane aircraft', and Michael made his first flight in a Hurricane (N2522) on the afternoon of 23 April. He liked it immediately. 'A dream aeroplane, absolutely super. I loved the marvellously springy undercarriage, a beautiful softness of feel.'

Over the next eight days, Michael flew 17¼ hours in eight different Hurricanes, practising formation flying, aerobatics, air to ground gunnery, formation attacks, and mock fighting. On 5 May he was told to take Hurricane N2522 and carry out a height test. 'One of the things in getting to know the aeroplane was to go up high – to get the feel of the thing at height.'

On reaching 30,000 feet, Michael decided to see just how high the Hurricane would go. 'I flogged my way up and eventually got to 33,000. Then I thought: let's see how fast it will go downhill, so I rolled it over on its back and went straight down with the engine full on. I thought it would be fun to see 400 mph on the clock. I got the thing up to 400 by the time I was passing 20,000 feet. Then the engine blew up.'

There was no violent explosion, just a muffled 'woosh'. Michael had plenty of height and he glided into North Weald, but unfortunately ended up on the other side of the main road which bordered the aerodrome, smashing through a hedge and dispersing the usual crowd of Sunday sightseers. 'I fairly scattered them and got a left and a right of bicycles – one on each wheel,' he later wrote to his mother.

Michael was in danger of being sent on the dreaded Brighton B Course for this incident – a disciplinary course for wayward officers – along with Barry Sutton, who had committed the unpardonable sin of landing the 'Führer's' Hurricane with the wheels still retracted; but the danger passed, 'although we thoroughly deserved it', and the following Thursday, 9 May, Ian Soden informed Michael that he was now considered fully operational.

At first light on the morning of 10 May 1940, the German Luftwaffe carried out heavy and co-ordinated attacks on airfields in Holland, Belgium and north east France. The German armoured thrust through the Low Countries had begun, violating the neutrality of Holland and Belgium in a plan to outflank the French Maginot Line and avoid the static trench warfare of 1914–1918. The so called 'phoney war' was over.

An integral part of the German plan for the offensive was the use of intensive air support, Luftflotte 2 and 3 providing the equivalent of a creeping artillery barrage in advance of the armoured columns; employing nearly 4,000 aeroplanes, four fifths of the entire strength of the Luftwaffe. Facing this huge armada were just over 650 Allied aeroplanes, of which only 60 were RAF fighters: 40 Hurricanes and 20 Gloster Gladiators.

News of the German offensive came through to 56 Squadron on the morning of 10 May, and A Flight flew to Gravesend, refuelled and flew a patrol three miles off the coast in the Ostend to Zeebrugge area. The flight saw no enemy aeroplanes and a patrol the following day also brought no sightings. On 12 May the squadron flew to the advanced airfield at Martlesham Heath, taking off from there to cover a low level attack by Fairey Battles of 12 Squadron on the two vital bridges near Maastricht.[1] The Hurricanes patrolled the Bergen op Zoom, Breda, Zundert to Turnhout area. Groundfire was heavy and accurate and

1. All five Battles failed to return and two posthumous VCs were won.

the CO's aeroplane and another were hit. Michael flew on neither of these patrols, fuming at being still considered 'last reserve'.

By the middle of May the remnants of the RAF's Advanced Air Striking Force – mainly Bristol Blenheims and Fairey Battles, with token fighter escort – were retreating in the face of the advancing German armoured columns, leapfrogging from airfield to airfield. 607 Squadron, equipped with Gloster Gladiators, the RAF's last biplane fighter, flew almost continuous sorties from the aerodrome at Vitry-en-Artois, near Douai, and destroyed a number of enemy aircraft; but the Gladiator was severely outclassed and 607 Squadron suffered heavy casualties. The Hurricane squadrons of the AASF fared little better, Nos 1 and 73 Squadrons losing nineteen aeroplanes and twelve pilots in seven days.

On 16 May, while the 56 Squadron pilots were at lunch, the 'Führer' came into the Mess with Group Captain 'Paddy' O'Neil, the Station Commander. Ian Soden was told to gather his flight in the anteroom. The news caused general excitement: A Flight was to remain at North Weald, but B Flight was to stand by to fly to France that afternoon. Ian Soden chose Tommy Rose, Barry Sutton, Peter Down, Taffy Higginson and Cliff Whitehead as the pilots who would fly to France, and they took off in the late afternoon, watched enviously by the others and wished godspeed by Paddy O'Neil and Group Captain 'Beery' Bowman, who had come down from Group HQ to see his old squadron off to the scene of his triumphs of the last war.

After refuelling at Manston, the flight flew to Vitry-en-Artois, where they were greeted by a lugubrious old sentry, who informed them with some relish, 'There were six killed on Sunday, and more the next day, and many yesterday. They're all getting killed.' With this cheerful greeting ringing in their ears, the pilots walked into Vitry – 'more like a very large farmhouse than a village' – found an estaminet and had a meal of pork chops, washed down with a rough red wine. Their first impressions of France were identical to those of a generation before: 'Cobbles everywhere, no kerbs, lots of straw and smell.'

By an ironic stroke of fate, Vitry-en-Artois lay almost exactly in the middle of the area covered by the first patrols of 56 Squadron when it had arrived in France in 1917, and later, in 1918, when stationed at Valheureux. In the next three days of fierce fighting, B Flight, 56 Squadron, 1940, more than upheld the glorious traditions of their predecessors: Ball, McCudden, Gerald Maxwell, Bowman, Rhys Davids and others – names still very much in evidence on the squadron honours board and a constant source of inspiration. Ian Soden and his flight were soon to write their own page – no less epic – in the history of 56 Squadron.

The airfield at Vitry had no runways, the grass was long and a crashed Blenheim lay in the middle of the field. A dilapidated wooden hut served as a flight office: it had no furniture, only a telephone linking the pilots with Wing HQ in Vitry and the operations hut on the other side of the aerodrome. B Flight had teamed up with a flight of 226 Squadron, commanded by Flight Lieutenant Freddy Rosier, an old friend of Ian Soden, and the two flights intermixed at readiness and scramble.

On 17 May B Flight took off at 5.00 am on its first patrol. They saw no enemy aeroplanes, but ran into heavy anti-aircraft fire east of Lille. Cliff Whitehead's Hurricane was hit in the tailplane, and Ian Soden lost a wingtip.

Soden, Down, Rose and Higginson took off again at 8.00 am, leaving Sutton and Whitehead behind to stand at readiness with a section of 226 Squadron. The four Hurricanes returned safely at 9.20, the pilots flushed with success. Soden had shot down a Junkers Ju 88 and Higginson a Dornier Do 17.

At noon, Soden, Rose, Down, Higginson and Whitehead flew another patrol and met with even greater success. They sighted a formation of eight Heinkel 111s ten miles east of Cambrai, and attacking from directly astern all five shot down a bomber, with Rose and Whitehead sharing a sixth damaged and Down damaging another. The Hurricanes were then jumped by a formation of fifty Messerschmitt Me 109s.[1] The others dived into the cloud cover and escaped, but Soden turned and fired into the mass of enemy fighters, shooting one down before half rolling away and diving for home. Soden was later awarded a posthumous DSO for this action, one of the first to be won by Fighter Command in the second war.

The next 'bit of excitement' came in the middle of the afternoon. A Dornier 17 attacked the aerodrome, dropping a 500 lb bomb, which luckily did no damage. Soden, Higginson and a pilot of 226 Squadron were on duty as 'flap flight' and lost no time in getting off to chase the Dornier, which had turned for a second pass across the aerodrome. Seeing Soden's Hurricane climbing towards him, the German pilot

---

1. Although technically inaccurate, the Messerschmitt Bf 109 and Bf 110 have been designated Me 109 and Me 110 to avoid a conflict of the terms used in Michael's diaries.

quickly turned away, but Soden was on his tail at once and the watchers on the ground heard the Hurricane's eight Brownings open fire before the two aeroplanes disappeared behind the trees bordering the aerodrome. Soden landed twenty minutes later, having shot down the Dornier, which had crashed in a field near Douai.

B Flight patrolled the Brussels to Ghent area the next day, destroying a lone Dornier between them, and around lunchtime a number of pilots from other squadrons began to arrive at Vitry, awaiting transport to take them on leave. Among these were two ex-56 Squadron stalwarts, Sergeant Hillwood and Pilot Officer Leonid 'Minney' Ereminsky, and, red tape being swept aside, they were taken back into 56 Squadron. Ereminsky, a white Russian who had lived in England since childhood, had left the squadron earlier in the year, volunteering to go to France with No 615 Squadron, a Gladiator squadron.

In the afternoon, Tommy Rose, Barry Sutton, and Pilot Officer Dillon from 226 Squadron, took off from Vitry to meet and escort a formation of bombers. They had barely retracted their undercarriages when they were jumped from behind by Me 109s. Barry Sutton, wounded in the foot, and despite his low height, half rolled away and managed to return to Vitry, his Hurricane badly shot about, but Tommy Rose was shot down and killed at Brebières, east of the aerodrome. Dillon was also killed by the 109s.

That evening Soden shot down another Heinkel from a formation of three, and at 7.00 pm, Taffy Higginson, Cliff Whitehead and Minney Ereminsky engaged a force of Messerschmitt 110s south of Vitry and destroyed four. But while the Hurricanes were fighting the 110s, which were evidently a decoy force, a number of Dorniers attacked their base at Vitry. One Hurricane was destroyed on the ground, but Ian Soden ran to another, belonging to 226 Squadron, and took off amidst exploding bombs and petrol drums. He was never seen again. In two days of fighting Ian Soden had shot down six enemy aeroplanes: an airfighter in the great tradition of his squadron.

By 21 May the AASF had virtually ceased to exist as a fighting unit: most of its aeroplanes had been lost in the fighting or destroyed on the ground and the pilots and ground personnel were ordered to make their way back to England. B Flight 56 Squadron had evacuated Vitry at 11.00 pm on the night of 18 May, and flown to Norrent Fontes. After a night spent sleeping in a barn, Higginson was told to return to the aerodrome at Vitry and destroy what aeroplanes and stores remained. He and Whitehead found only one flyable Hurricane still at Vitry and it was flown off by a pilot of another squadron before they destroyed the rest by firing repeated revolver shots into the petrol tanks. They then destroyed the petrol stores, setting thousands of gallons ablaze. Higginson and Whitehead finally left Vitry when the advancing enemy was only three or four miles from the aerodrome.

While these stirring events were taking place Michael was still at North Weald, miserable at not being with the flight in France. He had ferried a replacement Hurricane to Glisy on 16 May, returning to North Weald in an Anson, but had taken no other part in the operation. Although he realized he was the least experienced of the flight, and therefore the least fitted to go, he longed to join the others instead of kicking his heels at North Weald, acting as adjutant.

When the telephone rang one morning, the speaker announcing himself as Group and asking for news of B Flight, Michael saw his chance. After answering Group's question he began to extol the virtues of an extremely promising young pilot officer, by name, Constable Maxwell. By some oversight this young pilot officer had been left behind and really should be allowed to join the rest of his flight in France. Group listened patiently, asking all manner of questions about this brilliant young pilot. Michael, who above all 'wanted to chase Germans', had no qualms regarding false modesty, and shot a terrific line. 'Of course, he was leading me on ... I didn't care two hoots about the private line shoot, or being modest. I was using any means, fair or foul, of joining my flight.'

At the end of the conversation, when Michael had exhausted the not inconsiderable list of virtues possessed by this amazing young pilot, the unknown officer at Group asked if by any faint chance the speaker happened to be the Constable Maxwell in question. Michael was forced to admit that he was. Group roared with laughter and rang off. Unbeknown to Michael he had been speaking to 'Beery' Bowman, Gerald's old companion and fellow flight commander of 1917, who had himself used similar unscrupulous methods to get back into action when forbidden to fly as a squadron commander in 1918. Bowman no doubt reflected that fighter pilots had changed very little in twenty five years and that the traditions of his old squadron were in good hands.

Taffy Higginson, Ereminsky and Peter Down finally arrived back at North Weald 'loaded with bottles, dirty, unshaven and worn out'. Michael was extremely upset by the news of the deaths of Ian Soden and Tommy Rose, but 'absolutely thrilled' by the sight of Peter Down: 'We'd heard he'd been killed, but to my joy he gets out of a battered plane, laden with champagne and a four day beard.' Michael, eager

and keen, asked Higginson if there had been any of the thrills, the
sense of fun and glamour of the last war.

'I will never forget his words. He looked at me with steady eyes.
"No", he said. "It was just sheer bloody hell and terror from start to
finish".'

Michael made his first operational flight on 23 May: an offensive
patrol in the Merville, Lille, Arras, Bethune area. The Hurricanes
were attacked by three Me 109s over Merville, and chased a He 126
between Calais and St Omer before losing it in the cloud cover. They
then attacked twelve Messerschmitt Bf 110s, a twin engined, two seat
fighter a little faster than the Hurricane. Michael chased one of the
110s without result. 'I let off a thousand rounds or so but he got into
cloud.' Turning back, Michael found himself in the middle of six of the
enemy fighters and lost no time diving into the cloud himself. He later
wrote to his mother:

> You may remember the Ballad of Culloden – 'Cannon and drums,
> the Frasers are leaving'. It was fascinating seeing a German plane
> for the first time. It was just like a first shot at a goose. You fire and
> presume it will come down – of course, it doesn't!

Events in the ground war in France had now reached a crisis. By 20
May the German 2nd Panzer Division had thrust to the coast at
Abbeville, trapping the BEF and three French armies, and it
advanced north during the next three days, capturing Boulogne and
isolating Calais. With the annihilation of the Allied armies within his
grasp, General Guderian, commanding the 2nd Panzer Division, was
ordered by Hitler to halt his advance, and Lord Gort seized the
opportunity to establish a perimeter defence around the small port of
Dunkirk. When the German advance recommenced on the morning of
27 May, the exhausted but resolute troops in the perimeter held off the
German army for seven days, while over eight hundred strangely
assorted ships evacuated the troops from the beaches of Dunkirk.
Tugs, motor launches, yachts, pleasure steamers, lifeboats, drifters,
trawlers – any vessel capable of carrying a cargo of troops, however
small, was pressed into service. Together with the destroyers and
capital ships of the Royal Navy this flotilla of small craft brought
338,226 troops – mainly British – home to England.

Keith Park maintained a constant shuttle of fighter patrols over the
beaches of Dunkirk, using his forward airfields in Kent. 56 Squadron
was engaged in sweeps behind the beachhead and saw little of the

actual fighting over the beaches – although Michael remembered the huge column of black smoke from Dunkirk which stretched completely across the Channel, thinking that if he were bounced he could easily escape into it and fly all the way home – but on 27 May the squadron patrolled between St Omer and Calais in an attempt to engage the enemy aeroplanes before they could reach the beaches. Taking off from Mansion at 3.30 pm they attacked ten Heinkel IIIs near Dunkirk. Squadron Leader Knowles shot down one, claiming another as inconclusive, and Baker, Fisher and Ereminsky shot down another between them. Michael was shot down.

Michael had first seen the Heinkels at 10,000 feet over Ostend. He was slightly behind the rest of the Hurricanes and he attacked a lone Heinkel a hundred yards behind its companions. Michael closed to 250 yards, just below the enemy bomber, and fired a ten second burst. Smoke began to pour from the Heinkel's fuselage, both its wheels came down and the gunner in the turret under the fuselage stopped firing. As Michael turned away a great deal of oil from the stricken Heinkel suddenly covered his windscreen, obliterating his forward vision, and he lost sight of the bomber.

Events then happened with startling suddenness. An Me 109 made a hurried and unsuccessful pass at the Hurricane and Michael had no sooner evaded this, and was chasing after the enemy fighter, when there was an 'almighty bang and smoke all round'. The Hurricane fell away, refusing to answer the controls. Michael decided it was time to leave. He slammed back the canopy and as the Hurricane turned over onto its back he was shot out – 'like a champagne cork'. Tugging at various parts of his parachute harness, Michael finally found the ripcord and pulled hard. His parachute blossomed out above him, checking his descent with a violent jerk.

Gliding gently down, Michael was surprised to feel quite calm and detached. 'What a fool', he thought. 'I ought to have made sure where the ripcord is *before* departure.' Below him a battle appeared to be in progress, and he watched the gun flashes with interest while he calmly timed his descent – fourteen minutes. On hitting the ground he was dragged twenty or thirty feet before he managed to free himself from his harness and struggle to his feet. He was startled to find himself surrounded by a number of unshaven and ferocious looking soldiers in unfamiliar uniforms. A ring of rifles pointed at him and everyone looked extremely unfriendly.

Michael explained, in French, that he was an RAF pilot, but his speech brought nothing but blank, hostile stares and a slight but menacing movement of the raised rifles. An officer now appeared, and Michael realized with relief that the soldiers were Belgian, and probably spoke only Flemish. His troubles were far from over, however. The officer was equally suspicious. Tales of fifth columnists and saboteurs were rife and he insisted that Michael show some proof of his identity. Michael had no papers and had left his identity discs at North Weald. Before taking off he had changed into an old tunic and had not even an initialled handkerchief to show the suspicious Belgians. On Michael's confessing this, the rifles were immediately lowered, there were broad grins all round and he was enthusiastically hugged and kissed on both cheeks by the bristly troops.

'You *must* be English,' explained the officer. 'Only the English would go to war like this'.

The troops had seen the Heinkel crash in a field a short distance away and they all set out to view the remains. But on the way a car drew up, and after exchanging a few words with Michael's new friends, an officer in the car informed Michael that His Royal Highness, Prince Charles of the Belgians, would like to see him. Feeling the situation was becoming a little unreal – in the space of twenty or thirty minutes he had shot down a Heinkel, been shot down himself, baled out of a Hurricane, nearly been shot by friendly troops, and was now being summoned to an audience with royalty – Michael was driven to a nearby anti-aircraft battery. Here he found Prince Charles, who was in charge of the battery and who apologized profusely for being the cause of Michael's predicament. His guns had been firing at enemy aeroplanes all morning, he ruefully admitted, and Michael's Hurricane was the first aeroplane they had managed to hit.

General conversation continued for a while in a friendly, relaxed fashion, until Michael mentioned that his parents had had the honour of once meeting those of the Prince. Prince Charles evidently considered this overstepped the bounds of protocol a little and, although still polite, became a little distant. Michael sensed this change of attitude in the Prince and hastened to explain the circumstances of the occasion. On a visit to Scotland some years before, the King and Queen had stayed with his uncle and aunt, Lord and Lady Lovat, at Beaufort Castle, and Michael's parents had dined there with them. The Prince relaxed once more. He remembered the visit and recalled how much his parents had enjoyed it.

Prince Charles was extremely worried by the rapidity of the German advance and the grave situation which was now developing. He advised Michael that it was imperative that he lose no time in making his way back to England. He placed a car and an officer at Michael's disposal, gave him a pass, and Michael set off for Ostend, reaching the port in the late afternoon. Michael's companion found a trawler. It was not leaving until after dark, he explained, to avoid the German E boats, but he must get back to his battery. Before leaving could he have a souvenir of the occasion – perhaps Michael's parachute? Michael pointed out that a parachute cost £80. Converting this into francs, the officer agreed that this was rather a lot and suggested Michael's flying helmet instead. 'I said that this was not worthy of him (costing only 40/-) and gave him my pipe. He was delighted.'

While Michael waited to board the boat, Ostend was twice dive bombed by Stukas, Michael watching with professional interest as the Stukas screamed down on the harbour. 'I rather enjoyed it as I could see the bombs before they got down and thus could see if they were likely to be close.'

Boarding the trawler at 10.30 pm, Michael was astonished but delighted to find the captain was a Highlander, who had been Head Forester on the Lovat estates before the first war. On learning Michael's identity the captain insisted that he have his own cabin for the journey – the only cabin on the tiny boat – brushing aside Michael's objections that there must be people aboard more deserving than himself. Among the troops, VIPs and refugees aboard the trawler was a young army lieutenant, and he shared the cabin with Michael, although the captain insisted that Michael had the bed and the young lieutenant the chair. In the event they had no sleep. No sooner had they left Ostend, dodging the flares dropped by German aircraft, than the trawler was attacked by a German E boat, which fired two torpedoes. Luckily the trawler had a shallow draught, the torpedoes passed harmlessly underneath her, and all aboard opened fire with rifles, the ship's Lewis gun, and a captured German machine gun. Under this fusillade the return fire from the E Boat stopped and it hove to. Michael was all for taking it prisoner, but wiser counsel prevailed – the captain pointing out they were only half a mile from the coast – and the trawler continued on its course for England, reaching Deal the next morning.

On landing they learnt that Belgium had capitulated a few hours before. They had escaped just in time.

Michael was astonished and gratified at the warmth of the reception he received on his safe return to the squadron. He was heartily congratulated on his escape and drinks pressed into his hand. The CO suggested that he take the next day off and Michael rang Gerald.

'You've been posted missing,' said the delighted Gerald. 'We all thought you were dead. You'd better ring mother'.

Michael's mother had been entertaining guests when the telegram had arrived in its dramatic blood red envelope marked 'Priority'. She excused herself and quietly opened it.

'Regret to inform you that your son', read the first page . . . she turned to the second . . . 'Pilot Officer Michael Hugh Constable Maxwell is reported missing as the result of air operations on 27 May 1940. Letter follows. Any further information will be immediately communicated to you.'

Michael's mother refolded the telegram and returned her attention to her guests. She said nothing to them. She had no wish to embarrass them or burden them with her private grief and anxieties for her youngest son.

While Michael had been making his way back from Belgium, the squadron had not been inactive. Later the same day it had flown another patrol, engaging forty to fifty Me 110s over Dunkirk. Squadron Leader Knowles shot down two, with Cooney and George Smythe both claiming inconclusive victories. Fish Fisher failed to return from this patrol, but he turned up later and was taken to hospital in Margate.

Twelve Hurricanes patrolled the beaches again the following day, but saw no enemy aircraft, and on the afternoon of 29 May, the squadron flew a combined action with Nos 151, 264 and 213 Squadrons. Patrolling between Dunkirk and Furnes the squadron attacked a large force of Stukas, Heinkel 111s and Me 109s, and George Smythe shot down a Stuka. Pilot Officer Dryden was shot down and forced to crash-land on the beach, later making his way back to England by boat. A similar patrol, later that evening, met with the same varied opposition, with Taffy Higginson and Minney Ereminsky each claiming an Me 109. Coghlan attacked two Junkers Ju 88s, causing both to smoke, and they were classified as inconclusive. 'Charlie' Baker attacked a Heinkel 111, which also smoked before he lost sight of it. To offset these successes Sergeant Elliott failed to return and was posted missing.

Michael flew two patrols on 30 May, but although 56 and 151 Squadrons patrolled the Dunkirk beaches no enemy aircraft were seen. On the last day of May, 56 Squadron was withdrawn to Digby for a well earned rest, returning to North Weald on 4 June. A patrol was flown on 6 June, which saw an indecisive skirmish with a number of 109s, neither side gaining any result.

On 8 June 56 and 151 Squadron flew as escort to a formation of Blenheims which were to attack targets in the Abbeville area. Michael had been told that elements of his old regiment, the 4th Camerons, were still fighting in the St Valery area – they capitulated the next day – and as the Hurricanes and Blenheims roared over the enemy coast, amidst continuous anti-aircraft fire, he was thrilled to think he was part of this force which was helping to protect old friends, some of whom he had helped to recruit and train.

Landing back at Manston, the forward base, the squadron was told that another escort had been laid on for the early afternoon. The Hurricanes took off at ten to four, but the Blenheims had missed the rendezvous and gone on ahead. The Hurricanes flew to Le Treport, hoping to meet the bombers on their return, but were bounced by a number of 109s, which made a quick pass before climbing away. Without warning, cannon shells smashed into Michael's Hurricane, the splinters wounding him in the leg and foot. Anxiously trying the controls, Michael found that the Hurricane was still flyable – just – and he decided to try to make it back to North Weald. The Blenheims now appeared and Michael closed up with them, hoping they would report his position if he were forced to land in the sea, but their guns swivelled round in his direction and he hurriedly banked away. Michael soaked his handkerchief in the blood from his leg and again closed in to the bombers, waving it at them. The nearest crew now realised his predicament and allowed him to tuck in close to them.

Arriving back at North Weald, Michael found that the Hurricane was difficult to land. 'Instead of easing back the stick as the speed got down to approach speed, I had to get it further and further forward, because the nose wanted to rise. I landed with the stick almost fully forward. I had only one elevator and only half a tailplane.'

George Smythe was one of the pilots watching as Michael brought the crippled Hurricane in to land. The rest of the patrol had been split up by the attack of the 109s and had all landed earlier. 'It was obvious that his aircraft had been badly shot up. One of his tyres burst on landing and he slewed towards the hangars and finished up near our maintenance hangars. We all rushed across from dispersal to help get him out. The maintenance crew from the hangar got there first. By the time I arrived he was out of the cockpit and being helped down the wing. He had been slightly injured in one foot and blood was oozing out of his flying boot, leaving bloody footmarks on the wing. One of the young groundcrew who was helping him down noticed this and said in an awed voice. "Blimey, I fort it was blue." Constable Maxwell glanced down at his foot and replied somewhat ruefully. "Oh no, my dear fellow, I can assure you it is good ordinary red stuff – always has been." '

Wing Commander Victor Beamish, now Station Commander at North Weald, was also on hand to help Michael from the badly damaged Hurricane and he warmly congratulated him on successfully bringing the aeroplane back in such a state. A man could stand with his head and shoulders through the smashed tailplane, and Michael readily admitted that it was 'rather tatty'.

Michael was taken to Epping hospital to have his wound attended to. George Smythe recalls: 'He had unbelievable courage amounting, in our view as staid 26 year old NCO pilots, almost to foolhardiness. He would, tackle anything German that flew with unquenchable enthusiasm and in the early stages frequently came off worst, arriving back at base with his aircraft riddled.'

After the capitulation of the Belgian forces and the evacuation of the BEF from Dunkirk, the fighting in France continued for a further two weeks, the German army mopping up the remainder of the Allied forces. Those that escaped, including the remnants of several RAF squadrons, did so from ports in south west France, but the final cost was high. The RAF had lost nearly a thousand aeroplanes in the battle of France, in addition to the sixty six lost in the ill fated Norwegian campaign: nearly two-thirds of its total allotment since the beginning of hostilities.

On 18 June, the French asked for an armistice. The war in France was over. Great Britain now stood alone.

With the German forces now in command of the coast of Europe, from Norway to the tip of Spain, invasion of Great Britain seemed inevitable. In the eyes of the German High Command, and to many neutral countries, Great Britain's position seemed hopeless; defeat merely a matter of time. At a meeting of Hitler and his Chiefs of Staff on 20 June, it was agreed that as a prelude to a successful invasion of the southern coast of England, air superiority was a prime essential.

For the air attack on Britain the Luftwaffe mustered three Luftflotten: Nos 2, 3 and 5. Luftflotte 2 moved into bases in Holland, Belgium and north-east France; Luftflotte 3 to north-western France; while Luftflotte 5 – which was to undertake only a minor role in the operations against Britain – operated from bases in Norway and Denmark.

Luftflotten 2 and 3 – the RAF's main protagonists – had a total of

1,800 aeroplanes with which to launch the attack. This massive force consisted of 1,000 bombers and dive bombers, 650 single-engined fighters and 160 twin-engined, long range fighters. Between this vast armada and defeat for Great Britain stood RAF Fighter Command with just over 500 operational and serviceable aeroplanes. In July 1940 the survival of Great Britain and the civilized world rested with the skill and courage of just over 1250 young fighter pilots; the groundcrews that kept them flying, and the generalship and prescience of their leaders, primarily Air Chief Marshal Hugh Dowding and Air Vice Marshal Keith Park. It would be a long, hard and bloody summer.

CHAPTER XII

Battle Over Britain

'Never in the field of human conflict was
so much owed by so many to so few'.

Winston Churchill August 1940.

'The Prime Minister must have been thinking
of our Mess bills.'

Pilot Officer, 56 Squadron. 1940.

Michael rejoined 56 Squadron at North Weald on 9 July. The squadron was now commanded by Squadron Leader G. A. L. Manton and there were several other changes. Flight Lieutenant John Coghlin now led A Flight and Michael's new flight commander was Flight Lieutenant E. J. Gracie. Gracie – known as 'Jumbo', which suited his shortlegged ungraceful waddlings admirably – was popular from the very start, despite his outspokenness and intolerance of unsuccessful pilots, however hard they tried. Effort counted little with Gracie; results were all that mattered. On his arrival at 56 he had quickly absorbed its traditions and upheld them to the great benefit of the entire squadron. If his faults were obvious his qualities as a leader were thrown into greater relief. 'He has great guts, not much fear and a wonderful persistency and continual keenness. He has the elements of greatness in him'. Squadron Leader Manton, being inexperienced, deferred to 'Slim' Coghlin and Jumbo Gracie, who virtually commanded 56 Squadron between them. All three got on well personally – 'which did credit to the three of them'.

Old friends were still much in evidence; the sergeant pilots still a solid nucleus, Taffy Higginson, George Smythe, Cliff Whitehead and Peter Hillwood being now pilots of considerable experience. Barry Sutton, recovered from his wound, had rejoined, and new arrivals included Pilot Officers Geoffrey Page and P. S. 'Squeak' Weaver.

In July 1940, with the Luftwaffe not yet fully established in its new bases, its main attacks were mounted against shipping in the English Channel and the Channel ports. This tactic had a dual purpose: to deny the Channel to British shipping and secondly, to draw the

British fighters into the air to protect the all important convoys, and thus into combat with the escorting German fighters. It was essential that the German fighter pilots met their opponents under circumstances favourable to themselves. The British would certainly refuse to commit their fighters over France, where any losses – both in terms of men and machines – would be irretrievable, and the best the Luftwaffe could expect would be to meet the British fighters over the Channel, whose waters would close over friend and foe alike. Given the numerical superiority of the German fighter force, this would in time had the desired effect of decimating the British fighters.

Michael's first operational patrol on rejoining the squadron was a convoy protection patrol on the afternoon of 15 July. Fighter Command was now flying continuous protection patrols during the hours of daylight, the squadrons operating from the forward airfields on the Kent and Essex coasts. Each squadron was at readiness throughout the day, flying back to its main base in the evening, their companion squadron being on duty the following day. 56 Squadron, at readiness at Manston, was scrambled at 1.30. The Kent radar stations had plotted a raid building up and 11 Group ordered up three sections of Hurricanes.

The clouds at 2,000 feet were extremely thick. The three Hurricanes – Gracie, Higginson and Michael – had difficulty in finding the enemy bombers, but Michael suddenly saw them.

I suddenly see huge black shapes dive down at the convoy. There's a shout of 'There they are' and we are off at them flat out. It is the most sickening and awful sight seeing those angels of death diving upon the ships. There is a huge burst of flame from the biggest ship and a smaller one from another. I have a horribly strong fear of an unexpected attack from behind with the sickening crash of cannon and machine gun fire that I experienced over the Somme.

Luckily the heavy cloud frustrated the efforts of the fighter escort and the three Hurricanes drove off the enemy bombers – Dornier Do 17s from KG 2. Higginson and Gracie each claimed a probable from a confused combat in the clouds.

On Saturday 20 July B Flight was again ordered off on a convoy patrol: Gracie leading Michael, Page and Weaver. Michael's propeller refused to move from fine pitch and he was forced to return, but the others caught a Ju 88 of KG 4 and shot it down to crash near St Osyth, all four of the crew being taken prisoner.

Michael flew an interception on 23 July, the flight being vectored to ten miles south east of Clacton at 12,000 feet, but seeing no action. He flew a convoy patrol on 24 July with a section from A Flight, but again saw no sign of enemy aircraft.

Sunday 28 July was fine after the summer storms of the previous day. In anticipation of heavy raids, 11 Group moved eight squadrons to its forward airfields in Kent. 56 Squadron flew patrols throughout the day to protect a damaged destroyer which was being towed to Chatham.

> We take off at 4.20 – while still dark – and go on patrol over a damaged destroyer off N. Foreland. The whole of B Flight go. I am on Gracie's left with Page on his right. We cross the coast and find the destroyer being towed by a tug. We stay there for an hour and then go to Rochford. We continue the patrol throughout the morning and when we are relieved at 1.30 it had almost reached Chatham and safety. I feel we have done a good and complete morning's work. I rather enjoy the whole operation.

There was a relative lull in the airfighting during the first week in August, brought about mainly by British tactics. Dowding and Park had realised German intentions in respect of their fighter force and the convoys now sailed mainly at night – especially through the Straits of Dover. By day, free chasing groups of Me 109s roamed at will along the Channel and over south-east England, attempting to draw Dowding's fighters into the air, but he frustrated these aims by ignoring the provocation. Bombers were the important targets for Fighter Command and until these appeared in force the British fighters would stay on the ground. Meanwhile, Dowding used this hiatus to build up his strength in aeroplanes and pilots. In late July, Fighter Command began to make good its deficiencies. By 1 August it had improved its numbers of operational pilots by an additional 214, to a total of 1414, and allied with increased output from the aeroplane factories, this showed a considerable improvement in the strength of Fighter Command for the stern task which it still faced. But if there was an improvement in quantity, the quality still gave cause for anxiety. Many of Fighter Command's pilots were inexperienced. The fighting in France, and during July, had drained the squadrons of over eighty experienced squadron and flight commanders – men of the calibre of Ian Soden – and this became one of Dowding's chief causes of concern as the battle wore on.

Michael flew two patrols during the first week of August, neither of which saw any action, but on 11 August the flight was scrambled to intercept a Dornier. The Hurricanes failed to find the enemy bomber and were vectored to guard a convoy. Sergeant Baker became separated from the others and was next seen going down with glycol pouring from his aeroplane. He baled out and was seen to land safely in the sea.

Three of us try to help him. Weaver circles round, keeping him in sight – a most difficult thing as the turning circle of the Hurricane is too big and the aircraft is on the verge of spinning all the time. Another tried to get the ships over, while I fly above watching for any hostile aircraft. It is extremely hard to keep an eye on a Mae West in the water as it is so small and one is unable to circle it slowly enough. After a destroyer failed to reach him a motorboat picks him up, largely through the efforts of Weaver. He is in the water for an hour and does not recover.

August 12 dawned fine. With the forecast of continued fine weather the Luftwaffe stepped up its attacks during the day, mounting raids against the important radar stations on the south coast. These attacks were relatively successful. Three stations were put out of action for six hours and during this period the German bombers attacked Fighter Command's forward airfields at Lympne and Hawkinge.

At 12.50 eighteen Dorniers from KG 2, escorted by Me 109s, attacked the advanced airfield at Manston. Manston, on the North Foreland of Kent, was used by those fighter squadrons of 11 Group whose bases were further inland, and the Spitfires of 65 Squadron were actually taking off as the Dorniers and Messerschmitts swept over the airfield, leaving a swath of destruction in their wake. Over a hundred and fifty bombs were dropped on the station, destroying the workshops, two hangars, and badly cratering the airfield itself.

Fifty-six Squadron was scrambled at 12.45, but arrived too late to catch the raiders and the Hurricanes landed at Rochford, refuelled and came to readiness.

Rochford, near Southend, was a pleasant airfield, the dispersal consisting of a bell tent, a telephone and a number of chairs and tables. After lunch the pilots lounged in the chairs or lay in the grass in the hot sun, talking over the events of the morning and waiting for the next raid to develop. The long, hot afternoon dragged on and the tea wagon was a welcome diversion. Michael, Taffy Higginson and Geoffrey

Page, sat at a small table, Page amusing himself by dropping dollops of strawberry jam on the wasps attracted by the remnants of tea, voicing his two expressions of 'jolly good' and 'bang, bang' each time he scored a hit. Michael and Higginson laughed at this game, dryly observing that he might well come to a sticky end like the wasps.

Then, with startling suddenness, the telephone rang. Gracie snatched off the receiver: 'Scramble! Angels One Five.' Almost before he had finished shouting everyone was running hard for the Hurricanes, the Merlins already bursting into life. Parachutes lying ready on the tailplanes were slipped on with a practised movement; into the cockpit from the port side as the groundcrew leaves on the starboard; goggles and helmet snatched from the gunsight as the straps are tightened. Within minutes the Hurricanes were off, climbing rapidly towards the Thames Estuary, Gracie leading with Michael No 2 and Page No 3.

Over the Estuary they sighted the enemy bombers: Dorniers of Luftflotte 2 escorted by Me 109s.

It is a wonderful sight. A huge black mass in three vics of nine each. It is an exhilarating moment. There is no chance of missing them; we will soon be in battle, a feeling one would get after starting down the Cresta.

The Dorniers bore slightly north. We go into Echelon Right and come at them from the port side. Before we reach them we are astern and Gracie goes flat out at them, diving slightly below – and then up up up.

Michael glanced across at Geoffrey Page. Page grinned back and gaily thumbed his nose, echoing the 'sign of the Romans' painted on his Hurricane: his 'precious Little Willie'. Michael saw the Me 109s above, but concentrated on the bombers, leaving the escorting fighters to be tackled by the three rear sections of Hurricanes.

The formation of the Dorniers is superb. No Hendon display was better. Close and tight, their fire control is perfect. Two second bursts of tracer from every gunner converge on Gracie. Gracie breaks away. Page and I attack when suddenly an Me 109 passes me on my left, quite close. He is painted yellow and going fast, straight at Page. I turn at him and give him a long deflection shot. Suddenly he jinks violently and breaks away downward. I see a parachute, but follow the 109 down. It may be Page, it may be the

109. I go down some thousands of feet, but am left behind. I avoid another 109 but do not get a shot at him. I had a shot at the bombers and a long burst at the 109, so go down to sea level and then home, thinking I am out of ammunition, and anyway, too far below.

Page had been hit by the concentrated fire from the Dorniers. The header tank above the engine blew up and filled his cockpit with flames. Page, burnt on the hands and face, kicked at the stick as the Hurricane rolled over and fell out. His trousers and one shoe had been blown off and he was wounded in the leg. With his badly burnt hands he had some difficulty in pulling the ripcord, falling 14,000 feet before he finally succeeded – a thousand feet above the sea and ten miles north of Margate. He was finally rescued by the Margate lifeboat, vainly trying to swim, blinded by the swollen and blistered flesh around his eyes, his hands burned to the bone. Michael had recorded Geoffrey Page as the keenest member of the squadron: 'He hates going on leave and can only think of fighting. He has done well, getting several planes down, and is very self-confident,' but behind this brave front Page had written to a friend: 'It's only an hour before dawn. To me it will mean just another day of butchery . . . it makes me feel sick . . . how will it all end?'

Barry Sutton, his Hurricane streaming glycol, force-landed at Manston. Squeak Weaver landed safely, but his Hurricane, 'Oswald' was badly damaged and written off. 56 Squadron claimed two victories from this engagement: a Dornier by Weaver and a 109 by George Smythe.

August 13, – 'Eagle Day' to the Luftwaffe, the day designated for the beginning of the major assault – was mainly fair, but cloud developed as the day wore on, with large formations of bombers attacking Sheerness and Eastchurch in the morning. The German fighters carried out their customary free chases during a later raid against Odiham and Farnborough, and during the afternoon a massive formation of nearly three hundred bombers and fighters attacked Southampton and the airfields at Middle Wallop and Warmwell. Further to the east the Ju 88s of Luftflotte 2 mounted an attack on Rochester. 56 Squadron had been at readiness on the airfield since 12.30 and was scrambled at 3.30.

With Gracie leading the squadron, Michael flew in the second section with 'Dopey' Davies and George Smythe.

We come up through the clouds at 5,000 feet on the south side of the river. There, right above us, are the Bandits. As soon as they are shown to Jumbo, who never sees anything, he turns to the right and climbs up into the sun. Davies carries on after doing an S turn to gain height, then straight in after the Ju 88s. There are twenty of them in wide formation going south, diving slightly. We follow Dopey, steaming on, his eyes glued to the bombers. I have my plug out, but the cautious Dopey keeps at plus 2 boost to be on the safe side. We cross the bombers' slipstream. It annoys me to an astonishing degree that Germans are using British air. It is my first real feeling that the Germans are trespassing.

There are a large number of Me 109s above us. Smythe and I both tell Davies, but he does not hear, perhaps we did it together. My eyes are glued on the 109s above and as soon as I see them starting to dive on us I break away and up hard. Smythe does the same. The last I see of Dopey is his well masked and goggled head crouching intently as he gazes at the receding Ju 88s. I turn right round and face the diving 109s, which hurtle past and then up. After several of their attacks I go down a few thousand feet in a spiral. The bombers are out of sight. Straight above are about forty 109s and one Hurricane. The whole sight is so commonplace and natural. Forty odd aircraft are wheeling aimlessly, slowly, like so many plovers on a windy day. Yet it is a fight for life.

The Ju 88s were scattered by the squadron's attack, jettisoning their bombs over Kent, but the Hurricanes had been roughly handled by the escorting Me 109s. Joubert had bailed out, slightly wounded; Peter Hillwood, shot down over the Thames Estuary, swam two and a half miles to the shore; Dopey Davies had baled out near Rochford, badly burned; and 'Boy' Brooker crash landed at Hawkinge. Although one source gives credit to 56 Squadron for damaging seven Me 110s, Michael's diary makes no mention of the twin engined German fighter, and it seems more likely that the squadron's successes were three Me 109s of JG 51: one crashing, the two others crash-landing at Calais and Coquelles.

The squadron was scrambled again the next day, patrolling Manston at 20,000 feet. No enemy aeroplanes were sighted, but Michael, overshooting on an inside turn and making a quick circuit to regain position, caused some chaos, everyone thinking the enemy had been sighted.

August 15 was a day of heavy and concentrated attacks, the Luftwaffe flying over 2,000 sorties (each aircraft being counted as a sortie) and it was a day of heavy casualties, later known to the Luftwaffe crews as 'Black Thursday'.

Fifty-six Squadron was scrambled from Rochford at 11.20 am. A large raid was building up and the squadron was again ordered to patrol Manston at 20,000 feet. Some Me 109s on a free chase suddenly appeared, the first sections climbing away, but the rear attacking the Hurricanes, shooting down a South African pilot, L. W. Graham, damaging Mounsdon's aeroplane and 'frightening Brooker'.

The squadron flew to Rochford early the next day and throughout the morning flew convoy protection patrols. In the evening, talking over with Wing Commander Victor Beamish the combats of the last few days, the pilots bemoaned their casualties, offset by very little success.

'Don't worry', Beamish assured them. 'Your luck will change.'

As he spoke the telephone rang, the squadron were ordered to readiness and forty minutes later the Hurricanes were climbing hard towards Chelmsford, the controller's calm voice informing them: 'Forty bandits approaching from south east.' Then, a moment later, 'Seventy bandits approaching from south.' And then, yet again: '*Many* bandits approaching.'

The twelve Hurricanes climbed up through cloud, Michael flying with Taffy Higginson and Barry Sutton.

> We go up and up. We emerge through the clouds at 6,000 and there, straight above us, is a veritable armada. There are seventy plus signalled and they seem to go up in layers and layers.

Squeak Weaver, leading, ordered B Flight to tackle the escorting fighters, A Flight the bombers, and the fight broke up into scattered actions.

Michael and Taffy Higginson engaged a pair of Dorniers, separated from the others, Michael attacking the bomber on the right, Higginson the one on the left.

> I get below and come up firing from 250 to about ten yards, nearly hitting it. I turn hard right and he turns hard left. I again get on his tail and rain bullets at him. It is a Dornier Do 215 and for a heavy bomber does staggering aerobatics. He does a stall turn, steep turns and a half roll. I fire off 2,000 rounds from twenty five yards, but do not appear to do him much damage. He half rolls and I am going too fast and overshoot and he goes down past another

Hurricane and then vertically into the clouds. This is depressing as I don't seem to have done much harm, but Wicks reports shooting down a badly damaged Dornier, which is possibly the same one.

Taffy Higginson succeeded in shooting down his Dornier, but his Hurricane was badly damaged by the rear gunner's return fire, and Higginson force landed at Whitstable, the Hurricane skidding and smashing along the ground for a hundred yards before stopping and bursting into flames. Higginson scrambled clear, unhurt.

Barry Sutton claimed a 109 and another damaged from this action, the squadron claiming nine victories in all for the loss of one pilot, L. W. Graham, who baled out slightly wounded. The squadron's luck *was* changing.

Michael did not fly on the 18th, but the squadron continued its run of good luck. Patrolling the Canterbury area in the morning, it attacked a formation of Me 110s of ZG 26, part of the covering escort for a number of raids being carried out on Biggin Hill and Kenley. Peter Down, Squeak Weaver, Mounsdon and Robinson all shot down an Me 110, while Innes Westmacott, a recent arrival, shared another with Cliff Whitehead. Patrolling Manston later in the day, the squadron intercepted a large force of Dorniers and Heinkels over West Mersea. Weaver claimed a Heinkel and Sergeant Robinson damaged another. Higginson shot down a Dornier; and Gracie, the CO, Westmacott and Mounsdon each damaged a 110 from the escort. There were no casualties.

The squadron was scrambled to intercept an 'X' raid on 19 August, but failed to make contact in the heavy cloud and returned to North Weald. Michael flew a convoy patrol the next day with Cliff Whitehead and Peter Hillwood, followed by an offensive patrol in the afternoon, but neither patrol saw any action, a pattern which was repeated the following day. Another convoy patrol was flown on 22 August. Michael recorded:

It is pleasant to find the nights getting longer, entailing later risings and earlier off duty in the evenings. It will be much better in the autumn when everything is concentrated into a shorter period. It is the ages of waiting which gets on people's nerves – a battle does more good to the nerves than a week's rest. It really lets off steam and you feel better.

At a conference on 19 August, the Luftwaffe high command had

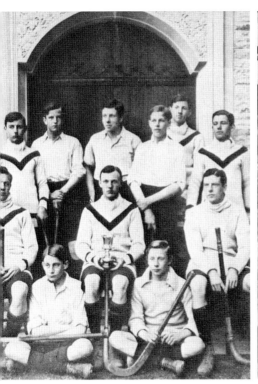

Left: Downside School. The hockey team of 1913 with Gerald second from the left. Immediately in front of Gerald is his great friend Dick Stokes, who served as a Privy Counsellor and minister in the Labour government of 1950. *Right:* Ready to leave for France. Gerald poses in front of his SE5 A 4863 at London Colney on the morning of April, 7 1917.

Nov. 1916 Date and Hour	Wind Direction and Velocity	Machine Type and No.	Passenger	Time	Height	Course	Remarks
8AM-8.12AM 11.12.16	W	M.F.L6701	Capt Hawey	12 min	500	✓ Turnkouse Hawthan	2 landings
11.12.16	W	MF.L6701	Capt Hey	10 -	"	✓ " "	2 landings
11.12.16	W	"	Solo	6 -	500	" "	" "
Total time in air for week 11/11/16: 28 min							
"	" Solo	= 6					
"	" in air since Commencement 28 -						
"	" " Solo	= 6					
12.12.16	W	MF.L6701	capt Hawey	4	500	"	1 landing
12.12.16	"	"	Solo	9	500	"	1 landing
13.12.16	"	"	"	14	900	"	1 "
13.12.16	"	"	"	20	900	"	1
13.12.16	"	"	"	20	1100	"	3 landings
13.12.16	"	"	"	13	400	"	3 "
13.12.16	"	"	"	14	400	"	4 "
14.12.16	N	"	Solo	12	700	"	1 "
14.12.16	"	"	"	14	900	"	1 "
+.12.16	"	"	"	14	1200	"	1 "
15.12.16	W	"	"	16	1200	"	1 "

Page from Gerald's logbook showing his first solo flight after only twenty two minutes of dual instruction.

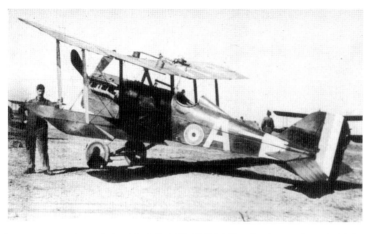

'My SE5' Gerald flew this SE5a B.502, for several months in the late summer of 1917. His rigger, Corporal Ferguson, stands by the wingtip.

Gerald taxying out at Estrée Blanche in the late summer of 1917. A photograph taken by one of his fellow Flight Commanders in 56 Squadron, Captain J. T. B. McCudden.

Airfighters. Captains J. T. B. McCudden, I. H. D. Henderson and Gerald Constable Maxwell at Estrée Blanche, August 1917.

Gerald in the cockpit of his SE5a while a fighting instructor at Ayr, Scotland. Note the camera gun on the top wing.

The Brothers. Ronnie, Ian and Gerald pose in front of a Sopwith Camel of the RNAS.

Fighting Instructors at Ayr in 1918. *L to R*. Leacroft, Atkinson, Gerald, Taylor, Le Gallais. The aeroplane is a Bristol MC1.

In the spring of 1918 the No. 1 School of Aerial Fighting at Ayr included several high scoring fighter pilots. In this group Gerald (27 victories) is on the far left, front row. Fifth from the left in the front row is Lieutenant Colonel W. B. Rees VC, commanding the school, and Captain J. T. B. McCudden (57 victories) is second from the right. Third from the left in the second row is Captain E. D. Atkinson (8 victories).

Gerald's SE5a Flight at Ayr, 1918. Gerald, with characteristic modesty, has seated himself off-centre in the group, fourth from the left. Of interest are the two members of the WAAC, the forerunners of the WRAF.

Gerald in 1918.

Three instructors at Ayr: J. T. B. McCudden, Gerald and E. L. Ziuk.

Gerald outside the mess at Valheureux during his refresher course with 56 Squadron in the summer of 1918.

A formal portrait of Gerald, now a Major, in the newly designed RAF uniform of 1918.

Left: On board the Northland for the Victory Bond tour of America in 1919. *L to R.* Captain A. W. Beauchamp-Proctor VC, DSO, MC and Bar, DFC (54 victories); Major S. E. Parker; Major F. Holliday DSC, MC, (8 victories); Gerald Joseph Constable Maxwell MC, DFC, (27 victories); Major P. F. Fullard DSO, MC and Bar, (46 victories). The photographer was the other pilot in the group, Captain H. W. Woollett DSO, MC and Bar, CC, L de H. (35 victories). *Right:* 'Carrie' at Saranac Lake, 1920.

Between the wars Gerald flew his own Hornet Moth.

Michael and Jock at Farlie.

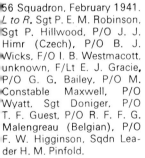

56 Squadron, February 1941.
L to R. Sgt P. E. M. Robinson,
Sgt P. Hillwood, P/O J. J.
Himr (Czech), P/O B. J.
Wicks, F/O I. B. Westmacott,
unknown, F/Lt E. J. Gracie,
P/O G. G. Bailey, P/O M.
Constable Maxwell, P/O
Wyatt, Sgt Doniger, P/O
T. F. Guest, P/O R. F. F. G.
Malengreau (Belgian), P/O
F. W. Higginson, Sqdn Lea-
der H. M. Pinfold.

Three of the Few. Sgt Pilot
Peter Hillwood DFC, Flight
Lieutenant E. J. 'Jumbo'
Gracie DFC, Pilot Officer
F. W. 'Taffy' Higginson DFC,
DFM.

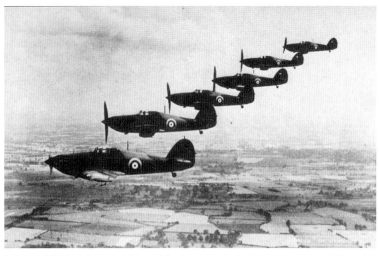

Hawker Hurricanes. 'A dream aeroplane; absolutely super'

Hawker Hurricane N.2479, 56 Squadron, April 1940.

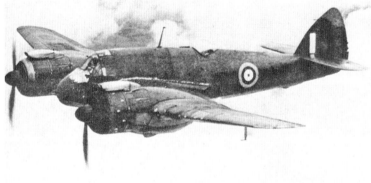

Bristol Beaufighter 1F. After the Hurricane, 'a tub like bus'.

Beaufighter 1F T.4638 of 604 Squadron painted in Special Night Finish. With its immense firepower the Beaufighter was a formidable opponent for the night flying bombers of the *Luftwaffe*.

Outside the Pheasant Inn, 604 Squadron. Flight Lieutenant C. Hartley and Michael. Note the top button of the tunics are left undone in the tradition of the 'fighter boys'.

Leaving 604 Squadron to join 264 Squadron in December 1942. John Quinton and Foster check John and Michael's personal effects before they are loaded into their Beaufighter. Note Michael's bicycle: passed on to Michael by his father, it served Michael well throughout his school and Oxford days and throughout the war years. It is still in service with Michael's son Hugh.

604 Squadron Middle Wallop, Autumn 1941. Michael (left) with John Selway.

Top Left: Flying Officer A. M. Stanley (left) and Flying Officer R. M. Muir outside the 264 squadron mess at Ashwick Hall, Colerne. Tony Stanley failed to return from a Night Ranger on March 11, 1943. *Lower left:* Mosquito NF11s of 264 Squadron at Colerne, 1943. *Right:* Back from a Ranger. Michael sitting on the wing of his Mosquito, with John Quinton leaning against the fuselage. 264 Squadron, Colerne 1943.

Fighter pilots of two wars: Gerald with Roderick 'Rory' Chisholm (later Air Commodore R. Chisholm CBE, DSO, DFC) at Ford in 1942.

Michael in 1942.

Gerald while commanding Ford, September 1941.

Gerald and Michael together at Ford in the late summer of 1943.

Michael (centre) while commanding 84 Squadron, Seletar, 1945.

Mosquito VIIs of 84 Squadron on Seletar aerodrome, 1946.

Mosquitos of 84 Squadron over Singapore. Michael's aeroplane is marked X.PY.

John Quinton and Michael in a Mosquito VI of 84 Squadron, 1945.

Last days in command of 84 Squadron. Michael (third from the left second row) with his pilots and navigators in front of his trusty 'X'. Seletar, December 1946.

60 Squadron at Butterworth, Penang, 1947. P/O K. Nixon, F/L C. F. Griffiths, Michael Constable Maxwell, F/O R. C. Bridges, F/O T. W. F. De Salis, F/O G. Worral.

Left: 56 Squadron reunion, 1953. Three airfighters of the first war meet again. *L to R.* Gerald, Major E. J. L. W. Gilchrist and Squadron Leader Duncan Grinnell-Milne. Gilchrist commanded 56 Squadron from May 1918, handing over command to Grinnell-Milne after the armistice. *Right:* Gerald at the end of World War II.

Carrying on the tradition. William 'Billy' Michael Constable Maxwell, Gerald and Carrie's eldest son.

Left: Gerald explains the SE5a to H.R.H. the Duchess of Kent after the presentation of the 56 Squadron standard in April 1956. *Right:* After two wars. Gerald relaxing at Alresford.

The Constable Maxwell brothers as Gold Staff Officers at the coronation of Queen Elizabeth II in 1953. David, Gerald, Ian, Andrew and Michael.

Gerald in the cockpit of his SE5a 56 Squadron, Estrée Blanche. September 1917.

"Forty Two years
So much love
Gerald. X
19

Forty Two Years On. Echoing the pose of 1917, Gerald in the cockpit of the rebuilt SE5a in 1959.

decided on a change of tactics. It was considered that the British fighters had not yet been brought fully into combat; that a strong force still existed, despite the casualties inflicted. The Luftwaffe was aware that the main fighter force was grouped in the approaches to London and a more concentrated form of attack was advocated. Ceaseless attacks on ground targets would bring the British fighters into the air, and airfields and aircraft factories would be continually bombed. The fighter force of Luftflotte 3 was transferred to the Luftflotte 2 area of operations to provide overwhelming numbers of Me 109s to escort the bombing attacks. Plans were made for the Me 109s to fly almost continuous free chases over the Channel, twenty miles out to sea, making frequent feint attacks on the south coast radar stations. These would bring the British fighters into the air to meet the empty threat, and while they were refuelling the bombers could raid their targets unmolested.

Although there was no shortage of aeroplanes, Fighter Command had suffered heavy casualties between 8 and 18 August, with 94 pilots killed or missing and 60 wounded, and lack of pilots was now the main cause of concern to Dowding and his commanders. Those pilots who were still operational were desperately tired and battle weary. Life on the airfields of Fighter Command was a continual round of danger, hard work and fatigue. Groundcrews worked miracles in keeping Hurricanes and Spitfires ready for combat, and servicing had been developed into a fine art, with the fighters refuelled, rearmed and ready to take off again within eight to ten minutes of landing from the last scramble.

August 24 saw the first implementation of the new German tactics. The cloudy weather of the last few days had broken and the day dawned fine and clear. By 8.30 am a massive raid of forty Dorniers and Ju 88s, escorted by sixty Me 109s, began to build up over the French coast and throughout the day raids were made in strength on airfields and towns on the south coast and southern counties. Manston was attacked twice, with devastating effect, finally deciding Fighter Command to evacuate the airfield. Ramsgate, North Weald, Hornchurch: all came under heavy and concentrated attack; and further west, Portsmouth and Southampton were heavily bombed.

At North Weald, 56 Squadron was scrambled twice during the morning, but no contacts were made. At 2.10 a convoy patrol was flown, but despite fifty plus bandits being plotted the Hurricanes were directed to stay with the ships and saw no action, landing at Rochford to refuel. At 3.45 the sirens were heard wailing in nearby Southend.

We had got down twenty minutes before, so think this is a great joke. It's the first time I have heard this wailing noise. We all laugh. There is a distant sound of engines – a squadron – no, many squadrons – our laugh becomes hollow. North Weald is rung up. No orders yet from Group, but we stand by. The noise of many engines gets closer. We get to our planes at very high speed. There are still no take off orders. About 120 enemy aircraft pass almost overhead. 'Take off!' I join Higginson and Smythe, Innes' machine being U/S. We climb up and up.

As the Hurricanes climbed away from the airfield the Me 109s were suddenly among them. 'Look out, they're blitzing us,' Smythe shouted over the RT. Higginson, Michael and Smythe managed to avoid the 109s, which climbed speedily away, but were too late to engage the bombers. Twenty succeeded in reaching North Weald, but the main force was turned back by determined attacks by Hurricanes of 151 and 111 Squadrons, over fifty British fighters harassing the enemy bombers as they retreated over the Thames Estuary. The Me 109s had gone, having come to the end of their petrol endurance, and only the Me 110s remaining prevented a massacre.

Fifty-six Squadron claimed four victories for no casualties. Squeak Weaver shot down a Heinkel of KG 53, killing Hauptmann von Lonicer and his crew; and Wicks, Marston and Manton each shot down an Me 109 of JG 51 over the Estuary. 151 Squadron claimed three victories and another damaged, but suffered a pilot killed and another seriously wounded during the day's fighting.

The damage at North Weald was not as extensive as at first feared. A hut from which Michael had just moved was completely destroyed – 'luck!' – and Peter Down saved all the cars in a blazing garage. He basked in the glow of congratulations on his heroism until he happened to mention that his own car was at the far end!

A number of workmen and airmen had run into the woods during the attack, an action which infuriated Victor Beamish, who had himself flown with 151 Squadron during its attack on the bombers. Michael wrote:

Beamish announces over the blower that he will shoot anyone who leaves his post, and means it! The flight mechanics in both squadrons were superb. It is only some of the AC2s and clerks who can't take it.

Michael had flown seven sorties during the day; only five minutes short of six hours of combat flying. Little wonder that he recalled: 'Tiredness is my main memory of the Battle of Britain, even more than fear.'

Fifty-six Squadron was scrambled only once on 25 August. The German raids were concentrated further west during the morning and it was not until 6.00 pm that a raid was reported to be building up over the Pas de Calais. Park put six squadrons into the air at 6.25, including 56 Squadron – Michael flying with Grade and Whitehead – but only 32 Squadron made an effective contact, shooting down a Dornier and a 109, but losing a pilot in the process, thereby reducing its effective strength to only eight pilots. It was withdrawn from the front line two days later.

The German attacks on 26 August followed much the same pattern as the previous day, with the addition of attacks on the airfields at Biggin Hill and Kenley. 56 Squadron was scrambled at 11.40 to intercept a raid of over fifty Heinkel IIIs and Dornier Do 17s, escorted by eighty Me 109s and 110s. The airfighting ranged from Canterbury to Maidstone, Manton shooting down two 109s and Mounsdon another. 56 lost two Hurricanes in the fighting: Wicks was shot down near Canterbury by a 109, but baled out unhurt, and George Smythe force landed at Foulness.

Michael had no successes during the day's fighting, but his luck changed on 28 August. Dover control reported a heavy raid building up over the Pas dc Calais at 8.20 am and 56 was scrambled with four other squadrons. It was a frustrating interception. 'We get to the right height, up-sun, etc and then someone's RT sticks at send. It upsets everything and we don't pick them up. Everything in our favour and a detail wrecks it.'

It was a different story just after midday when the squadron was again scrambled to intercept thirty Dorniers flying up the Thames Estuary to attack Rochford.

'We take off again at 12.30. Andrew is talking to me on the telephone. "Must go – flap". "Rochford 15,000," says our telephone. We take off and proceed towards Rochford but are vectored to the south side of the Estuary. Suddenly we see them. Twenty seven bombers are going north west from Manston, a huge black pack of them; they look extraordinarily sinister.

'I have taken recently to wearing goggles and gauntlets – while every pilot who has been hit in the legs wears flying boots! This gives great extra confidence, while a piece of white heather from the home of my fitter gives the Highland touch.

'We approach the bombers. "Line astern, line astern – go." I am in the last section with Flight Sergeant Higginson and Hillwood; the whole squadron is in front of me and has the deadly appearance of a female wildcat whose litter is in danger. It is the supreme moment of the fighter squadron – the moment for which pilots are trained, thousands of people are employed, the moment when the squadron which has been directed by its controller has sighted a big enemy formation over its own land. The object of the fighter is purely the destruction of the invader. Often mistakes occur, sometimes identity is doubtful – sometimes there is no doubt. Now there is no doubt. A big formation such as this can only be German and it is attacking England.

'For a moment the squadron remains in formation, then gradually two sections dive away and B Flight (my own) continues to climb.

'We have turned north now and the enemy are straight ahead. We are well above Manton and his flight. Still above us are the hostile fighters. It is our job to keep them off the six machines below us while they split up the bombers.

'There are three enemy fighter squadrons – thirty to forty aircraft. Our odds are better than they often are, but six Hurricanes can only do the job of disorganizing so many. Gracie leads his section at one lot of fighters and we continue on after, and above the other flight.

'Then appear two 109s going down in a turn, slowly, apparently unaware of our presence. Many friendly machines must make it harder for the Hun to pick us up.

'I am in the rear of our section and see about six 109s on our right and slightly above. I turn and face these while the other two dive on down and destroy the two below.

'We all circle round. The whole thing becomes quite natural and almost peaceful. The thought of practice fights and the thought of Gerald both come to my mind. The Mes do not appear to be very aggressive, but do not leave me an opening. Large amounts of yellow in these planes make them look weird when seen quite close.

'I see a Hurricane diving down on the tail of an Me with another Me chasing it. I am much too far away to chase or warn, and am too occupied to give it more than a thought.

'These Mes seem concerned largely with self protection. Two of them go off after their bombers. I then find two in line astern below me and another above and in front, but turning and climbing to the right.

I feel it is hopeless to chase him, but to gain height and watch him as I do so. To my surprise and joy I find that by climbing steep at 150 mph at full bore I can keep on a smaller radius circle and gradually get closer. The two below present an ideal target, but the plan is obvious. I should attack them and be then a sitter for the higher ones.

'I follow him round in a long steep turn, gaining ground all the time. Either he is not at full throttle or is acting as a decoy. I try and keep out of sight of the pilot.

'This climb is exhilarating. I realize that I am getting closer and while turning fairly hard can watch my own tail.

'Two fifty yards – he is in range – I keep on to make sure of my judgement. He is well inside my sights and more than fills the cross piece. At 200 yards, after another rear glance, I aim, carefully allowing for his turn, from a perfect quarter position. A two second burst – a piece of his cowling comes off – he turns straight away from me. I get in another three second burst. Flashes of fire come from his rear – are they guns or my own deWilde?

'Suddenly he turns over onto his back quite slowly and goes vertically downwards, glycol pouring from the front. I watch him for a sec. and then look for the other two.

'I notice spots of oil on my windscreen. I presume it is from the Me. There is a Dornier below me; after another look for the fighters, I approach to fire, but my windscreen is covered in oil and I see nothing.

'I got the Me at 18,000 feet and the Dornier was at about 14,000. There are a lot of Mes still about so I dive in a straight spiral down, down, down.

'I am clear of everything at 2,000 feet – over water. I appear to be midway over the Estuary. I turn south and head for the distant shore. My oil pressure is now zero and the temp. is off the dial.'

The Merlin was now running unevenly, and although Michael was using almost full throttle the Hurricane was rapidly losing height. Deciding against baling out over the sea, Michael tightened his straps and lowered his seat. The land looked very far away.

As the Hurricane approached the coast at Herne Bay the engine began to 'jump about like a mad thing' and gradually ground to a stop. The beach below was covered in anti-invasion obstacles, making a force landing impossible and Michael realized that he had no choice. To bale out now would mean the Hurricane crashing into Herne Bay itself, causing civilian casualties. It seemed just possible to reach the fields beyond the town, but by that time he would be to low to bale out and would be committed to a crash landing with wheels up.

As the crippled Hurricane cleared the last of the houses, the glycol exploded, clouds of white smoke pouring from the engine and completely obliterating Michael's forward view. He was now too low to bale out and the glycol going usually portended flames and explosion in fifteen seconds. He had to get down – quickly. He saw a field, lowered the flaps and turned into wind.

'I see nothing in front and hardly anything from the sides, just clouds of smoke and fumes. There is a road and telegraph posts. Will I clear it? I turn gently as my speed is about 95. A tree looms up – I have to turn harder – the controls go limp, the right wing begins to drop. The only thing to do is a crash landing on the wing. She is almost out of control, but enough to keep the nose up and the right wing down. I go down in a terrific sideslip, thinking as I go of my beautiful US.U. I can just hold the nose up to prevent her diving in. The right mainplane hits, there is a crunch and I seem to go round and round.

'I end up standing on the left running board with wreckage all round. An awful moment of feeling caught – of losing all – the remains of the cockpit fall off me and I get out and clear. Where is the engine? A column of flame 25 yards away shows where I had left it. My noble "U – Archangel" is no more!'

Michael lay down in the stubble. It seemed impossible that he was not injured and his legs felt sore. A crowd gathered around him.

'Are you hurt badly?' someone asked. 'Do you want an ambulance?'

'I don't know', Michael replied. 'But you'd better get one in case.'

After a careful check he found he was not hurt and stood up. It seemed miraculous that he could have survived the crash without a scratch. A crowd of curious sightseers had now gathered around the wrecked Hurricane, but were being shooed back by a pompous colonel. Michael was annoyed at this intrusion on his preserves. ' "Excuse me Sir", I say sweetly. "But I wouldn't stand in front there. The guns are all at fire". A portly officer, a deer-like leap.'

Michael's sense of showmanship then came to the fore and he gave the delighted crowd a tour of the Hurricane, extolling its virtues and telling them what a marvellous aeroplane it was. He was sad at having to finally leave it – during manufacture someone had painted 'Good Luck' on the control column and he had become very fond of US U – but some officers of the 8th Fusiliers now arrived and gently led him away from the shattered Hurricane.

'Come on, old chap, you can't do anything.'

He was taken to the Fusiliers' mess, where hardly a word was said to him and no questions asked. He was not sorry. He was more interested in observing his own reactions. He was delighted to find that he was not suffering from any kind of shock and was not depressed at having crashed. Shooting down the Me 109 had given him tremendous confidence and he was eager to get back into the fight. He made his excuses to the Fusiliers and a lady drove him to the local station, Michael gracefully declining her offer to drive him back to North Weald – 'I hate seeing you boys risk your lives and then just sent off in a train' – being much more frightened of her driving than he had been during his crash landing.

Unshaven, dirty, his uniform ripped and torn, wearing his scarf and flying boots and carrying his parachute, Michael was the centre of attraction as he trudged through the crowds at Victoria Station. But the stares were friendly, affectionate, and he felt extraordinarily close to the people around him. A porter proudly carried his parachute, indignantly refusing a tip, and the taxi driver from Victoria to Liverpool Street was equally emphatic in refusing his fare. 'You've risked your life for us, I wouldn't dream of taking your money.'

Michael arrived back at North Weald at 9.30 pm. He was given a warm welcome and his Me 109 was credited as a probable. During the afternoon the squadron had again been scrambled and Weaver and Smythe had each claimed a 109. Weaver had also been shot down in the morning's action, at the same time as Michael, but had baled out and returned to take part in the afternoon's fighting. He and Smythe had shot down Feldwebel Schöttle and Unteroffizier Kleeman of JG 54. Smythe had in turn been shot down by one of his victim's comrades, but had baled out safely. Barry Sutton had also baled out, slightly burned. From a study of German losses for the day, it appears that Michael's victory was an Me 109 from JG 3, possibly Leutnant Landry.

Michael was at readiness the next day. His various aches and bruises made him a little slow in running to his Hurricane, and the CO was mildly sarcastic about his lack of speed before remembering his crash of the previous day. Apologizing, he told Michael to take a few days' leave and Michael left North Weald the next day.

In the last few days of August, 56 Squadron fared badly. On 30 August Gracie shot down a Dornier which was bombing Luton, Wicks and Innes Westmacott each claiming an Me 110 from the escort, but Brooker had to bale out and Jumbo Gracie crash-landed.

On the last day of the month the squadron was scrambled to

intercept a raid approaching North Weald, the twelve Hurricanes meeting the escorting Me 109s and 110s over Colchester. No victories were scored and the squadron lost four pilots: Cliff Whitehead baled out unhurt, but Innes Westmacott and Mounsdon were both wounded. Tragically, the gallant Squeak Weaver was shot down and killed. He was chasing the Me 109s out over the sea, giving a running commentary on his radio, when the transmission abruptly stopped. Just before take-off he had been told of his award of a DFC.

Jumbo Gracie, who had flown with a stiff neck, legacy of his crash the previous day, breezily bounced into Epping Hospital, jokily diagnosing that he had a broken neck. He returned to North Weald in the evening, white as a sheet. 'It really is broken', he announced shakily.

With these losses 56 Squadron virtually ceased to exist as a fighting squadron and was withdrawn to Boscombe Down in Hampshire, where the few remaining pilots of experience could train the replacements.

CHAPTER XIII

Victories and Circuses

Michael rejoined 56 Squadron at Boscombe Down on 5 September. He found many changes. Squadron Leader Manton had been posted and the new CO was Squadron Leader H. M. Pinfold. Jumbo Gracie was in hospital, as were Innes Westmacott and Barry Sutton. The sergeant pilots still remained: the solid, never changing backbone of the squadron: Taffy Higginson, Cliff Whitehead, Peter Hillwood and George Smythe. Of the officers, only Michael, Boy Brooker and Brian Wicks remained of the 'pre-blitz' strength.

The training of the replacement pilots progressed well and no contact was made with the Luftwaffe until 14 September, when a lone Ju 88 was seen at 20,000 feet. Michael, practising fighting attacks with two of the new pilots, Edwards and Heslop, climbed hard to intercept, but the Ju 88 peeled off into cloud and eluded the Hurricanes. Thirty minutes after landing, Michael and Taffy Higginson took off and were vectored to Ringwood. Michael suddenly saw a Dornier Do 17, slightly below and to their right. The two Hurricanes went in to the attack, but the Dornier pilot was warned of their approach and dived into cloud. Higginson stayed above the clouds, Michael below, both watching for the emergence of the Dornier. It finally broke cover above the cloud and Higginson shot it down into the sea, forty miles out from Southampton.

On 27 September the squadron was scrambled at five minutes past eleven to intercept a raid heading for the Filton works of the Bristol Aeroplane Company. As the Hurricanes reached 20,000 feet the instructions were modified, sending them to the Bournemouth area, but Michael realized that his oxygen supply had not been connected properly – 'a fool me, a fool my mechanic' – and he peeled off and returned to Boscombe Down.

Ops gives me permission to go off and I go again to join them. All the airmen have their tin hats on and the 'new boys' are standing about wishing they could fly. It is moments like this that a pilot realises that the ground staff are vital only up to the last moment and that finally and at last the whole business is his.

Michael was reminded of his own days as a 'new boy', watching people take off, and he felt a representative of them all as the Hurricane hurtled over the grass and into the air. He climbed rapidly, heading for Bournemouth. He could hear the controller, 'Bandy', calling up 'Boffin Leader' – 56 Squadron's call sign – giving him a vector to steer, and information that the enemy formation was approaching Salisbury from the south east. Michael was undecided as to his best course of action. He knew it was unlikely that he could find the other Hurricanes, yet 50 plus bandits seemed rather large odds for a lone Hurricane. He had turned towards Bristol, in the hope of finding the squadron, when the RT again crackled into life. 'Bandits approaching Bristol'. Michael decided to get into position to the south of the city and attempt to intercept the enemy bombers as they turned for home.

'I climb up to 15,000 feet about twenty miles south of Bristol and then see a lot of aircraft above me at 21,000 to 26,000 feet. They seem to be mainly fighters and are being attacked by Spitfires – all very high. Then there appears a black mass four miles north of me and 2,000 feet above me. I climb up full bore. I think of doing a head on attack, but decide this would be unwise for there would be many guns able to get a shot at me just as I passed. As a result I keep them on my right, and by this time just below me, and as they pass I turn in to attack from behind.

'There are twenty-five to thirty Dorniers in open formation and I do a stern attack on the rear aircraft. There does not appear to be anything behind in the way of 109s so I take a careful bead on the fuselage from 250 yards and give a three second burst. Tracer comes back from the rear aircraft and a piece of junk falls from the left side of the cockpit of the Dornier, but the rear gunner continues to fire back. I close up slightly and fire another burst at the port engine. Part of the cowling comes off. I break away hard to the left. On turning right again I see the machine diving down with a cloud of black smoke coming from the port engine.

'Up to date I have had a number of fairly easy shots at enemy aircraft and have usually seen very little result. On seeing wreckage come off this Dornier my reaction is purely that of surprise!

'Another Hurricane gives it a burst as it goes down – I think he might have gone for one of his own. I follow down in a steep dive. They manoeuvre for position. I try to do a head-on attack, but at the last moment he turns away. I follow round and get in a long burst from 100 to 70 yards from the inside of the circle. The Dornier then dives right away down – we are at 6,000 feet – I follow and suddenly feel almost sick. No one has got out and it appears to be going to dive into the ground. He pulls out, however, and circles slowly – I notice that his port engine has stopped. I am just going to give him another shot when I realise that he is just trying to land.

'For five minutes I watch him from a vantage point of some 500 feet above and on his right. The other Hurricane does the same just behind me. The EA tries to land in a field ahead of him, but overshoots and opens up his one good engine. There are trees in front – I could not desire a friend to clear those trees more than that German. He gets over and I am delighted. On we go at 140 mph. Suddenly he slows up – I do so too and nearly stall. I lose him for a second – there is a hill in front of him but he has not cleared it. I turn and see a huge great silver thing lying broken on a grassy bank between two woods. There is a black hole to one side where it must have hit the ground. The nose is askew – broken at the base – the whole plane is steaming but is not on fire – it is on its belly but seems otherwise all right. No one gets out.

'The other Hurricane, TM-R and I fly together for a moment – thumbs up and waving joyously at each other. I return, but can't find the machine. It crashed about thirty miles south of Bristol and twenty miles west of Salisbury.

'The shooting of the 109, my first solo bag, had been impersonal. The aircraft had simply shed glycol and the pilot could have baled out or made a forced landing. In addition there were plenty of other aircraft about to keep my attention. The case of this Dornier was different. While attacking the formation I was frightened and excited, but once it left the others I began to experience the most wonderful, jubilant excitement imaginable. I took a joyful pleasure in the thought that I had made it leave the formation, and all I wanted to do was to close in and kill. I had no fear of his bullets, even though a shower of tracer came at me whenever I got within range, and I felt no compunction in shooting something damaged. I just felt a primitive urge to chase and to kill. It is this instinct that makes men and animals hunt, the instinct to destroy and kill. Suddenly all this changed. I saw that he had had enough and merely wanted to land. The fight was over; he had given in, and all he wanted was a safe place to get down.

'Four humans were in that plane. They were up in the air and in a damaged machine that the pilot was heroically trying to land. This last few minutes was the most unpleasant I have experienced in this war. I was safe, they were in danger of death. They crashed and no one got out.

'When Soden was killed I thought that I would feel hatred when in the air. I did so on the ground, but in the air I never felt any. The only emotion I felt was impersonal and technical – the wish to destroy certain parts of the enemy aircraft in order to put it out of action. There was no fear, there was respect, but not hate.

'When this aircraft got separated the instinct of the chase caused excitement and an almost savage desire to kill. When the fight was over the German aircraft was no longer capable of hurting this country – it was weak and only interested in self preservation. I felt they were just airmen who were in a dangerous plight and one I could well imagine, for I had experienced the same thing myself ... It was beastly and unpleasant.'

Michael's 'Dornier' was in fact an Me 110 of ZG 26, the crew, Oberfeldwebel Tipelt and Unteroffizier Brosig, both being killed. ZG 26 lost six of its Me 110s in this raid, and another crash landed at Cherbourg. Manston claimed one of the 110s and Higginson and MacKenzie damaged others.

The following evening, at a party, Michael met a local solicitor, who on being told of the action, remarked, 'Oh, how absolutely splendid of you. I hope they were all killed.' Michael, who always said a prayer before firing his guns in anger, and had had a mass said for the German crew, was profoundly shocked and angry at this callous attitude. 'This is the filthiest remark I have ever heard and I was staggered by its bloody sadism.'

Fifty-six Squadron now flew to Warmwell each day to co-operate with the Spitfires of 152 Squadron, and on 30 September the two squadrons were ordered off to intercept a free chase by a mixed formation of 109s of JG 2 and JG 53 and 110s of ZG 26. The British fighters were scrambled too late, however, and failed to gain sufficient height before meeting the enemy fighters.

The result is hopeless. We meet twenty four Me 110s slightly above us and we turn too late and are too low to break them up. It is a rather wonderful sight seeing those 110s passing us quite close – at about 600 mph passing speed.

They go up and we go down – there being dozens of 109s spreading up into the upper air. I stay with Higginson, but some five hundred yards behind. Sometime later – still with Higginson – I feel and hear a rushing clattering noise. I have never shifted quicker and down I go on my back, warning Higginson on the RT. Defensive action in a Hurricane, to anyone who heard cannons coming from behind, means stick full over and then back with full strength and both hands, and also full rudder. When you recover from the blacking out you are going down in a violent aileron turn with the clock approaching 400 mph. It was a single 109 which neither of us saw. He put two bullets in my port mainplane from below. This was lucky!

After lunch the squadrons were again scrambled to intercept a raid of forty Heinkel 111s of KG 55, escorted by Me 110s, which were to attack the Westland factory at Yeovil. Michael flew in the rear section with Boy Brooker, and the Hurricanes were roughly handled by the Heinkels: Michael, Sergeant Fox, Squadron Leader Pinfold and Wicks were all shot down.

'The CO does a quarter attack, but is too late with his turn in. We have only just got height but could have done a head on, which is good against He 111s, otherwise we should have turned in quicker. He has had very little experience of fighting, but is exceptionally good. There are a lot of Me 110s above. I come in with Brooker, carefully watching the fighters. They don't even come down very quickly. When I am about four hundred yards from the 111s there are two sections in front attacking them. I hear a "Phut" and oil begins to cloud my windscreen – a stray bullet from the bombers.

'Herne Bay! I think of having a crack but remember how quick the oil goes and go down in a spiral, shutting revs to fully coarse and throttling back. Below some cloud I cannot see land. My windscreen is obliterated and all my instruments are covered. I can't see my compass. It is a bad moment as I cannot clean my compass and goggles together – one is clear and the other oils up. I fear taking my goggles off and there is a shower of oil coming out.

'At last I see where is north and set off, carefully nursing the engine. Land is nearer than I thought. Once I am in gliding distance of it I stop the engine and then pull my goggles up.

'All now is quiet; all is peace. But there is something sinister in the easy quiet of my machine.

'There is a long narrow strip of coast and beyond it a lagoon and then fields. The latter is the best place, but it is a bit far and there are hills. The strip may be mined and it is very narrow!

'I never thought I would long to jump by parachute. What an easy solution! I am near the coast, while a 'dead-stick' Hurricane, as I found at Herne Bay, is hell to control, and as hard to land safely.

'I decide that the beach is the place, and with reasonable height and a mile to go, I try to remember the wind direction of Warmwell.

'I intend at all costs to keep up speed. At 120 and near the coast, I pump down the flaps. There is enough height to get in, but not much to spare. I do my turn in at 110. Even at that speed the controls are very dead. The difference between a prop turning and one stopped is a big one.

'Round she comes, and now into a probable wind, but find it partly across, so lower a wing slightly. I try and judge the new touch down position, the wheels being up. The hold off takes an age then she drops gently onto her belly.

'Gosh what a jerk! She seems to tip right forward and to be turning over, but no, a cloud of flying shingle is sprayed up. With a grating slither she slews round and pulls up. Out I get like hell! I cannot find the bullet hole and the damage seems small. A wing tip is bent slightly, the prop is broken on one blade only; the radiator is ruined and the bottom dented. The whole cockpit is covered in thick black oil. Oh joy to be safely grounded!'

Michael had crash-landed on Chesil Bank, a long narrow strip of shingle to the west of Portland. He stayed by the Hurricane, being uncertain whether or not the bank was mined, and amused himself by looking for any bullet holes in the engine area. After a while a number of Durham Light Infantry arrived, and leaving a guard on the Hurricane, Michael walked back to the north end of the bank, a long trudge of two miles in flying boots. On reaching the coast he was met by a pair of officers, taken to tea in their mess, and later returned to Warmwell by truck.

It had been a bad day for 56 Squadron. Marston and Ray had been shot down in the morning, and five others in the afternoon, Edwards being hit by an Me 110 of the Heinkels' escort. Squadron Leader Pinfold and Wicks had managed to land at Warmwell, with glycol pouring from their Hurricanes. Both Fox and Edwards had baled out. Only Sergeant Ray was injured, but the actions of the day did little for the squadron's morale. A lighter side to the day's events was recorded later by Michael.

During a flap, Brooker (with five others) is sent up and finds 100 fighters above him. 'Do you want to attack, Blue Leader?' Sergeant Whitehead, leading B Flight, replies: 'I don't want to commit suicide yet.' So down they go. Nosowicz, the Pole, is furious. 'But did you not see them? They were straight above you, hundreds of them, hundreds of them!'

Michael was next in action on 7 October. Another raid was mounted against the Westland works, this time by Ju 88s of KG 51, escorted by fifty 110s of ZG 26. Flying in the third section with Taffy Higginson and Peter Hillwood, Michael saw the enemy formation at 15,000 feet. The Hurricanes were at 18,000, but Brooker, leading, took them inland to gain more height and got them in a good position to carry out a quarter attack. The first section of Hurricanes went straight through the enemy formation, the second attacking from the quarter, with Michael's section attacking from quarter to astern.

Michael attacked a 110, getting good bursts into the fuselage and silencing the rear gunner before the enemy pilot broke away into the glare of the afternoon sun. Michael glanced quickly behind. He had mistakenly identified the 110 as a Dornier; he felt sure its escort would be somewhere near and he had no wish to be bounced. When he looked for the 110 again it had disappeared.

ZG 26 lost six of its aircraft during this raid and Michael's opponent was possibly one of them.

On the way back to base, Michael was 'blitzed' by a Spitfire, but the Hurricane turned inside the Spitfire 'with the greatest ease'. A pilot of 152 Squadron ruefully admitted later to having attacked a 109 which had turned out to be a Hurricane.

The following day saw the return of Jumbo Gracie and another new pilot, Tommy Guest. New arrivals were quickly indoctrinated into the traditions of the squadron, Michael and Ken Marston always congratulating them on having been posted to 56. An essential part of the welcoming ceremony was an inspection of the Squadron Honours Board, complete with a piece of shrapnel from North Weald days, and with Gerald's name being mentioned as one of the 'most famous' of the first war pilots.

With the onset of winter the air battles in the south east, which had reached a climax in September, finally petered out. The Luftwaffe had been met and defeated. The Battle of Britain had been won and the threat of invasion was over. The victory had not been lightly won. It had cost the lives of nearly 500 young fighter pilots, with another 420 wounded and injured, many with disfiguring burns. The fate of the civilized world had rested squarely in the hands of 1500 young men and they had proved more than equal to their awesome task. A picture is sometimes painted of their lighthearted and willing acceptance of the appalling odds, but the truth is far less simple. If the pilots of Fighter Command began the battle full of the lighthearted confidence of youth, ten days or a fortnight of heavy fighting over the southern counties of England, with its attendant heavy losses, brought home the realisation that this was a grim and deadly business. Many unknown and unsung young pilots, too inexperienced to last long in action, made the supreme sacrifice after scoring one or two victories, while the survivors battled grimly and resolutely on.

Michael was one of the lucky survivors. Too inexperienced to have been thrown into one of the most fiercely fought and critical battles of history, he had survived by a combination of luck and determination. He had been shot down four times and wounded once. His cousin, Lord Eldon, Lord in Waiting to King George VI, relating Michael's exploits to the King, had credited Michael with having put a penny on the income tax. The King was amused, but the grim reality remained that Michael had narrowly escaped death or appalling injury four times.

Attacking a formation of bombers, with tracer converging on him from perhaps fifty rear gunners, Michael found that he was strangely unafraid, even exhilarated; but the fear of cannon shells suddenly smashing into his aeroplane from an unseen assailant never left him. It was a primeval, almost superstitious fear. The fear of being attacked while walking through a wood at night; of an unknown terror leaping from a dark doorway. Like all pilots he had fought his personal fear, and pushed it down, but it had taken 'some pushing'.

As winter set in over Europe, air activity slackened. 56 Squadron was scrambled to intercept an 'X' raid on 1 November, but failed to make contact. With the 56 Squadron Hurricanes at 23,000 feet, others at 26,000 feet and Spitfires at 27,000, it was an ideal combination, a far cry from the outnumbered days of the summer, but the thirty plotted enemy aircraft turned for home. 'Unfortunately. I really felt like a scrap'.

A few days later Michael flew to Heston in a Tiger Moth, a type he had always wanted to fly. 'I am amazed at the tiny wings and really quite scared as I open up its baby "clock". It floats off like a glider and I really feel I am flying.'

After lunching at Heston, Michael flew a Spitfire for the first time. It felt very different from the Hurricane taxying out, but Michael thoroughly enjoyed the flight 'rocking cheerfully' as he pumped up the wheels on take-off. 'The Spitfire is a lovely aeroplane. It goes so effortlessly through the air and climbs far faster than the Hurricane.' Michael climbed to 8,000 feet, did a slow roll – 'rather nervously' – and a few stall turns. The greatest difference from the Hurricane was the acceleration of the Spitfire in a dive, and the resulting 'freeze up' of the ailerons, which Michael found a little alarming. At the end of the flight, after a careful analysis, Michael was still undecided which of the two fighters he preferred, but considered that Hurricanes vs fighters and Spitfires vs bombers would be the best combination.

After a visit to Farnborough, and a look at a captured Heinkel 111 and an Me 110, Michael returned to Boscombe Down, arriving at dusk. 'Someone beats up our dispersal in a Hurricane, diving at 250 or so. I do the same at 70. They are all watching. I can almost hear the cheers.'

The following afternoon the hooter went and the squadron was scrambled to engage a group of Me 109s on a free chase. Wicks led the squadron, with Michael leading Radwanski and Sergeant Heslop in the rear section. The Hurricanes climbed to 15,000 feet, north west of Southampton, but the 109s were suddenly among them. 'Look out, 109s above and left', someone shouted. The Hurricanes split rapidly, Michael following Cliff Whitehead's section, but losing it in the ensuing commotion. Finding himself alone, Michael circled round, keeping a wary eye open for 109s. A Hurricane flashed by, trailing glycol, followed by another. Feeling sick after his circling, Michael returned to Boscombe Down to find that Tommy Guest had shot down a 109. 'We were both frightened, lost and hurrying home. I gave the 109 a burst and eventually it crashed into the sea. Oh hell, I forgot to turn my sights on!'

The squadron was ordered off twice the next day, but no contacts were made and Michael left the following morning on a week's leave. He motored up to London in the trusty Ford, and on leaving Staines could see an air raid in progress over the capital, quite enjoying the spectacle until a battery opened fire almost in his ear.

After dining at the Dorchester with his brother Andrew, 'a good dinner and an even better cigar', they caught the night train for Northumberland to stay with their sister Joan and her husband at Harehope Hall, always associated in Michael's mind with going home from Ampleforth for the Christmas holidays. As he settled into his sleeper he reflected that it almost made the war worthwhile to be able to relax in a bed with no duties for a whole week. 'I hardly like to sleep and so miss the pure joy of it.'

Michael returned to Boscombe Down on 15 November, and continued with training the new boys, practising formation fighter attacks and formation flying. On 28 November, the squadron was vectored to 23,000 feet over Southampton, but it saw only contrails at 30,000 feet. After this 'maddening and cold' attempt at interception, the squadron was moved next day to Middle Wallop. Michael was sorry to leave Boscombe Down. The squadron had arrived there in a holiday mood, despite the casualties of August, and had enjoyed the 'camp by the wood'. The pilots found the new mess at Wallop very agreeable, with good food and, above all, warm. Michael shared a hut with Ken Marston and they soon settled into their new quarters.

December saw a forecast of the future, with Michael flying an Anson early in the month, the first twin engined aeroplane he had flown. The Anson seemed a trifle sluggish after the Hurricane, but Michael enjoyed the new experience, finding the Anson easy to fly and with an amazing turning circle.

The winter weather having set in there was a fair amount of free time at Middle Wallop. Alresford was only twenty-six miles away and was home from home for Michael and any of his friends who wished to stay. There was nearly always a party somewhere in the evening, and one such demonstrates the cosmopolitan make-up of Fighter Command.

On the way home we all sing. Don MacKenzie, Maori – which he does rather well; Ken, English; Francis, French; and self, Gaelic. After that we all sing Highland songs. Don's father has taught him most of the best in New Zealand. It is a pleasant journey home.

Michael was given the 'day' off on 10 December. Before returning on the 17th he was advised that the squadron had again moved, to North Weald. The final stages of the journey back to the old aerodrome brought back many vivid memories of the pre-blitz days and the many good friends who had gone, but on arriving at the aerodrome Michael was shocked to learn that his friend and roommate, Ken Marston had been killed in a collision in the circuit.

Michael was glad to be back in what he considered to be the front line, ready for the 'spring blitz', which he then thought would be the inevitable continuation of the attacks of the previous summer. 'After three months "rest" it is good to get back.'

Everyone seemed pleased to see 56 back at North Weald, including Wing Commander Victor Beamish, who was still Station Commander. The squadron shared the aerodrome with 249, another Hurricane squadron, and took over 23 Squadron's dispersal, which was excellent – 'two stoves, plenty of chairs and big enough'. The weather was still poor and no operational flights were made until Saturday, 21 December, when the squadron patrolled Maidstone with 249 Squadron. Spitfires in the top cover chased an Me 110 at 25,000 feet, finally shooting it down, but the Hurricanes saw no action.

Michael was given Christmas leave the following Monday, which he spent at Alresford. To his delight it was a real family Christmas. His mother was there, his sisters Betty and Ursula, his brother Andrew, and of course, Carrie and the children. To everyone's delight Gerald arrived soon after and the party was complete. 'We work up all the best home for Xmas holidays atmosphere. There is something unique about it. It gives many wonderful and quite ga ga memories.'

Michael saw in 1941 at North Weald, drinking with a stranded pilot. As he reflected on the events of the old year he remembered the last New Year's party at the FTS at Hullavington, where he had drunk a toast: 'A Merry New Year, you won't live to see another!'

Three days after these celebrations, Michael and Jumbo Gracie flew an afternoon patrol over Clacton. There was a lot of snow on the ground. As Michael looked down on the black mass of houses, squatting comfortably among the whiteness, he was struck by how peaceful it all looked, and a sense of responsibility for the safety of the people below flooded over him. The thought of the two Hurricanes – his own and Gracie's – guarding the peaceful little coastal town, with its families still celebrating Christmas, gave him a sense of power. 'This power is a joyful power and causes a strong and healthy pride.'

56 Squadron suffered a sad blow on 7 January, when Jumbo Gracie was posted. He had been virtual leader of the squadron in the air since his arrival in July 1940. The squadron gave him a great farewell lunch and old times were recalled and laughed over; in particular Gracie's penchant for succinct remarks over the RT. He had been known to tell control to 'pull your bloody finger out', and on one occasion, having lost the squadron coming home in the dusk, had called up to ask where he was. 'You lost us, you find us,' said someone. His memorial tankard was inscribed: 'My body is posted, my soul never.'

Returning from an uneventful convoy patrol on 9 January, Michael was delighted to find Gerald at dispersal. The news had come through that 56 and 249 were to take part in the first 'circus' operation in the morning, carrying the offensive into Nazi occupied Europe. Michael was excited at the prospect of going over to the offensive, but as a precaution decided to paint the crest of Saint Philomena on his Hurricane, an especial wish of his sister Ursula. Saint Philomena was an early Christian martyr, who had deflected the arrows of the bowmen trying to kill her by turning them back onto her attackers. Michael rather hoped her crest would do the same to the cannon shells of any 109s he might happen to meet on the morrow, and to the amusement of the groundcrews he painted $\rightleftharpoons$ P $\Leftarrow$ in red under the cockpit of his Hurricane.

With the closeness of brotherhood, intensified since the beginning of the war, Michael felt Gerald's sadness at no longer being an active participant in the air war. 'It is a job he used to do and tomorrow I will be doing it. I think he really regrets that twenty years have passed and that he is now out of the front line.' Being in the 'front line' meant a great deal to Michael, the feeling of being in the forefront of the war. The operation planned for the morning, the beginning of the offensive, was the 'result in action of a nation's effort. Like a goodnight to Gerald. I feel I have taken over from him the work he did so well in 1917.'

That night Michael walked alone through the quiet woods of Epping. What would the morning bring? Me 109s? Flak? What else? He felt no fear, only a quiet excitement, very unlike the wild enthusiasm, and later loathing of war, of only a few short months before.

January 10 dawned fine, but a haze delayed the start of the operation until later in the morning. 56 and 249 took off from North Weald at 11.50 in company with Douglas Bader's 242 Squadron, which had flown in at 10.30, and formed up with six Blenheims of 114 Squadron over Southend. In all, six fighter squadrons flew escort for the Blenheims. With 56 flying close escort, the Hurricanes of 249 and 242 Squadrons providing top and flank cover, and with the Spitfires of 41, 64 and 611 Squadrons higher still, it was a far cry from six short months before. As the force roared over the waters of the Channel, Michael and Peter Hillwood weaving gently in position just below the Blenheims, Michael felt particularly secure. 'I am closest to the bombers so am personally protected by 107 fighters!'

The formations crossed the French coast at 12,000 feet near Gravelines and flew south, its target the ammunition dumps near the

Fôret de Guines. A flurry of AA came up among 249 on the right, but there was no sign of any other opposition. Every nerve tense with excitement, Michael was weaving continually, watching behind and longing to see the bombs drop. Where were the 109s? the AA?

So intent was he in watching for the enemy fighters to appear that he suddenly realised that he was dangerously close to, and just under the Blenheims. As he throttled back, the bombs dropped, 'looking black and sinister' and he felt a pang of compassion for those below. Their bombs released, the Blenheims turned for home, noses down. A little more AA came up as the formation neared the coast, but it was not heavy and they were able to fly through it without loss.

Suddenly it was over. They were across the Channel and the white cliffs of Dover were a welcome sight in the sunshine. 'How peaceful they look, and oh how friendly.' As the aircraft thundered over Kent countryside Michael relaxed and began to enjoy himself. It was thrilling to be returning from a daylight raid over enemy territory, and the whole affair had gone so smoothly. Safely inland, the Hurricanes formed up in their best 'pansy' formation – 'close and perfect, but operationally useless' – and waved to the Blenheim crews as the bombers turned away to land at Hornchurch.

Back at North Weald everyone was full of the raid; all talking at once and feeling on top of the world. The only enemy aeroplanes seen had been some Me 109s which had attacked 249 Squadron near Dover, shooting down Pilot Officer McConnell, the only casualty. McConnell had baled out, breaking his leg, but his life had been saved by Victor Beamish who had been flying with B Flight, 'as usual not in correct position, but in position, again as usual, to protect his pilots'. Beamish dealt with the 109 and it was seen to crash into the sea. The Spitfires had claimed another couple of 109s and a Pole of 249 Squadron, frustrated by the lack of action, had 'lost' his squadron and attacked an enemy aerodrome, shooting down a 109 in the circuit and groundstrafing some Henschels.

All in all it had been an exciting and satisfactory day, rounded off by listening to the story of their exploits on the BBC news that evening. For once the news story was accurate, even to the statement that McConnell's aeroplane had 'crashed on landing'.'It went into the Dover cliffs head on – so it was literally true!' Michael commented dryly.

The weather was now bad, with snow and almost continuous fog, and the squadron did little operational flying. There were several changes. Squadron Leader Pinfold left, being replaced by Squadron

Leader Norman Ryder DFC; and Taffy Higginson, commissioned in September, took command of B Flight, fulfilling the first part of Michael's impression at their initial meeting in April the year before that he would one day be a leader.

Michael flew a lone patrol at dusk on 16 January, and three days later set out with Innes Westmacott on a 'mosquito' raid over France.

Innes Westmacott had recovered from his wounds and rejoined the squadron in early November at Boscombe Down. One of the first people he saw on the evening of his return was Michael, who gave him a warm welcome and suggested over a pint of beer that Innes join him in visiting some friends who lived nearby. Innes, tired and dirty after the long train journey, was reluctant to go, but Michael assured him that they need not stay long and he finally agreed.

Michael's friends, the Hollender family, had two daughters, and that evening Innes Westmacott met Babette Hollender, who later became his wife. The Hollenders kept open house for members of 56 Squadron, and over the next few weeks Michael and Innes Westmacott were frequent visitors, striking up a close friendship. They also developed an expensive acquaintance with the various pubs and clubs in the Salisbury area. Innes Westmacott recalled: 'At one we discovered they still had some bottles of Cockburns 1912 Port and we bought the lot, had it set aside for our use and managed to drink it all before the squadron returned to North Weald.'

Mosquito raids, later called Rhubarb, were a new idea to carry the offensive into enemy occupied Europe. Two fighters would cross the French coast at low level, and strafe any ground targets that presented themselves – trains, transport, aerodromes etc – darting back into the cloud cover on completing their attacks. It was essential for the success of the operation that low cloud existed over France, and weather conditions had to be exactly right.

When Innes and Michael set out on 19 January, the cloud was very low at North Weald, but they hoped it would be higher over France. As they crossed the Channel, however, it became increasingly obvious that the cloud was, if anything, even lower, and they were forced to return. It was during this flight that Innes Westmacott, who was leading, 'realised what a really fine pilot he (Michael) was. Many a pilot would have found it difficult, if not impossible, to keep formation on his leader in such conditions, but Michael stuck meticulously to my right wingtip merely remarking "not very nice" after we had landed.'

There was a chance to relax during the inclement weather. Norman Ryder, Taffy Higginson, Tommy Guest and Basil Hudson went to

London nearly every night, getting back in time for readiness next morning. On these sorties into town, if funds were low, much capital was made out of being 'poor fighter boys' and drinks were stood by admiring listeners to 'line shoots'.

Michael was given a week's leave at the end of January and he spent it at Horsey Hall, home of his sister Mary, motoring up with his mother. While at Horsey Michael had the strange experience of meeting the Luftwaffe on a more personal level. Returning from church on Sunday they saw a large fire a mile or two away and drove over to investigate. As they approached the scene a sergeant jumped on the running board of the car and announced that the fire was a crashed German aeroplane and that the crew had escaped. A few hundred yards further on they found the four German airmen.

They are dirty and unshaven – like us on dawn work – but also very muddy. One has hurt his knee. I stop people talking to them and take them in the car to the local military. The officer puts Mae Wests on the seats and they wipe their boots.

Walking in the quiet of the Norfolk countryside, Michael reflected on what the coming spring and summer might bring. He felt the German attack would be all or nothing, and although confident that the RAF would again stop the Luftwaffe he realized that the cost would be high. He felt a quiet determination to defend 'landscapes such as this before me', his only fear that of being injured and no longer able to be in the vanguard of the defence.

Michael arrived back at North Weald on 1 February, complete with four mallard which his sister Mary had given him for the mess. He flew two patrols the next day, but saw no action.

Another circus operation was laid on for 5 February. As before, Bader's 242 Squadron flew to North Weald in the morning, staying for lunch, and on arrival it followed the usual form of putting on a show for the host squadron – 'every squadron shows off when visiting as a matter of course'. The 56 Squadron pilots were singularly un-impressed.

Michael commented:

They are a good squadron and formate well, but are known as 'The Bullshit Squadron'. They do a pansy fly past and land in a manner which would be super if done properly – as it is it is much too close to allow for errors and one overshoots, nearly hitting our hut.

After lunch 249 Squadron took off, followed by 56, but Bader's aeroplane refused to start and 242 stayed behind. Forming up, 249 and 56 climbed steadily, crossing the French coast at 18,000 feet west of Calais and turning east. All was quiet. Suddenly, Sergeant Jones, flying No 2, broke violently away from the formation and dived towards the French coast. Michael watched him go. The angle of the dive was not excessive and nothing appeared wrong, but the Hurricane simply vanished. The whole squadron 'wobbled unevenly' as everyone looked round to see if any enemy aircraft were near, but there was nothing, and they flew steadily on. The formation ran into a fair amount of flak east of Gravelines, but although accurate it was fairly scattered and no damage was done. Below lay Dunkirk, 'the beaches gleam golden in the sunlight. The port looks so normal and seems to have returned to the haven of the Channel steamer of peacetime – the port whose name has made history!'

The Hurricanes recrossed the English coast without having seen any action, a few contrails high in the south and east the only sign of any enemy aircraft. Back at North Weald they found that 242 had gone home. There was no news of Sergeant Jones and he was posted as missing.

Michael flew another escort for the Blenheims of 114 Squadron on 10 February. It was to be his last operational flight with 56 Squadron. The bombers arrived over the Weald at noon. The Hurricanes had taken off ten minutes before and the two formations quickly sorted themselves out and made for the coast. Michael was impressed, as always, by the Blenheims.

> They look so vital, so sinister, so powerful, but so unprotected. It thrills me that these big machines are defenceless and depend on us for defence. A Hurricane looks so small alongside them.

Fifty-six Squadron again flew close support, with 249 and 41 Squadrons behind and above, crossing the French coast at 12,000 feet near Gravelines.

'Look out Doctor aircraft, 109s.' The voice of Victor Beamish came suddenly over the RT. As usual he had been first to see the enemy. Looking up, Michael saw 249 Squadron's Hurricanes break up, wheeling like gulls on a windy day.

> They look unconcerned, unhurried. It is a death fight and they are my friends. An aircraft is spinning, another is diving and is being

pursued by another; smoke is pouring from a fourth. I watch for upwards of a second, but all is vivid and stationary. It occurs to me in a flash how like the last war it looks – again just inconsequential pictures which portray great deeds of valour and emotion are but shadows – this air battle of my friends is real. They protect us.

A blazing mass hovers in the air. It is a blazing plane. A pilot is in there – no, it does not drop. A burning parachute – no, it burns too long. A furnace in space. This mass is probably a signal to the 109s to retire. Poor old 249 get AA now. We get a touch but all is calm.

The Blenheims dropped their bombs and turned for home, noses well down at 230 mph. With the raid over everyone's energies were concentrated on getting home. 'There is flak coming up from the ships, the fear of an attack from a hive of 109s. The rush of the dive; it is exciting; I really enjoy it; it is grand.'

The British aircraft crossed the Channel without incident – 'so narrow, so peaceful, it does not look a formidable obstacle. It stopped Napoleon; it stopped the Germans. It is amazing that so small a belt means so much.'

Making their usual rude signs of farewell to the Blenheim crews – 'one pilot is wearing a tin hat!' – the Hurricanes turned away for North Weald, landing after only 1 hr 25 mins flying.

On 16 February, a Rhubarb sortie was laid on for Michael and Taffy Higginson. Michael was keen and excited, particularly at the prospect of being led by Higginson.

Taffy is grand. Very solemn, twisting the last inch of his whiskers, talking in a lugubrious voice, saying he intends to take no risks whatever. He is a wonderful pilot and fighter, but is absolutely mature in matters of business. He is very much the same as McCudden was.

But Michael was again disappointed by the weather, which clamped down, making the operation impossible, and they stood down later in the afternoon.

Three days later Michael was talking at tea with Wing Commander Beamish, who told him that a few selected pilots were going to a new OTU at Debden for a change. Michael, unsuspecting, and wondering who would go, made several suggestions, and it came as a shock when a short time later 'Ginger' Neil of 249 Squadron burst into Michael's hut and announced without preamble: 'You're posted!'

'Of all the awful blows I have rarely had a worse.' Michael immediately went to see Beamish, but the Station Commander was firm. The old policy of only sending tired or unwanted pilots to the OTUs had proved to be a failure, he explained, and only keen and experienced people would now be sent. He pointed out that Michael had been in the squadron for nine months and that was long enough for anybody at a stretch. In vain Michael protested that he did not want a rest and was perfectly happy where he was. Beamish was adamant. 'It is for your own good and for other people's good', he explained. Michael was heartbroken. It seemed so ironic that now, when he felt so confident, so much more experienced than in the previous summer, when he would have been glad of a rest, he was being posted. To leave all his old friends in 56 and his new ones in 249 was an awful wrench.

'Ginger' Neil, who slept in the hut adjoining Michael's – 'we have a standing joke due to each occasionally waking the other up with nightmares' – Michael found highly strung but ever keen to discuss airfighting, and they had had several long talks together.

> He is a nice person and we get on well together. On the fateful evening he is rude in the Mess about my departure so we have a battle royal, only ending when a big armchair falls on top of me who am already on top of him! Both stuck, we have an armistice. We sit round and quench our thirst while everyone pulls my leg at my noisy lamentations.

Victor Beamish came into the mess later and confided to Michael that the people who were to go to the OTU had been picked personally by himself and the AOC. He again emphasized that the posting was not a 'stooge' job, but a compliment, and that anyway, Michael could come back to 56 Squadron in two or three months. 'Depression is only slightly stayed.'

The day finally arrived for Michael to leave 56 Squadron: 21 February, headlined in block capitals in his diary as 'BLACK FRIDAY'. He went down to the hangars to say goodbye to the troops, especially to his special hut, the armourers. He had always insisted that the hut was the tidiest and best appointed in the squadron and on this last visit he was delighted, as were the groundcrews, to be joined by Victor Beamish and Norman Ryder, Beamish commenting that the hut did him credit.

Michael said goodbye to all the people who had been through so much together the previous summer and autumn.

Flight Sergeant Brown, of B Flight and Dowling of A – both close friends – also a host of riggers and fitters. I find them all being paid so stand on a soap box and say goodbye to them all. They all cheer as my Ford takes me away.

On arrival at Debden, Michael found that nobody knew anything about a new OTU so he awarded himself a forty-eight hour leave. 'Where do I go? Of course, North Weald!'

A party was arranged and a good time was had by all, the festivities finally breaking up in the early hours. When Michael went into the mess next morning for breakfast he was amused to see his last night's companions looking very much the worse for wear.

I thoroughly enjoy laughing at the 'fighter boys', who take the form of a bleary eyed Taffy, drunken looking Tommy Guest, crass Innes and dour Ryder – having their somewhat meagre breakfast at 9.00 am after doing 1½ hours' readiness. An hour later they agree I will be sat upon – nay, even shat upon!

With these dire threats ringing in his ears, Michael left 56 Squadron. He was determined to return.

CHAPTER XIV

Back to War

Gerald had been recalled to the RAF on 24 August 1939, having previously been commissioned as a flight lieutenant in No 930 (Hampshire) Squadron, Royal Auxiliary Air Force in May. April 1940 found him serving in the Administrative and Special Duties Branch at the Air Ministry, and during the later stages of the Battle of Britain he was made an acting wing commander and appointed Wing Commander Tactics at Fighter Command. Visiting Michael soon after Michael's joining 56 Squadron, Gerald had been horrified at the tactics being used. All the early mistakes of the 1914–1918 war were being repeated and the lessons of that war, so dearly bought, had been forgotten and ignored. Michael had urged him to make his ideas known, and at first Gerald was reluctant – perhaps his ideas were no longer valid, the style of airfighting changed so much since 1918 – but events proved him right. The Air Ministry thinking, that all aeroplanes would move about in large formations, 'like ships at sea', were, in Gerald's own words, 'all wrong; when fighters met other fighters or bombers they at once got split up and dogfighting started just as it did in 1914–1918.'

With Wing Commander J. Kayll DSO DFC, Gerald toured the fighter squadrons, giving useful information and learning of their troubles and requests. He initiated a change in tactics in respect of fighters flying in unwieldy threes or line abreast, suggesting instead that fighting partners, or pairs, should be standard, as flown by 56 Squadron in 1918, a lesson not forgotten by the Luftwaffe and developed during the fighting in the Spanish Civil War.

On 2 June, 1941, Gerald was made Station Commander at Ford in Sussex. Activities at Ford were many and varied and Gerald took the opportunity to fly practically every type of aeroplane which used or visited the station. Under his guidance Ford was an extremely happy station. Air Commodore Roderick Chisholm, later in command of a small experimental section at Ford, recalls that the spirit of the station was a direct reflection of Gerald's personality, his keen interest in people and his human approach. Having been a fighter pilot himself,

Gerald both understood and sympathised with the sometimes prima donna attitudes of the flying crews, and he earned their affection by sharing their healthy disrespect for those in higher authority who were not directly involved in promoting the furtherance of the war to a successful conclusion.

One example of Gerald's approach typifies this. A young Australian pilot at Ford was caught red handed by the MPs while filling his car with aviation spirit. This was a 'crime' committed by nearly everyone on the station with a car, but Group decided to make an example of the young Australian, and he was placed under open arrest awaiting court martial. Gerald was upset: not only by this treatment of a youngster who had come over 10,000 miles to fight for the Mother Country, but by the waste of his training, for it seemed certain that he would be reduced to the ranks. After some thought Gerald summoned the culprit to his office.

'You know what the charge is?' he asked.

'Yes, sir'.

'Will you accept my judgement?'

'Yes, sir'.

'How do you plead?'

'Guilty, sir'.

'Very well. You are sentenced to two hours' detention in your room. Dismiss.'

The youngster still stood before Gerald, obviously puzzled.

'What will happen about the court martial, sir?'

'As your commanding officer I have the right to try and sentence you, and I have done so,' replied Gerald. 'You cannot be tried twice for the same offence, so you cannot be court martialled now.' As the delighted young pilot left the room he failed to hear Gerald's *sotto voce* comment ... 'but I can'.

When Gerald took command at Ford there was still a great deal of work to be done in bringing the station to a more efficient operational state, but within a month of his arrival the perimeter track had been completed and the landing ground showed a marked improvement. In August 1941, Gerald's old RFC boss of 1917 days, 'Boom' Trenchard, visited the station, flying in again in December, and he and Gerald talked over old times and refought old battles.

Ford was an excellent aerodrome. Its approaches were good from both east and west, and the River Arun, the castle and church at Arundel, all provided good landmarks. In his book, *Cover of Darkness*, Air Commodore Chisholm recalls that the weather at Ford was often better than in other parts of the country, murky or overcast conditions frequently clearing once the downs to the north had been passed.

Quite apart from the advantages enjoyed by Ford from the purely flying aspect, the station was also ideally situated for Gerald personally. Arundel Castle, the home of his cousin, the Duke of Norfolk, was only a mile or two to the north, and Alresford only just over an hour's drive away.

With typical generosity, Gerald threw open Alresford House to the operational flying crews, and they were able to relax for brief periods in the calm, unhurried atmosphere of the old house and its beautiful grounds. But not for long. At the outbreak of war Carrie had turned the flower gardens into two acres of tomatoes and vegetables in aid of the Dig for Victory campaign, but there were still acres of seemingly useless bush covered and marshy land. It was suggested that, if spring water could be found, watercress might be a possibility, and on his next leave Gerald sank a two inch pipe into the ground. At twenty feet he hit clear spring water and around this the first trial bed was laid. All the pilots who visited from Ford then lent a hand in the construction of the watercress beds. John Cunningham, 'Rory' Chisholm, Michael, and a host of others, helped to clear the ground. Hundreds of tons of earth were moved and concrete paths, dams, spillways and drains were laid, more pipes being sunk down to the water supply. Gerald and Carrie found an expert helper from nearby Sutton Scotney in Mr J. Biggs, who together with his father had been growing watercress for over fifty years. Under his expert guidance the beds were laid and Alresford became a successful watercress farm, continuing to the present day.

CHAPTER XV

604 Squadron

The beginning of October 1941 found Michael at No 60 (Night Fighting) OTU at East Fortune. He had now been off operational flying for eight months and was anxious to get back to a squadron. After leaving 56 Squadron, Michael had spent a month at No 52 OTU, Debden before leaving at the end of March for a six weeks' instructors' course at the Central Flying School. As had many pilots before him, he found the course at the CFS a rewarding experience in the art of flying. Flying accurately, he found, was all important – keeping to the right speed and height, and combining all manoeuvres with the appropriate 'patter' for the benefit of the pupil – and with his usual self-critical and analytical approach he was able to refine and improve his flying. His landings, which had always been 'purely a safe way of coming home for tea', now became the conclusion of a systematic approach which was later to stand him in good stead, and he passed out the course with a good rating, Wing Commander H. 'Speedy' Holmes considering he would make an excellent instructor and asking him to come back. 'I thank him kindly, but say that is the *last* thing I want.'

While at Upavon, Michael was able to spend the occasional weekend at Alresford, where Carrie was always happy to see him – 'a perfect sister in law' – and he also visited Middle Wallop, the home of 604 Squadron, famous for its night fighting successes. At the end of the course at CFS he dined with Rory Chisholm, 'Pop' Geddes and John Cunningham, all of 604 Squadron, and found them good company and charming people. In fact, he found a wonderful spirit in 604 Squadron as a whole, and although his diary reveals that he still considered himself a member of 56 Squadron, an alternative to rejoining 56 began to take shape in his thoughts of the future. He disliked the idea of flying a twin engined aeroplane – 604 Squadron was equipped with the Bristol Beaufighter – but the job and the company seemed agreeable and rewarding.

Back at Debden, Michael carried on with instructing, finding it 'rather fun', the pupils improving quickly and the work constantly changing. The course at the CFS had given him a new confidence and he found the thrill of being competent and sure of his instructing techniques a gratifying experience. Instructing was not without its drama and excitement. Watching a pupil take off for his first flight in a Hurricane, Michael was horrified to see another taking off in a Master.

It is a terrible sight. At 100 feet the Master starts doing a climbing turn to the right. Higher and higher goes his nose, steeper and steeper the turn. The Hurricane goes straight on. Suddenly there is a crash – a cloud of debris come off – both aircraft go on!

The Master pilot put his nose down, did a circuit, despite having only half a tailplane, and landed safely, but to Michael's horror the Hurricane began to turn.

It is bound to stall. Making a noise like fifty racing baby Austins over revving it makes a sagging circuit at 90 mph. He gets round, puts wheels and flaps down and lands safely. Half of each of the three prop blades are off. Someone said that no instructor could have done it – only an inexperienced pupil. We all had pups!

Fifty-six Squadron still exerted a pull, and in June Michael motored over to North Weald for lunch. He was given a friendly welcome and was especially glad to see Taffy Higginson again, looking well and in good form. Taffy loaned Michael his Hurricane II for a forty five minute local flight and he found it a great improvement over the old Mark 1. It was pleasant being back in the atmosphere of an operational squadron again, and many old friends were still present, but Michael later recorded sadly: 'It is the last time I see Taffy.' Just under a week later he returned to North Weald for a party and was stunned to hear that Taffy, 'Junior' Harris, Robinson and another pilot had all been shot down. Of all the pilots in 56 Squadron, with the possible exception of Ian Soden, Michael had the greatest respect and admiration for Taffy Higginson, considering him *the* pilot of the squadron, and he was both saddened and angered at the news of Taffy's loss. Saddened at the loss of a friend; angered because Higginson had been fighting, with no rest, since the early days of the war. The long convoy patrols; the detachment to France in May 1940; the Battle of Britain; the later fighter sweeps over France, nearly two years of continuous operations. 'Those responsible for not sending him away are fools – bloody fools.'[1]

At the party, Michael had a talk with 56 Squadron's new CO, 'Prosser' Hanks. Michael was impressed by Hanks, 'tough looking and flat out for the squadron', who told him that before Norman Ryder had left he had advised him to get Michael back into 56. Michael was delighted to hear this, but at the back of his mind was the first faint glimmering of a hankering for night fighting. During the course of the evening he had a long talk with 'Spekie' Speke, a much loved member of 604 Squadron, who advised him very strongly to try for a posting to 604 Squadron, pointing out that it was an interesting and pleasant existence. Michael looked round the room; at all the old 56 Squadron faces: Fisher, Barry Sutton, Mounsdon, Peter Down, 'all in various stages of repair', and memories of the pre-blitz 56 came flooding forcibly back: of Tommy Rose, Ian Soden, Taffy, Ken Marston. Could he possibly be happy in any other squadron?

In the middle of June, now promoted to flight lieutenant, Michael spent a few days at Alresford, visiting Ford with Gerald. Gerald showed him over the Fighter Interception Unit (FIU) and after tea they collected Rory Chisholm from Tangmere. Chisholm, an old Amplefordian and a long standing friend of the Constable Maxwell family, was a leading member of 604 Squadron and had had some success at night fighting, shooting down two enemy aircraft in the course of a single patrol three months before. Looking at Chisholm's Beaufighter, squat and ugly, sinister in its black camouflage, Michael wondered if he could ever give up the joys of a Hurricane for such a 'tub-like bus'.

A 56 Squadron pilot forcelanded at Debden in late June and Michael took the opportunity to fly him back to Duxford in the OTU's Domini. One disturbing piece of news learnt at Duxford was that Michael's recent promotion to flight lieutenant rather precluded his getting back into 56 Squadron, which already had its allocation of flight commanders, with no change envisaged in the foreseeable future.

On his arrival at 60 OTU at the end of July, Michael was interviewed by Wing Commander Edwards-Jones as to his plans for the future, and this new circumstance prompted Michael to reply that he would like a posting to a twin engined night fighter squadron. Michael wrote to Gerald, telling him of the interview, and Gerald wrote back to

1. Happily, Higginson was not dead. He escaped from captivity and later led a Wing.

say that he had almost arranged Michael's posting back to 56 Squadron, but that in view of his letter was now working on a posting to 604 Squadron. 'What a life', Michael wrote. 'This is depressing as I would have liked 56 but, failing that, 604.'

Michael stayed a little over two months at East Fortune. Although he enjoyed his life there he felt bored with instructing, and despite having flown fifteen hours at night felt he was doing less flying than he would have liked. He was therefore feeling a little jaded and one evening in the ante-room, when asked if he would like to be posted, replied a little offhandedly, 'Yes, but to a certain squadron'.

'Well, you're posted to 604,' replied Wing Commander Cole, 'and you're to get there as quickly as possible.'

No 604 (County of Middlesex) Squadron was an Auxiliary squadron, formed at Hendon in March 1930. Mobilised at the time of the Munich crisis in 1938, the squadron had been sent to North Weald, returning to its home base at Hendon as the crisis passed and re-equipping with Bristol Blenheims at the end of the year. At the outbreak of war the squadron went again to North Weald to serve as a day and night fighter squadron, standing at readiness with Nos 56 and 151 Squadrons. But the excellent forward view, navigational capacity, longer duration and the general unsuitability for day fighting, made the Blenheims the natural selection for night readiness duties and despite their lack of experience in night flying, the pilots and gunners of 604 readily accepted their new role.

It was a frustrating role. Night after night the squadron's Blenheims took off to attempt to intercept the German night raiders, chasing after rumours and false alarms before returning, often through bad weather, to the small, ill-equipped airfields. In those early days there was a far more deadlier foe than the Luftwaffe: Sir Isaac Newton. In the mess of a later night fighter OTU a large picture of Sir Isaac was flanked by a tiny picture of Hitler, with beneath them both the caption 'Relative Dangers'. Gravity was the implacable enemy to the crews of 604 Squadron, learning their trade during the winter of 1939–1940.

With the refinement of a radar set small enough to be carried in an aeroplane, events were to change rapidly. Work had been progressing steadily since 1936, when the world's first airborne radar had been carried in an Avro Anson, but it was seen merely as an air to surface (ships) radar and it was not until May 1939, a bare three months before the beginning of the war, that the first Air Interception (AI) flew in a Fairey Battle. 604 Squadron received its first AI Mark III set equipped Blenheims in the early summer of 1940, the squadron's airgunners becoming reconciled to their new role as radio operators, but the AI Mark III was an inefficient set and it was not until the arrival of the Beaufighter Mark 1, with its vastly improved AI Mark IV, that the squadron had its first success against the night raiders, John Cunningham shooting down a Ju 88 on the night of 19–20 November 1940, for the first success at night in a Beaufighter.

The temperament and intellect of the 604 Squadron crews perhaps ideally equipped them for their task of seeking out the German bombers in the vastness of the night skies. As Auxiliaries they were older than most pilots and aircrew of the regular RAF, drawn from the world of business and the City: mature men, used to getting results. Not being regular officers they had no inhibitions in speaking their minds to senior officers when attempting to obtain the latest equipment; 'civilians in uniform' they adapted themselves to this new art of fighting in the night skies: pooling ideas, thinking out new gadgets, systems, tactics, endlessly experimenting, arguing, talking shop. As in a business enterprise, nothing was allowed to stand in the way of success and by the summer of 1941 they had brought the task of night interception by airborne radar to a fine art, developing a system which put the squadron in the forefront of night fighter squadrons.

When Michael joined 604 Squadron on 8 October 1941, the CO was John Cunningham, formerly a flight commander, who had been with the squadron since 1935, a not uncommon occurrence in 604. Twenty four years of age, with a DFC and bar and DSO, Cunningham was the RAF's leading night fighter pilot and had scored the squadron's first victory at night to be won in a Beaufighter fitted with AI Mark IV radar – 'the magic box'. Quiet, unassuming, he was the ideal leader for 604, interfering little, knowing that the members of the squadron were keen, conscientious, and needed no driving to the job in hand. A pre-war test pilot for the de Havilland Company, Cunningham was a natural pilot, never happier than when flying, and Michael recorded after a flight with him: 'He is the finest pilot whom I have ever seen and it is a joy to be with him. One flight with him and you see why he has done so well.' An integral part of Cunningham's success was his operator, Jimmy Rawnsley – 'the quiet little voice from the back'. A peacetime electrical engineer, Rawnsley was a modest and friendly person, 'the perfect natural gentleman'. Small in stature, he affected an Irwin flying suit several sizes too large, and devotedly nursed his weak-eyed white Sealyham terrier. Michael thought him 'one of the kindest and most thoughtful people I have ever met'.

Roderick Chisholm, who had taken over John Cunningham's flight on the latter's promotion to commanding officer, had joined 604 in 1930, but had left when his job as an oil technician had taken him to Persia. Returning to England at the beginning of 1940, he had to take a full refresher course before rejoining the squadron. Unlike Cunningham, Chisholm was not a natural pilot, which added to the considerable hazards of flying at night. A lesser man would have asked for a posting to a day fighter squadron, but Chisholm was made of sterner stuff. By sheer determination, application and raw courage he improved his flying, and mastered the art of instrument flying at night. With his patient approach and clear brain he was a teacher of great natural ability, able to explain the intricacies of the magic box to the new people, spending many hours with pilots and their operators until they had mastered the new theories and techniques.

John Selway, another 'B' Flight pilot, was a great imitator of the myriad excuses made by the airmen. 'Not my job, sir ...Well you see, sir ... Sorry, sir, he's gone to tea, sir'. Selway was teamed with Derek Jackson, a peacetime university professor, famous for his work in astro-physics. He had a varied life style before the war, from lecturing at Balliol to riding in the Grand National, and he brought a scientific approach to the problems of night interception with airborne radar. With his outlook on life in general, and his brilliant, if at times unpredictable personality, Derek Jackson was at first treated as something of an oddity until his worth was realized. Originally paired with Vernon Motion, with whom he had frequent and heated arguments, Jackson finally teamed up with John Selway who, realizing Jackson was something of a genius, did as he was told, laughing at and with his new operator. They made a perfect pair and the result was excellent.

Vernon Motion, at thirty-seven a lot older than most pilots, had several thousand hours of flying in his logbook, both civilian and military. Tall, dark and slim, he first appeared to Michael as a typical film villain, but despite this initial impression he later found Vernon Motion to be one of the most kindhearted and tolerant of men, with a superb sense of humour, usually directed against himself. Given to painting his own character in the blackest of colours, Motion would describe his matrimonial career as 'two confirmed, one probable'. Nicknamed, not unnaturally, either 'Perpetual' or 'Commotion', he was a fine pilot, with plenty of courage, and ready to fly in all weathers. Along with Pilot Officer Thwaites – 'Twaites' because of his inability to pronounce his own name – Mickey Phillips, and Hadji

Baba, Chisholm's dog, 'Captain Hadgi', these personalities composed B Flight in the autumn of 1941.

A Flight also had its share of squadron personalities, all of whom had an influence on Michael in various ways. The flight commander, Squadron Leader Stanley Skinner, son of a successful publisher, had scant regard for senior officers – 'those senior bunglers' – and was justly famous amongst the groundcrews for his telephone conversations with exalted people at Group. Any order from Group of which Skinner did not personally approve, would occasion an immediate telephone call. He would ask to speak to the most senior officer present. 'Is that you . . .? Skinner here', would set the tone of the conversation. He then usually demolished all opposition with a devastating 'Don't be silly old man, it's no . . . use', and several wing commanders, overawed by his imperious manner, had been known to call him 'sir'. Skinner believed that the war should be fought in as comfortable a manner as possible and did everything in his power to expedite this. Another member of A Flight was Edward Crew, a successful night fighter pilot with five or six victories to his credit and a DFC, plus the dubious distinction of having shot down a Hurricane at night, probably mistaking it, as Michael caustically remarked, for a Ju 52, the large, three engined German transport aeroplane. Short, thickset, and, despite his shyness, a great character and personality, Crew was an ex-Cambridge University Air Squadron pilot and he and Michael had many acquaintances in common. Good company, with a keen sense of fun, under the influence of several pink gins or port, either of which he enjoyed in immoderate amounts, Crew became even more dignified and quiet. When Michael and Crew shared a room Michael's nightly duty was to take away Crew's book after he had fallen asleep. One night Michael neglected to take away the book, just to see what would happen. Crew was most hurt, pointing out that it was the prerogative of anyone sharing a room with him to take his book, tuck him up in the approved manner and switch off the light.

With these and other pilots, and their respective navigators, Michael quickly realized why the squadron had become so successful and he soon felt at home in his new surroundings, the thoughts of 56 Squadron receding as he applied himself to the new tactics and techniques of fighting at night.

Rory Chisholm gave Michael his first flight in a Beaufighter on the evening of 9 October, Michael standing behind Chisholm in the small well formed by the floor of the escape hatch. The Beaufighter,

Chisholm's own 'O' for Orifice, seemed to Michael to take a long time to leave the ground, going up slowly, 'like a lift', at 160 mph, but he was impressed by the smoothness and fascinated to hear Sergeant Ripley working 'the magic' from the rear. The following day he flew with John Cunningham and Jimmy Rawnsley, appreciating for the first time Cunningham's ability as a pilot – 'he seems to treat the Beau like a biplane' – and becoming accustomed to the 'twin fans'. After these two flights, Michael was longing to fly the Beaufighter himself, but Chisholm first checked him out on a Blenheim, showing him the 'taps' on a circuit before allowing him to fly it solo. Michael found the Blenheim an easy aeroplane to handle, and after landing he and Chisholm motored over to Alresford for the evening, with Chisholm explaining on the way the stages of development of the AI radar. 'He has a wonderfully clear brain and expounds forcefully – not to say loudly – and simply.'

Returning to Middle Wallop next morning, Michael flew the Blenheim again and had another flight in Chisholm's Beaufighter. He was now champing at the bit, and asked John Cunningham if he could take up a Beaufighter, but the CO insisted that he do another two hours' solo in the Blenheim. Michael, impatient to get his hands on a Beaufighter, flew the Blenheim for two hours that evening, doing dusk and night landings, and this keenness brought on a fatigue spell, common if a new type of aeroplane is flown too much at the outset. On the final landing Michael found that he was lost on the aerodrome, finally ending up in 93 Squadron's dispersal. On getting back to the 604 mess he found Cunningham and Rawnsley at supper. Cunningham was encouraging about Michael's flying, amused at his getting lost, and gave his blessing for taking a Beaufighter solo next day.

On 14 October 1941, after a fifteen minute circuit checkout by Chisholm, Michael flew a Beaufighter for the first time. The takeoff was a little bumpy, owing to the beginner's usual error of not getting the tail up quickly enough, but once airborne he found it a pleasant aeroplane to fly and very smooth. He had flown nearly eight hours on twin engined aeroplanes by this time and found the Beaufighter easy enough to handle, but it was obvious that it needed care and concentration, that any mistake would be difficult to rectify. It was far from the delightful 'toy' the Hurricane had been.

The next afternoon, after a solo flight in the morning, Michael flew for two hours with his newly appointed operator/navigator, a fair-haired young sergeant named John Quinton, whose shy stammer on the ground disappeared completely as he interpreted the blips on the cathode ray tube of his AI radar. Michael and John Quinton, out-wardly so different, got on well from their first meeting and made an excellent team in the air, but neither could have foreseen that it was the beginning of four and a half years of friendship and shared dangers.

Ten days after his initial solo flight in a Beaufighter, Michael flew the type for the first time at night. Take-off and final touchdown presented no problems, but after the Hurricane, Michael was unac-customed to the side view from the cockpit being obscured by the massive Hercules engines, and the large turning circle made getting into the Funnel – the approach lights – a little tricky. This problem soon disappeared with familiarity. Three days later Michael flew again at night, this time with the added responsibility of a passenger – John Quinton as operator – but all went smoothly and he found Mother, the radar beacons, a great help. That night he entered in his diary. 'I am now operational.'

Michael had put in a great number of hours in a relatively short period, benefiting beyond measure from the guidance and tuition of Rory Chisholm who, good teacher that he was, took endless trouble and interest. Michael was now at home in the Beaufighter and becom-ing appreciative of its many qualities. It was a comfortable aeroplane, safe and easy to fly, as long as flown in the prescribed manner, but it was not an aeroplane in which to let off steam; no expensive toy to be thrown around the sky in a lighthearted manner. Fast, with an immense endurance, and packing a terrific firepower – with its four 20mm cannon and six .303 machine guns it was the most heavily armed fighter in the world – it was an aeroplane designed for a job, which it did superbly. Flying the Beaufighter was a rewarding and maturing experience, finally giving more satisfaction than a single engined fighter.

Michael quickly analysed and came to terms with his new environ-ment. The differences between day and night fighting were fundamen-tal: people took on the characteristics of the aeroplanes they flew and adapted to the different type of hazards they faced. The atmosphere in 604 Squadron was entirely different from that of a day fighter squad-ron. The most dangerous part of a day fighter pilot's existence was fighting, the actual flying an incidental which was safe in comparison. The day fighter pilot had the contentment and joy of flying a high powered and relatively easy to control aeroplane, an aeroplane with which he could relieve his pent up emotions with aerobatics and generally showing off in the approved manner of all fighter pilots. His medium of expression was flying, which he loved, and the same spirit which made him land a little too close to his leader, showed itself on the ground in the corners taken a little faster each time in his car, and the lighthearted, schoolboyish jokes in the mess, where the whole atmosphere was gay, irresponsible and devil-may-care. Wine, women, song, flying, fighting – everything was undertaken 'flat out'.

The atmosphere of a night fighter station was very different: quieter, more mature, where people enjoyed life in a more grown up fashion. There were none of the high and low spots of a day fighter pilot's existence; no opportunities to relieve tensions with a line shoot or the exhilaration of throwing a high powered aeroplane about the sky. The aeroplanes of a night fighter squadron were weapons of war, designed for the job in hand; a less colourful job, where flying itself was a greater danger than the enemy. The Beaufighter *could* be thrown about by a good pilot, and often was, but the necessity to leave a greater margin of error robbed the exercise of its purpose. To let off steam in a Beaufighter merely meant making 'a dent in the ground', and flying it safely called for continuous concentration and care. Stanley Skinner's description of it as 'a brick with lights' was apt, but it matured boys into men by its demands and the responsibilities it engendered, changing their attitudes and way of life.

Michael benefited greatly from these changes. He still loved the Hurricane, but the satisfaction was waning. He was beginning to feel the need for something more demanding, capable of development. The only aspect of his new role he found disturbing was his responsibility for a passenger, his operator, but he accepted this readily after a while, realizing that he was now part of a team, a unit, self contained, no longer a mere number such as Red 2 or Yellow 3. He was maturing rapidly.

Michael and John Quinton were 'on flap' for the first time on the night of 28 October. Being at readiness again was an exhilarating moment for Michael. It was over eight months since he had last been operational and he pondered on what dangers and excitements this new type of fighting might bring. The night was dark and he looked to the south, wondering what was in store.

They were sent off at 9.25 pm, Michael flying through cloud on his instruments until breaking out into brilliant moonlight at 8,000 feet. It was an eerie but beautiful world, the strong, silvery light making the clouds far finer than by day. Michael was astounded at the immense distance he could see, by the vast panorama of this new arena. The voice of the controller at Sopley broke into his thoughts, advising him to 'hang about', and a little later came the quiet instruction. 'I have a customer for you.' 'Oh joy, oh thrill;' was their training to be rewarded by a combat on their first patrol? Michael chased the contact for sometime, but it turned out to be a friendly. A second contact brought the same frustrating result, and the Beaufighter returned after an hour and three quarters. Despite his disappointment at the lack of action, Michael was elated at being operational again, eating a hearty supper before he realized that he had had no dinner in his excitement.

Over the last months of 1941 and into 1942, Michael and John Quinton became increasingly proficient in their new trade, the only disappointment being the lack of material success. 604 Squadron's sector was to the west of London and it saw little action. As the squadron history relates, 'the peaceful days had come, when the Hun stopped coming for punishment'. It is impossible to assess to what extent 604 Squadron was responsible for this, but it was certainly greater than its personal score board.

This lack of action, however, did not preclude the possibility of casualties. Sir Isaac was still a cogent force. On 9 November the squadron suffered a great loss, and Michael a personal one, when Mike Staples, an old friend from Ampleforth, was killed while coming in to land.

Michael spent Christmas Day 1941 at Alresford with Gerald and Carrie. While out shooting with Vernon Motion a few days earlier he had been hit in the eye by a ricocheting pellet and, although not serious, the injury caused him to be stood down from flying. 'This needs a lot of laughing off as B Flight is on flap over Xmas.' Driving to Alresford – 'on one engine a bit tricky' – he felt the old thrill of going home for the Xmas holidays, and that evening the association was strengthened by Midnight Mass being broadcast from Ampleforth. Michael rang up Chisholm, who listened while at readiness in the hangar. Driving back to Middle Wallop on Christmas night, Michael found that his drug-treated eye worked very well at night and he arrived back in good time for dinner and a party in the mess.

In January, Rory Chisholm was posted to Group HQ, B Flight being taken over by George MacLannahan and Michael moving to A Flight, commanded by Stanley Skinner. On 8 March Michael and John came close to engaging their first enemy bomber at night. Taking off at 7.50 pm, a contact was soon made, the controller at Sopley warning them of trade coming in from the south south east and well out to sea. Michael orbited once and set off south, barely containing his excitement. Everything went according to the book, the Beaufighter approaching to within two miles of the contact before the controller's voice warned: 'Very sorry, friendly. Do not go any nearer.' Five minutes later they were infuriated to be told that it had been an enemy after all, but although Michael chased after it, he could not close the distance.

In March, John Cunningham broke the news to Michael that he was to be posted. Group had requested someone to take charge of the AI Flight at 60 OTU at East Fortune and Cunningham had decided it should be Michael. The fact that it would carry promotion to squadron leader meant little to Michael, who tried every ploy he could think of to avoid the posting. May he stay, in any rank? Even go out east? – anything to avoid another spell at an OTU – but Cunningham was firm. 'I have thought it out from all angles and I have made up my mind. You will soon be a squadron leader and will then have to go, so better you go now.'

Michael was very upset. He had greatly enjoyed his six months with 604, ideal in every respect save one: the chance of putting all the theories and training into practice. Now he was to leave without so much as having had a shot at an enemy aeroplane at night. Returning to the mess, Michael asked John Quinton whether he would accompany him anywhere he was sent. John readily agreed, but when Michael qualified the question with, 'Even to an OTU?', his face fell and he could hardly believe the news, thinking, like Michael, that they would have at least six months on operations. The squadron was loath to lose Quinton, but recognizing the value of the partnership finally agreed to his accompanying Michael.

Michael and John remained at East Fortune for the next five months, training the pilots and operators in the use of the AI and pairing them into teams. Although he felt deeply about each of his postings, Michael had the happy facility of adapting quickly and completely to each change, usually ending up quite content in his new surroundings. It was exciting taking up his first command, and starting from scratch – the OTU was being completely reorganized – made it doubly interesting. Michael was determined to promote the 604 Squadron method of interception against any opposition, but found on discussing it with his fellow instructors that they agreed wholeheartedly with his proposals, differing only in small details. With John Quinton's able help he found the task of sorting out the pupils into efficient teams a rewarding exercise, in which his keen judgement of human nature and personalities came into its own.

This pairing of pilots and operators was an extremely important and delicate relationship. Close friends off duty did not necessarily make the best team when flying, and often people of different and varied temperament evolved into successful crews.

CHAPTER XVI

Intruder

While Michael was at East Fortune, Gerald, still at Ford, was taking every opportunity to fly unofficially on operations. Only one account of such a flight survives, tucked away amongst Gerald's private papers, but there were 'several others'.

Half an hour after midnight on the night of 10/11 June 1942, a Boston 111, YP-W of 23 Squadron, took off from Ford. Pilot Officer McCulloch was flying the Boston, with Flight Sergeant Styles as his observer and Sergeant Clark as airgunner. The rear gunner of the Boston was Gerald. As the Boston crossed the enemy coast at St Valery, thirty five minutes after takeoff, Gerald called up McCulloch from the rear turret.

'How old are you, McCulloch?'

'Twenty-one, sir,' answered the puzzled McCulloch.

Gerald chuckled. 'The last time I crossed this coast was two years before you were born.'

The Boston flew first to the enemy aerodrome at Evreux and patrolled the area for forty-five minutes, hoping to engage any enemy bombers returning to their base, but there was no sign of any activity and McCulloch flew to Rouen, circling the town for nearly ten minutes until he saw some lights on the east bank of the river Seine. These were from the power station at Grand Quevilly, south west of the town, and the Boston attacked from 1,500 feet, dropping sixteen bombs. Several hits were seen, followed by explosions and blue flashes. Three searchlights then found the Boston, and a larger, diffused light held it for a minute and a half while McCulloch took violent evasive action. Successfully losing the searchlights, McCulloch headed for home, recrossing the French coast – again at St Valery – and landing at Ford at fourteen minutes past three. Gerald had anticipated Michael's later role as an intruder by just over six months.

At the end of August 1942, Michael was on leave, staying at Alresford and visiting Ford with Gerald. While at the station he flew a Hawker Typhoon for the first time, liking it very much and racing a

Spitfire, thrilled to find that with the Typhoon at cruising speed the Spitfire was flat out.

Flying over to Middle Wallop in the evening, in a more sedate de Havilland Hornet, Michael and Rory Chisholm spent the night in the old familiar surroundings of The Pheasant, but on returning to Ford next morning this pleasant interlude was terminated by Michael being recalled to East Fortune. On arrival he found that it had been decided to dispense with one night fighter OTU, and although considered by most people to be the better, East Fortune was to be dropped in favour of No 54 OTU at Charter Hall, the personal baby of the AOC, Air Commodore Vincent. Michael was furious. Not only were his own and John Quinton's hopes of returning to an operational squadron dashed, but their work of the last months was seemingly wasted, and it was with decidedly mixed feelings that they took up their new duties at Winfield, the satellite aerodrome of Charter Hall.

Michael came to feel that he was wasting his time at Winfield, doing little or no flying, and hearing of a chance to go out east with 255 Squadron he asked to be allowed to go, but Wing Commander Miller was adamant that he stay at Charter Hall to take command of B Squadron.

Training at 54 OTU carried on much as before and it was not until the middle of November that the welcome news at last came that Michael was posted back to 604 Squadron as a flight commander, and he motored south on the 18th of the month, reaching Andover after dark. After visiting the chapel and dedicating his new flight to St Francis and St Ignatius, he finally reached The Pheasant at 9.30 pm to find many old friends. 'Home at last!'

Michael was to spend only a month in 604 Squadron. The CO was now Wing Commander Wood, who after a few weeks told Michael that he was again posted. This time squadron politics had played a part. Gonsalves had previously been in command of B Flight, but was too junior to keep it, hence Michael's posting, but Gonsalves' promotion had now come through and he had been posted as a flight commander to 264 Squadron. Wood, knowing Gonsalves, was determined to keep him in 604, and had arranged for Michael to be sent to 264 Squadron in his place. It was a cruel blow.

Michael and John Quinton flew over to their new squadron at Colerne on 12 December, loading their Beaufighter NG-N with their kit and taking Pilot Officer Jack Foster with them to fly it back. Foster watched with mounting horror as Michael had loaded trunks, several suitcases, golf clubs, gun, kitbags and a bicycle, the last having to be dismantled and loaded through the escape hatch in the roof. After this, John Quinton's kit was put aboard! They staggered off successfully, flew round the coast – 604 Squadron was now at Predannack – and landed safely at Colerne. After giving Foster tea in the Mess, Michael walked back to the aerodrome with him and watched him depart in NG-N. As the Beaufighter taxied out, Michael reflected that it was his last link with 604, a good squadron, which he had now left for ever, and a Mosquito of his new squadron taking off failed to interest him in the slightest.

Feeling extremely low in spirits, he returned to the 264 Squadron Mess where his fellow flight commander, Squadron Leader Bryant-Fenn, introduced him to the others.

> He couldn't be nicer. Welcoming and anxious to show me around and meet the boys. It is nice of him, but it is maddening; I have no interest in this new squadron and fear it will show. I have worked up so much enthusiasm for 604 that a change means utter bathos and boredom.

Michael excused himself and went for a walk. Realising that this attitude of mind was thoroughly unproductive, that to mope about the situation was hopeless, he decided to forget the past entirely; never to think of Wood as being responsible for his having to again leave 604 Squadron and resolving to look only to the future and his service with 264 Squadron. He walked over to the chapel, turning these thoughts over in his mind, and when he returned to the mess he felt a different person. 'There are a few people about and it is an interest and a pleasure to meet them.' He had no premonition that his new posting was to prove one of the most successful periods of his service life.

No 264 Squadron was undergoing a period of change. Equipped with the DH Mosquito Mark 11 with the AI Mark V radar, orders had come through to strip six of its Mosquitos of their AI and fit additional fuel tanks. There was 'much rumouring and little knowledge'. The rumours finally coalesced into a new type of operation: Instep. The anti-submarine Sunderland flying boats, operating in the Bay of Biscay, were being lost to Ju 88 fighters, and an attempt to counter the threat with Beaufighters was not always successful. It had been decided to send Mosquitos and Mustangs to deal with the Ju 88s and Michael and Bryant-Fenn attended a briefing at Group HQ by the SASO, Air Commodore Rowley, to discuss the problems of operating

Mosquitos over the sea. Several navigators from a coastal Beaufighter squadron gave them all the tips they could, warning that it was imperative to leave a wide margin for error in their navigation. The Mosquitos were to operate from Portreath in Cornwall, where they would team up with the Mustangs of 400 Squadron RCAF, and Bryant-Fenn and Flying Officer Muir, with their respective operators, flew the first Instep patrol on 17 December. Apart from the return trip, when Bryant-Fenn was startled to see Ushant to the north of the Mosquitos, the patrol was uneventful, and the following day Michael and John Quinton, with Flying Officer Porter and his operator, flew to Portreath to carry out another, their escorts being Squadron Leader Woods and Flying Officer 'Pep' Pepper of 400 Squadron. Woods explained the form to Michael and John over lunch. The fact that they would fly at 300 feet above the sea, Michael found a trifle disconcerting, and he was amazed at the normal meal which the Canadian pilots ate, and their lack of apprehension at the prospect of flying over the sea for nearly two hours on one engine.

The four aircraft took off after lunch, crossing the Lizard in line abreast. After ten minutes Michael became accustomed to the 'general wetness all round' and settled down to watch for enemy fighters. The Mustangs looked very precarious with their single engine, but grandly pugnacious with their square cut wingtips and splendid streamlining, and Michael was glad of their presence as they entered the operating area of the German FW 190s.

In the event the patrol passed without incident. No enemy aeroplanes were seen, and the little force returned after two hours ten minutes. Michael, relaxed after the patrol, made a routine approach, coming across wind and lowering the Mosquito's wheels, but as he lined up for the final approach the port engine abruptly cut. In a pure reflex action, Michael opened up the other engine to maintain his speed and make sure of getting in, but with only seven hours on Mosquitos his reflexes were still atuned to the Beaufighter and, unlike a Beaufighter in a similar situation, the Mosquito simply surged ahead. Michael just had time to inform Control. 'My port engine has cut. I am coming in to land', before concentrating on the touchdown, the controller answering, 'Say again please.'

Michael ignored the request. He had his hands full of Mosquito. With the engine throttled back the flaps took a long time to come down and the aeroplane was going fast across the aerodrome, the stone wall at the end of the runway looking horribly close. Behind the wall, Michael knew, was a slope down to the cliffs, then a sheer drop into the sea. He applied the brakes, but they locked and the Mosquito careered on. Michael next tried to retract the wheels, but they stayed resolutely down and the Mosquito took the wall at high speed. 'There is an expensive noise as £30,000 of Mosquito reverts to its parent matchwood.' Michael and John quickly scrambled clear, conscious of the danger of fire, but after a moment, seeing no sign of flames, Michael crawled back into the wreckage, put on his helmet and called up control. 'I say again. My port engine has packed up, my starboard has now packed up too.'

Michael and John had escaped the 'landing' with little more than a bruise on Michael's bottom, and the MO gave them some tea and let them go. The stone wall had served a useful purpose in stopping the Mosquito just before the slope down to the cliffs and a three hundred foot drop into the sea. The aeroplane had left a perfect impression in the wall and earned Michael the nickname of 'silhouette'.

Michael spent the evening pub crawling with the 400 Squadron pilots, finding them such delightful company that he cancelled his hotel and passed the night at their dispersal. The next day being foggy, operations were cancelled, and after tea the crews went into Falmouth for a night out. Michael, having only flying clothes, was loaned the uniform of a pilot on leave and coached in Canadian to match the Canada flashes on his shoulders. He was to hail from Didsbury, Alberta, where his father owned the *Didsbury Chronicle*, with a weekly circulation of 500 copies – 502 when the family were at home! During the evening, one of the Canadians, forgetting Michael was wearing a pilot officer's uniform, made the error of calling him 'Sir', and Michael imposed the penalty of drinks all round on the culprit. When another forgetful pilot later hastily amended his 'Sir' to 'Sir Mike', a naval officer drinking nearby was intrigued enough to ask why the title. It was explained that Michael was of an old Scottish family, who had taken the title to the New World in 1680. After that everyone addressed Michael as 'Sir Mike' with impunity. Despite Michael's coaching by 'Hank' Hanton, the naval officer was puzzled by his accent being so slight, but it was explained away by Michael having spent a year at Oxford. By the middle of the evening, Michael was well into his role, speaking 'Canadian' without effort, and as the evening progressed, Hank Hanton, who at first could not understand why he and Michael had never met in Didsbury, began to recall various occasions on which they had, even good times they had shared in their home town in Alberta. At the end of the party a pretty girl came into the bar, announcing that she loved Canadians. Michael, as a good Canadian, felt it his duty to kiss her, the 400 Squadron boys forming up behind him. The girl was amazed at the number of Canadians in the queue, little realizing that it was circular!

After another uneventful Instep patrol on 22 December, Michael landed at the Overseas Air Dispatch Unit aerodrome at Trebelzue. 400 Squadron was moving to Trebelzue, but it was thought the aerodrome there might be too small for Mosquitos. Michael found it quite adequate and had his flight moved there from Portreath. It was decided to detach a flight of Mosquitos to Cornwall in the New Year, each flight staying four days.

Michael flew a night fighter patrol from Colerne on 24 December 1942, thrilled at being a guardian of his country on Christmas Eve. 'So many of the carols and Christmas legends talk of guarding on that night that is exhilarating to be doing exactly that myself.'

Michael had hoped to attend the New Year's party at Colerne, but on the morning of 31 December he was sent down to Trebelzue to fly an Instep patrol, the 'ground troops', led by the Intelligence Officer, Steve Stevens, having journeyed down the previous day. The patrol was uneventful and returned in good time to attend a New Year's party at the exotically named Stork Club in Perranporth. Twelve or thirteen aircrew piled into a small Standard van, the tight squash adding rather than detracting from their enjoyment in giving a lift to a couple of WAAFs on the way. Michael appointed the only teetotal member of the party to be sole driver of the van and they returned safely to the station in time for the sergeants' dance. Michael again borrowed a uniform, this time exchanging with a Canadian corporal, who made the most of his new found rank of squadron leader. Michael recorded: 'I never knew what you could do with a squadron leader's uniform. He marched up to one beauty, surrounded by eight men squabbling for her, told them to clear out, and took her off.'

Michael and Pilot Officer Tony Stanley flew an Instep on 3 January with Woods and Hanton in the Mustangs, and there was a brief moment of excitement when a strange aircraft was seen off Ushant. The patrol turned towards it, the Mustangs looking venomous as they went at it flat out, but it turned out to be a Beaufighter. In spite of warnings, Hank Hanton closed to within 300 yards before satisfying himself that it was not a Ju 88. Michael learnt later that the Beaufighter had been flown by William Hoy – nearly late of 604 Squadron!

Michael enjoyed his first week at Trebelzue, especially working with the 400 Squadron people. 'I really like the Canadians. We get on like two flights in one squadron. I call it the 2600 Squadron, which they like.'

After a welcome leave, Michael returned to Colerne on Friday, 15 January, and flew an uneventful night fighter patrol two nights later. Over lunch the following Monday, the CO, Hamish Kerr, confided that three Mosquitos were to be attached to Bradwell Bay in Essex to fly intruder patrols, and that he had picked Michael to lead the detachment. Michael selected John Mason and Tony Stanley, with their operators, Dicky Roe and 'Bimbo' Lawrence, to go with him, and despite the foul weather they left that afternoon.

At Bradwell the CO of 418 Squadron, Wing Commander Jimmy Little, and Squadron Leader Burton-Gyles explained the situation to them. The previous night the German bombers had been intercepted while returning to their bases by Hurricanes and Bostons, but these had proved too slow and it was hoped that the faster Mosquitos would be more successful. The plan was that the Intruder Controller at Fighter Command, with all relevant information, would dispatch the Mosquitos to the aerodromes being used by the raiders, to catch them on their return.

At the beginning of the evening the 264 crews were briefed in the operations room by Squadron Leader Burton-Gyles, who pointed out the locations of the various German aerodromes on the large scale maps which covered the walls. He gave them detailed instructions on the methods and pitfalls of intruding at night, particularly impressing on them that they must never fly directly across the enemy aerodromes, which were heavily defended by flak guns. At 6.15 pm the controller, Squadron Leader Salusbury-Hughes, telephoned, advising them to prepare three targets: the enemy aerodromes at Beauvais, Evreux and Creil. It was decided that Tony Stanley would take Evreux; John Mason, Beauvais; and Michael, Creil, the furthest south. Burton-Gyles briefed them on their respective routes, in and out, advised them to cross the enemy coast low and fast, and reiterated his warning of not to fly across the hostile aerodromes.

At ten o'clock the telephone rang again. Aircraft for Evreux and Beauvais were to take off at once.

'What about Creil?' Michael asked.

'No orders yet.'

Michael watched the others take off, hating to see them go while he, the flight commander, was still on the ground, but the orders finally came through.

'Creil aircraft to go via Gravelines.'

This change of the choice of route meant that Michael would possibly miss the returning bombers, and it was decided to stick to the original plan of going via Ault. 'Off you go. Good trip and remember what I told you,' Burton-Gyles admonished.

Michael and John Quinton were taken out to their Mosquito, Michael struck how sinister it looked in the darkness, the black shape powerful and threatening. 'Is it us who should fear it or the Hun.' It was only Michael's third night flight in a Mosquito and as he climbed into the tiny, crowded cockpit the worry of remembering the location of all the switches overrode any fears he had about the mission. They taxied out in silence: Michael concentrating on the take-off to come, John Quinton quiet with his own thoughts. Just before the runway, Michael stopped, ran through his cockpit drill, made the sign of the Cross and opened up the engines. The wonderful, full-throated roar of the twin Merlins and the beautiful controls of the Mosquito immediately dispelled all fears, both of flying and the dangers ahead – 'how lovely to be up at night in this carefree toy' – and orbiting once they climbed quickly to 1,500 feet.

As they crossed the Thames Estuary they flew straight through the balloon barrage – 'safer than turning' – and set course for Beachy Head. It was the first time Michael had flown low at night, and free of the instructions of a controller, but Beachy Head appeared on time and, rather to their surprise, exactly where they had expected it to be. Michael turned south, made out to sea, switched on the electric gunsight and settled down. 'Unless the aircraft gives trouble we are going intruding'.

The sea below the Mosquito's wings looked awfully vast, black and none too friendly. Michael checked his instruments. They had just over seventy miles to cover: at 240 mph, seventeen minutes of flying time. After the first few miles Michael's fears of flying low over the sea at night abated and he dropped down to 500 feet, but the time passed agonizingly slowly and it seemed an age before John broke quietly in on his thoughts: 'Five minutes more.' Michael put the speed up to 260 mph, the Mosquito's maximum in weak mixture, and three minutes later they saw a light on their port side. Suddenly the coast was there, 'black and sinister' and an inward voice whispered 'Go back home, an excuse is easy. That light is probably a trap'. 'You rotten little coward', said the other inward voice. 'Go on and do what hundreds have done before you.'

They crossed the coast between Le Treport and St Valery. 'Don't forget the cliffs' John advised quietly, as the Mosquito roared over in a shallow dive at maximum speed, a few searchlights probing the darkness behind them. Altering course, Michael headed for Beauvais. Now he had crossed the coast the inward voices had ceased. 'We are over France – low – at night. It is rather fun.' Crossing the Bresle, they picked up the landmark of the railway, and flying at 260 mph, weaving gently, they dropped lower still, Michael amazed at the amount of detail he could see of the dark countryside and the poor standard of the blackout. Skirting heavily defended Beauvais, the Mosquito turned to port and made for their destination, a small wood which surrounded the aerodrome on the outskirts of Creil.

As their estimated time of arrival approached, then passed, with no sign of the wood, they wondered what to do next. Michael had carefully memorized the features and plan of the aerodrome and its environs, but he recognized nothing in the darkened ground below. They circled the area 'rather shakily', remembering the warnings of not to fly over the enemy field. Would they do so without knowing it until the flak opened up? Intruding, which had seemed so easy, suddenly appeared a lot more difficult. They saw a town below them.

'That looks like Creil.'

'No it's not.'

'Well, what the hell is it?'

'Don't know. What do you think?'

'Well, we've had it now, we're miles beyond it.'

Michael turned north. 'More by luck than anything we see a wood. which looks like the one surrounding the aerodrome.' Closer inspection revealed that it was the enemy base and they circled it for half an hour, waiting for signs of the returning bombers, but there was no sign of life in the darkness below. Deciding the bombers must have returned while they had been searching for the aerodrome, they turned away and flew towards Creil itself.

As they approached the town a train was pulling out of the station. Michael watched it, 'climbing and puffing hard', and with the mental picture of the French driver in the cab all his childhood veneration of engine drivers came flooding back, making him reluctant to attack it. He returned to the enemy aerodrome, feeling that if he must shoot at something it should be something that could hit back, but all was still quiet on the darkened airfield and he returned to the train, deliberately making his first pass abortive to enable the crew to get clear. He need not have worried. His first 'real' attack was a failure, with too much deflection; the second with not enough and on the third pass he overshot. It was much more difficult than he had realized to get in position, his turning circle being so big that he lost sight of the target each time. In addition, judging the position of the ground during the attacks was far from easy. The Mosquito was down to 300 feet in the darkness and the ground was too low for comfort at that height.

On his fourth attack Michael carefully lined up the train and fired a long burst. The flashes from the cannon strikes were impressive, exploding everywhere, and steam showed evidence of some good hits. On the fifth attack a cloud of white smoke suddenly erupted, covering the whole engine. 'Got him, jolly good', exclaimed John.

Setting course for home, Michael realized that he was enjoying himself immensely, roaring over the badly blacked out houses, the people standing in their doorways easily discernible. 'Well, good-night, Messieurs. I can see them turn and look up.'

They recrossed the French coast by Ault, racing through a defile in the cliffs, praying that no flak would reach out for them, but all was quiet. The return journey was uneventful. The sea, seeming so hostile on the way out, was now friendly and welcoming, with no threat of groundfire or unknown hazards. Reaching the friendly coast, they climbed up into the moonlight, Michael warning John to keep a lookout for any Beaufighters coming up behind; suddenly the friendly voice of the controller at Tangmere was giving them a vector to Horn-church and hence to Bradwell, where they landed safely after three hours and ten minutes of flying.

John Mason and Tony Stanley had both returned safely, with only John Mason having seen any activity, when he had flown over Beauvais aerodrome and been heavily engaged by the ground de-fences. Tony Stanley had found no less than five aerodromes at Evreux, but had been unable to make up his mind which was the right one. The old hands of 418 Squadron, including Wing Commander Little, had waited up for them and were glad to see them back. They were not a little surprised that they had all returned safely. 'New boys on their first cross country don't all come back on a trip over enemy territory.'

Michael and John's next intruder operation was on the night of 20 January. Group rang in the evening with orders for the 264 detach-ment to cover German aerodromes in Holland, an order which horrified the highly experienced 418 Squadron crews. The enemy bases in the Low Countries were heavily defended and they con-sidered them far too tough for the inexperienced 264 crews. The very experienced Burton-Gyles tried to persuade Group to drop the idea, but it was keen for 264 to gain experience – a case of being thrown in at the deep end – and as Tony Stanley's Mosquito was unserviceable, Michael decided that he and John Mason would fly the operation.

Michael and John took off at 8.53 pm, flying to Lowestoft before setting out across the North Sea to Alkmar in northern Holland, 120 miles away and twenty-eight minutes of flying time. Michael, by now thoroughly at home flying low above the sea at night, dropped from 600 to 400 feet. John had seemed a little edgy and tense at take-off, but as they flew on above the sea he relaxed and was soon his usual self. Nearing the Dutch coast they were startled to see an appalling curtain of flak lighting up the night sky: streams of Bofors fire, with bursts above from heavier guns. It was the defences of Amsterdam firing at the RAF heavy bombers, and Michael, not for the first time, was filled with admiration for the bomber crews, reflecting that he could avoid heavily defended areas, whereas they had to fly to and into them. But if the guns were those of Amsterdam then the Mosquito was off course. The flak was only just to their right and Michael turned north, every instinct saying, 'Go home'. As the flashes died away behind them, Michael thought how easy it was to plan intruder operations, but how hard to carry them out. On the ground, when planning, the instinct of self preservation gave way to reason, but the positions were quickly and completely reversed when actually flying into hostile territory.

Michael took the Mosquito up to 6,000 feet to identify the coast. Finding their position he pushed down the nose and crossed at 2,000 feet, the ASI reading 390 mph. Suddenly, almost below them, the whole countryside lit up. Heart in his mouth, Michael instinctively pulled back hard and to one side on the control column and the Mosquito jinked like a snipe. John dropped all his papers, hit his head hard on something and swore volubly. The tension released, they both laughed at their fright, and almost immediately saw their first landmark ahead – Alkmar Wood. The lights were from a dummy airfield and were an excellent landmark, showing they were dead on course.

Michael turned the Mosquito south east towards Marken, a small island in the Zyder Zee, just off the coast to the east of Amsterdam. Reaching the island they turned to pass between the heavily defended towns of Amsterdam and Utrecht, but almost before they realized it a town appeared dead ahead. Their navigation was faulty and they were heading straight for Utrecht. It was too late to turn. Michael simply opened up both throttles and roared over the town at full speed. Unbelievably, no flak opened up and they flew on, reaching a river and turning due east for their next landmark of Arnhem. Arriving, they flew north east of the town – later to become so famous –

looking for their target: the airfield at Deelen. Suddenly the dark woods below were lit up as a system of lights was turned on for blind approach. It was the visual Lorenz system of the German aerodrome.

A few moments later John pointed out a German bomber going in to land, its lights all on. Michael at once turned to give chase, but it was obvious that unless they ignored the injunction of never to fly across an enemy aerodrome at night, they would never catch it before it landed. Discretion being the better part of valour, they let it go. A little later their patience was rewarded by seeing another, a little behind them and to their left, coming in with a couple of miles still to go. Michael turned hard right, letting the bomber pass the Mosquito, then hard again into position. It was curious coming in behind the enemy bomber. It looked so ordinary with its red, green and white lights: universal lights used on any circuit – German or British. Michael was conscious that it was a bogus impression, a lie, that the enemy aeroplane had no right to look so *friendly*, so harmless. It had just returned from bombing England. All at once he felt anxious to destroy it.

Both aircraft were at 2,000 feet, the Mosquito two miles behind. Michael opened up to 270 mph, rapidly closing the distance as the bomber lost height. They would catch it before it landed, but they would have time for only one chance; one quick attack. The Mosquito came in from the rear quarter at high speed. The enemy bomber was a black mass, filling the gunsight, coalescing into the shape of a recognisable aeroplane: a Dornier Do 217. Michael gently squeezed his triggers. The Mosquito shuddered and jerked as the 20 mm cannon opened up. There was just time to note three large flashes on the Dornier's fuselage before all the aerodrome lights went out and the bomber was on top of them. Michael broke hard to port, narrowly missing ramming the Dornier, and twenty or thirty streams of tracer came up at them, the enemy gunners ignoring the proximity of the Dornier in their eagerness to catch the intruder. At 600 feet Michael saw the hosepipe shape of the tracer coming closer and closer and he put the Mosquito over onto its back, half rolling down.

'Isn't the ground coming up a bit quickly?' John asked quietly. Michael had time for a quick chuckle at this classic understatement before rolling level, the Mosquito coming out below the level of some nearby trees, clear cut in the moonlight. Despite this violent manoeuvre the flak still followed them: just as accurate, just as intense, always just twenty yards behind the jinking Mosquito, following Michael's every move until he had put the aerodrome several miles behind them, when it suddenly stopped as abruptly as it had begun.

All the aerodrome lights were now out, the ground defences fully alerted. Michael circled, looking for any signs of the Dornier, but they could see nothing, the blackness below absolute.

They again approached the enemy aerodrome, but as they neared it the ground defences opened up again, and realizing they could expect no further joy in the vicinity, Michael flew away towards Arnhem. Just south west of the town they saw a train and made a series of attacks. The train stopped on top of an embankment and, lining it up like a golf tee, Michael attacked for the fifth time.

A steady squirt – a mass of steam and we just clear the telegraph poles. John thought we would hit the engine, so for his peace of mind it was lucky he never saw the telegraph poles, which I was watching.

Returning home, with the uneasy feeling that they were being followed, Michael climbed into cloud at 6,000 feet. Nearing the English coast they were advised they could not land at Bradwell, the weather being bad, and were diverted to Digby. Michael was glad to get down. The port engine had been causing him some anxiety, running roughly, and as they taxied in the temperature went up to 125°. Michael later wrote. 'I really enjoyed this trip. There is a satisfaction about a successful intruder trip which nothing I have yet experienced can give.'

A few days later the flight was sent to Ford, the weather forecast for the Bradwell area being poor. Gerald was away for the weekend, but Rory Chisholm was there and he and Michael discussed intruding, Chisholm being of the opinion that all the press-on types would get into intruder squadrons, the others concentrating on the more defensive role of night interception. As usual he swore at Michael's hat, making him promise to buy a new one if and when he got a squadron of his own. Michael readily agreed, laughing at Chisholm's optimism.

Despite the move the weather was little better at Ford, no operations were flown and Michael and John Quinton flew back to Bradwell after the weekend. The flight was now due to return to Colerne, and it returned to its home base on 26 January, despite Michael's pleas to be allowed to stay at Bradwell. 'The Free Fighting 264, as we call ourselves, is no more free and no longer fights', Michael wrote sadly.

At the end of January, Michael began another period of duty at

Trebelzue. On the last day of the month he flew to Ford, dropping John Quinton there for a Senior Observers Course and bringing back 'Bimbo' Lawrence from Colerne to act as his operator for the next ten days. After two uneventful Instep patrols, Michael and Bimbo Lawrence flew their first daylight Ranger on February 5, taking off at 2.10 pm.

The Mosquito kept well clear of the Ushant area, swinging round in a parabola to come in over Penmarck Point to the south of Brest, crossing the enemy coast at nought feet, lifting a little to clear the sea wall. The cloud was high and unbroken, offering no cover until 5,000 feet, 3,000 feet above the estimated safety limit, and Michael considered turning back as he climbed towards it. Deciding to go on, he flew inland towards Quimper, then south-east along the railway line, turning off east as Lorient appeared ahead. They were due to look at the enemy aerodrome at Kerlin Bastard (Curly Bastard) but in view of the lack of cloud cover Michael declined to poke his nose into this danger spot and flew up the Brest canal system to the power station at Guerledan, easily spotted by its large artificial lake. He attacked the power station at the bottom of the dam from 400 feet, watching with satisfaction as his cannon and machine-gun fire set the shed alight and collapsed the roof.

Turning, he next attacked the transformer, half a mile away. 'This is fun. Huge flashes are visible as the terminals of 32,000 volts touch, and you can almost hear the clatter of broken glass.'

As the Mosquito roared over the transformer, low enough for Michael to be able to read the signs, the oil coolant of the plant caught fire, burning with a bright orange flame, the black smoke rapidly thickening.

Bimbo Lawrence was a good, if inexperienced operator, but on the way out Michael had thought his outlook altogether much too serious, and he determined to relax his companion's obvious tension with a little judicious leg pulling. As they climbed away from the destruction at Guerledan, Michael sighed with exaggerated relief.

'How lucky, I thought the 190s would be here before this.'

'Yes', agreed Bimbo, with a rather forced smile, 'about time.'

'Well, let's do a few more just to see,' suggested Michael, turning north west for the power station at St Herbot, which he had picked because the name of the nearest town, Heulgoat (wholegoat) had appealed to him. They failed to locate the target, however, and after circling for twenty minutes trying to find it, they saw Brest dead ahead. Continuing his leg-pulling ploy, Michael drew Bimbo's attention to the sprawl of the town, saying in as scared a voice as he could muster. 'Look, how awful, almost over the 190 aerodrome. Let's go a bit closer and see what's there.' Bimbo Lawrence merely gurgled nervously, but a moment later, when Bimbo suddenly suggested they fly in and out of Brest's balloon barrage, Michael realized that his leg-pulling method of make or break was having the desired effect. 'It has worked, he has lost his serious outlook.'

Ten minutes later, however, Michael had a fright himself when the cloud, which had been ideal at 1,000 feet, abruptly cleared, leaving the Mosquito naked in the clear air. Michael hastily climbed towards the nearest friendly cloud and, still climbing hard, dodged in and out of the cloud banks until well out to sea and on the way home.

A few days later the flight received orders to move to Portreath in order to ease communications. Michael, always hating to move after having settled in, and liking the independence of being at Trebelzue, did everything possible to have the order rescinded, but although he persuaded the Station Commander at Portreath to agree to their staying at Trebelzue, the AOC, Air Vice Marshal Dixon, insisted they move, and the Mosquitos flew to their new base on 10 February.

The 264 Squadron crews made no secret of their dislike at having to leave their billet at Trebelzue, with its cosy mess down in the hollow, and the abundance of eggs, with their own pigs to provide the ham, but everyone at their new station did their best to please, even to meeting Michael's insistence that the new dispersal be painted. With the walls lined with Beaver boards and extra telephones installed, they had an even better dispersal than that at Trebelzue, and soon came to recognize the advantages of being on the sector station, with the sector Intelligence Officer near to hand, and meeting their controllers in the Mess. Soon after settling in, Michael walked round the aerodrome with Bimbo Lawrence. John Quinton was due to return the next day, with Bimbo rejoining his regular pilot, Tony Stanley. Bimbo was happy with Stanley, but confided to Michael that he thought him a little too carefree and apt to leave things to chance. In view of their recent experiences over Brittany, Michael suggested that Bimbo might find him the same, and was a little shaken by the reply. 'Oh no. You shoot a line about being casual, and even think you are, but underneath you are astonishingly methodical.' Michael hoped this were true, but his temporary operator was obviously a little more perceptive than he had thought.

Although a Ranger had been scheduled, the weather was bad the next day, being 'down on the deck' by mid-morning. Michael was wondering if a lunchtime drinking session was safe, and being ragged by two wing commanders from Group at the very idea of flying in such conditions, when John came into the mess and announced that the weather was clearing.

As the Mosquito taxied out at five minutes past three, the cloud base was well below the surrounding hills and it occurred to Michael how silly it was to be flying in such weather, but he took off, found the cloud base a little higher towards the south-east and crossed the coast at Start Point. Skirting the lighthouse south-west of the Channel Islands, they finally crossed the enemy coast at Cap d'Erquy, between St Brieuc and St Cast, going in low and fast on the approach to avoid any radar, the water hurtling past under them at 280 mph. As they crossed the coast, lifting slightly, Michael banked, first right then left. There was a small fishing village on their left and he watched for the first sign of flak, but all was quiet.

Flying north, pulling up every now and again to avoid the higher trees, the Mosquito covered thirty miles before the cloud began to disperse and blue sky appeared overhead. This was dangerous. Michael had just decided that conditions were too hazardous to continue when he saw a train a few miles to the east, on the line from Lambelle to Rennes, and he turned, coming in for a full beam attack. The cannon and machine guns made a few strikes, but Michael could see hits on the ground below and in front of the locomotive and he turned hard to starboard to come in again. The train had now stopped and Michael lined up carefully. The Mosquito vibrated violently as he pressed the gun switch. He saw a series of flashes as his cannon shells hit the wheels and engine, and suddenly the boiler exploded in a gush of steam and black smoke. The Mosquito flew through the debris, Michael instinctively ducking as a huge black shape flashed by the cockpit.

'I ask John what that huge bird beast was. He laughs like hell and tells me that it was the greater portion of the boiler.'

While lining up for this last attack, Michael had seen another train, coming from the opposite direction and he now attacked this from the north. 'A steady, gentle dive, the clatter of the cannon, the few sparks, the rush of steam, then the billowing mass of white.' But this train had teeth. As the Mosquito pulled away flak guns all along the train opened up and Michael jinked violently to spoil their aim. Pleased with their successes – 'both these engines were huge and both made a lovely pop' – they climbed to the cloud base at 2,500 feet and took stock of the situation. There was clear sky to the south, so that was out of the question, and Michael turned west, both he and John keeping a wary eye open for enemy fighters.

Approaching the coast they saw another train between St Brieuc and Lambelle and attacked from the port front quarter, causing the usual smoke to pour from the locomotive's boiler. After flying along the length of the train, their fire throwing up masses of sparks from the line of trucks, they finally turned away, Michael pushing down the Mosquito's nose and crossing the coast at 300 mph, well satisfied with the havoc they had wrought. The enemy coast receded rapidly and five minutes later was out of sight.

Crossing the home coast at Dodman Point, Michael flew straight to Portreath. Calling up the controller, Michael asked him if he knew what a Hornby was.

'Of course', replied the puzzled controller. 'I played with them as a boy'.

'Well', laughed the jubilant Michael. 'I've just broken three.'

Later in the evening Michael went for a stroll round the airfield and on returning to the mess found John in a state of 'jubilant intoxication', everyone standing him drinks in congratulations of the afternoon's operation. There was an uproar at Michael's appearance, drinks were again set up, and a short time later John appeared to Michael to be quite sober. 'The renewed rounds given us both were probably the reason.'

The next evening, Michael and John flew a Night Ranger, leaving the ground just after dark in their trusty 'X'. Hamish Kerr had arrived for lunch during the day and had given permission for only one more Ranger at night before Michael and John returned to Colerne, and they were determined to make it a patrol of note. Deciding to go south of the Brest peninsula and up to Rennes and Mont St Michel, they crossed the sea at 400 feet, following the same route as Michael and Bimbo Lawrence on 5 February, aiming to cross the enemy coast over Penmarck Point from the south. The last stage of the sea crossing was made at 250 feet, salt spray on the windscreen obscuring Michael's vision until a welcome shower of rain washed it off. The hostile coast was crossed dead on track and they noted some curious lights below them at Penmarck before joining the railway line to St Nazaire. There was no activity around Lorient, or the aerodrome at Kerlin Bastard, and they flew south east to the Focke Wulf 190 aerodrome to the north of Vannes. Michael longed to be the first to get a FW 190 in a Mosquito, but this airfield was also quiet and he flew on towards Redon. Here they saw a train, which stopped as they made their first attack. A residue of salt on the windscreen made visibility limited, in spite of the moonlight, and it was not until his fifth attack that Michael destroyed the engine. Turning away, they saw another train, going east. The fire box was open and Michael could see the crew in the cab, but his customary quick prayer for their safety was answered a little too spontaneously. 'Everything goes wrong at once – wrong position, bad shooting, and sudden cloud.' After circling for ten minutes, making abortive passes, Michael flew away. 'This train gives me much food for thought!'

Michael and John were now lost. After minutes of anxious flying they reached the bays of the coast, reorientating themselves and returning to Vannes and Redon, but they 'took the wrong turning' out of the latter town and were soon hopelessly lost again, an eerie sensation while over hostile territory. Michael was struck by the relative friendliness of the darkened countryside when sure of their position – 'in spite of things that go bump in the night' – to that of the threatening and sinister aspect of the same countryside when lost.

Not knowing whether or not they might fly over a defended area at any moment, they jinked hard at every village or small town which appeared, and after sometime the coast again came in sight. 'Oh, where can we be?' Michael flew west, hoping to pick up a landmark, finally leaving the land by a large bay, 'like a bat out of hell and as low as a swallow'. Setting a north westerly course, they flew for fifteen minutes until the friendly lighthouse of the Channel Islands appeared. They were closer to their original intentions than they had realized. The bay by which they had left the coast was that of St Michel. They finally picked up 'Eddie', the controller at Portreath, and were shaken to find they were off course and heading south of the Lizard. Correcting, they landed safely at Portreath at a quarter to one, and enjoyed a well earned supper of eggs and bacon.

Back at Colerne, Michael found a new arrival in Squadron Leader Ken Salusbury-Hughes. Salusbury-Hughes was a pilot of some experience, having commanded a flight in 23 Squadron and doing thirty seven trips before becoming an Intruder Controller. He was now attached to 264 Squadron between postings – an attachment Michael had arranged – and Michael outlined plans he had been formulating for intruding over Denmark and Norway, asking for Salusbury-Hughes' views. Salusbury-Hughes was politely interested, but more enthusiastic over his own, more ambitious ideas of intruding into the heart of Nazi Germany, perhaps even as far as Berlin itself to attack the flying training schools around the capital. Next to actually flying in air combat, Salusbury-Hughes loved talking about it, his eyes sparkling, admitting that in a tight corner, twitching with fright, he was blissfully happy. Older than most pilots at thirty-five, he was married, with a nine year old daughter and a 125 cc motorbike, 'Awful Agatha', which travelled everywhere with him in an Oxford. Over the next few months, Michael came to know Salusbury-Hughes very well, describing him in his diary in an ironically paradoxical entry as 'one of the most cold blooded killers and one of the most delightful companions I have ever met.'

After ten days at Colerne, during which Michael and John did no operational flying, Michael left for a few days' leave, returning on 9 March, and taking temporary command of the squadron while Hamish Kerr was on leave. Michael was excited by the power of being Squadron CO, however transient. Determined to make the best of it to stir things up, he took Ken Salusbury-Hughes to visit Air Commodore Basil Embry, SASO at 10 Group. Basil Embry, an old friend of Salusbury-Hughes, was already something of a legend in the RAF, having been shot down and escaping three times before finally making his way back to England.

As Michael and Salusbury-Hughes entered his office Embry got up from behind his desk and advanced upon Salusbury-Hughes in utter silence, like a cat stalking a mouse. Michael watched, fascinated, as the Air Commodore reached the respectfully giggling Salusbury-Hughes, seized hold of both ends of his huge handlebar moustache and pulled – hard. 'He has a weakness for my moustache', explained Salusbury-Hughes to the amazed Michael.

Michael soon found Embry even more of a character than Salusbury-Hughes. Soon after joining 10 Group, Embry had livened it up, keeping everyone on their toes. He had been known to arouse elderly officers, securely asleep behind their papers, by setting fire to their shield, or even, it was rumoured, on one occasion setting fire to an officer's hair. Only five feet tall, wiry, tough, with eyes that could beam, dance with joy at some schoolboy prank, then change to a cold, malignant fury when discussing ways to kill Nazis, Embry imbued all he met with his offensive spirit. 'Ken (Salusbury-Hughes) is one of the few killers I have met, but he is a lamb sucking milk compared with Basil,' Michael commented.

That night Michael was shocked to learn that Tony Stanley, Bimbo Lawrence, and Jerry Piers and his operator, Flight Sergeant Hill, had all failed to return from a night ranger in the Rennes area. As acting CO, Michael had the unhappy task of writing to their families, and he later visited Tony Stanley's parents, Colonel and Lady Mary Stanley, and Tony's sister Con, to give what comfort and news he could. Michael was dreading the meeting, knowing he could give them little or no hope, but it passed off easily. 'All three show the most astonishing courage, yet combine it with tender gentleness. Con has only one thought – to help in conversation and relieve her mother.' Lady Mary, daughter of the Duke of Westminster, had been paralysed from the hips down for twenty years, and Tony was her only son, but she thanked Michael for having been so honest with her and he left full of admiration for her courage and kindness.

Hamish Kerr returned to the squadron on 16 March, only to leave five days later on being replaced by Wing Commander W. J. Alington DFC. Before Hamish Kerr left he told Michael that he had recommended him for a DFC.

Michael and Salusbury-Hughes were anxious to impress their ideas on the new CO and buttonholed him at dinner, later taking him to see the operations room at work. 264 Squadron was now meeting with no little success in their offensive role, shooting up trains, power stations, and various ground targets during the Rangers, and on 22 March, nearly sixty Instep patrols were rewarded with the destruction of two Ju 88s off Bordeaux, three more only escaping by fleeing from the Mosquitos.

Michael flew an Oxford to Portreath after tea on 23 March, leading a flight of three Mosquitos on an Instep patrol the next morning. The weather was poor and they returned without having seen any action. On reaching the English coast between Land's End and the Lizard, they found the clouds were down to 100 feet, but Michael led them across the narrow strip to the opposite coast, flew up it until Portreath appeared, 'turned right' and landed.

Michael was surprised to find the C in C, Sir Trafford Leigh-Mallory, standing in the rain, waiting for their safe return and cursing Group for, as he thought, making them fly in such appalling weather. He congratulated them on their safe return and everyone walked down to dispersal, standing about with collars off and generally at ease. Michael took the opportunity to bring up his idea of the long range intruder missions, asking Leigh-Mallory his opinion. The C in C was interested and said he would take it up with his staff. This was exactly the answer Michael was expecting, staff having already rejected the idea when approached by Basil Embry. Salusbury-Hughes later visited Embry to tell him that the plan now had the C in C's approval, but Embry forestalled him, saying that he had just had a call from HQ to say they had withdrawn their objections. Embry was puzzled by this change of attitude, but Salusbury-Hughes airily told him that a certain Squadron Leader (Michael) had said that it was 'no good asking Air Commodores for what you want – you must go to the top'. This delighted Embry, who roared with laughter.

On Sunday, 28 March, Michael led Flying Officers Bouchard and Muir on another extended Instep patrol to the Bordeaux area. Michael and John were using John Mason's Mosquito and Michael was a little worried by the starboard engine, which, although well within the maker's tolerances, was a trifle low on oil pressure and high in temperature. His worries were well founded, if wrongly placed. After flying south from Portreath for an hour and forty minutes at the usual fifty feet above the sea, there was a sudden violent juddering and the whole aircraft began to shake. Michael throttled back the suspect engine, cursing himself for a fool for not having turned back before, but the vibration became worse. To his horror he realized that it was not the suspect engine that was giving trouble, but the other. He opened up the 'good' engine, throttled back the other and pressed the feathering switch. The big, black airscrew jerked to a stop and the Mosquito again flew smoothly. Still doing 200 mph, Michael eased the Mosquito into a climb. Calling up the other Mosquitos, 'an engine has packed up, I am returning', he turned to port. 'Butch' Bouchard got in the way during the turn and Michael roundly cursed him, the tension of the moment being broken by Michael's chuckles at Bouchard's profuse apologies.

The position was now extremely precarious. Too far out to be rescued, the only way to reach land was to fly – so fly they would. Michael asked John if he minded trying for home, as it would be relatively easy to fly to France – to safety, even if captivity. 'Good Heavens no', John replied, and Michael, who had expected no other answer, settled down to coax the Mosquito home.

Flying north at 160 mph, a hundred feet above the sea, Michael carefully trimmed the aircraft. At that speed the Mosquito held height comfortably and he reduced the engine revs to 2500 with plus 6 boost and gradually began to gain height. After an agonizing fluctuation the needle of the altimeter began to climb steadily, foot by foot, 'up three, down two!' It was hard work, requiring the utmost concentration, for any loss of speed meant loss of height, and height was a precious commodity when measured in inches above the threatening water, hundreds of miles from friendly land. Michael knew the Mosquito would fly on one engine, but that one engine was suspect. How long would it last with the extra demands being made upon it?

After the first frightening moment, and finding he could still cope with the aeroplane, all fear had left Michael and he knew that if they failed to get home it would not be his fault. He decided to give Ushant a wide berth, knowing that if they came down within range of the German FW 190s no Walrus of Air Sea Rescue could pick them up from the sea, and to lighten the Mosquito he began to fire off his ammunition. Slowly and steadily he coaxed the Mosquito up to 600 feet, managing to fire off all his ammunition in short bursts – short bursts because at each firing of the guns the Mosquito lost valuable speed. The jettisoning of the ammunition added a mere ten miles an hour to the Mosquito's speed, but it was better than nothing.

Everything is now set. The Mossie is going like a bird, is flying hands off, at a good safe speed, reasonable height – 600 feet – and the engine, although used more severely than a Merlin XXI should be, is well below maker's allowance of 2650 revs plus 7 boost. There is nothing to be done but sit back and pray.

Just off Ushant the RT crackled into life. 'Four aircraft to starboard, I think they are fighters,' came Mike Muir's voice. Then, a moment later. 'FW 190s at 3,000 feet, flying south east.' Michael immediately dropped the Mosquito to sea level and pushed the speed up to 220 mph, sacrificing his hard won height. One of his companions called the other. 'You stay with Red One (Michael) I will go at them if they attack.' One Mossie versus four FW 190s, thought Michael, a good show volunteering, but he resolved to land in the sea when the attack came, telling the others they would have more chance if not tied to the crippled Mosquito. John grunted agreement, but after an agonizing, never ending few minutes, the FW 190s were gone. They had failed to see the three Mosquitos, low down over the water.

As they approached the English coast, Michael requested Muir to climb up and obtain a homing, watching enviously as the other Mosquito soared effortlessly up to six or eight thousand feet. Muir passed on the fix. Flying on one engine, the Mosquito had been 'crabbing' and they had passed within ten miles of the FW 190 haunt of Ushant – not the forty or fifty miles desired. No wonder they had seen the enemy fighters!

Michael turned north, gradually climbing, overjoyed at being once more in RT contact with land. The Mosquito slowly gained height, Michael coaxing it to 2,000 feet as the dim shape of the friendly coast appeared ahead. 'What a super aeroplane.' Next minute the welcome sound of the controller's voice. 'Hallo Ocean Red. Everything is prepared for you at Predannack.' But now that safety was in sight, after four hundred miles on one engine, Michael was determined to go all the way. 'Thanks, chum, but I don't live there', he answered and flew on to Portreath. He did a right hand circuit, put down the wheels across wind and came in with a touch of flap, John pumping down full flaps on his hand pump. As they came steadily in, with just a touch of engine, there was a heart stopping moment as a Whitley was seen taxying out, but the bomber stopped. The Mosquito dropped lower. 'A very little engine, a careful hold off, a gentle bump, and we are on the ground.' Michael swung off the runway to avoid the Whitley, giving the pilot a good fright. 'We stop. All is safe. What a truly marvellous aeroplane'.

Two days later Michael and John took off after lunch in their own Mosquito, the trusty PS-X. Crossing at the customary point of Penmarck, they flew north, turning south east on sighting the railway and flying down the line to St Nazaire. Skirting Lorient, with the Ju 88 base just in sight, they picked up a breakdown train. Michael made two attacks, men jumping out of the trucks and 'running like mad' on his second. Lower than he should have been, Michael pressed home the second attack and the engine blew up in a satisfactory fashion. Just before Vannes they saw another train, four miles from the FW 190 base. Michael, conscious of the proximity of the enemy aerodrome, was determined to get the train in one pass. He made no mistake and the engine again blew up in the prescribed manner.

Crossing Redon at high speed, they were going too fast to get a shot at a Bofors gunner, leaning on the parapet of his emplacement and having a quiet smoke, but a few miles further on John abruptly announced that there was an aircraft ahead, at two thousand feet and going west. Michael gave chase, closing the distance at 260 mph, the aeroplane resolving itself into a Heinkel 111. It seemed an age as they closed the distance, but the Heinkel seemed to suddenly rush back at them. Michael fired a short burst, a cloud of black smoke poured out of the enemy's starboard engine and the Mosquito's windscreen was covered in oil. This was 1940 all over again! Michael broke away, attacking again from the port quarter. The Heinkel was losing height slowly and Michael's second attack slowed it down still more, its dive steepening.

Suddenly: 'There they are, 190s', John warned quietly. Behind, to the north, were four black shapes, flying south east. As Michael watched, all but the leader turned and dived towards the Mosquito, closing the distance rapidly. The FW 190s were at 3,000 feet, two miles behind the Mosquito, and with a height advantage of 2,500 feet. Michael pulled the emergency plug. At 3,000 revs and 14 lbs of boost the Mosquito headed for the nearest friendly cloud. They were at the bottom of the breakaway after attacking the Heinkel and had a straight climb. Could they possibly beat the fast German fighters, already gaining speed in a shallow dive? Michael recalled the last time he had been chased by the enemy, in 1940, when he had been pursued into the clouds by Me 110s. He had been thoroughly frightened on that occasion, but he was surprised to find that he now felt no fear; was more concerned in planning the best possible course of action if the 190s caught them before they reached the cloud. He would turn and meet the attack in good time. He had every confidence that the Mosquito could give a good account of itself if necessary, but he was conscious of the odds and was determined to make the cloud cover if at all possible.

Thoughts came clearly and quickly. 'Like old times, Johnnie.' Quinton just grunted. He seemed interested in the outcome of the race, but otherwise quite happy, knowing that Michael was doing all he could. Michael snatched a glance at the Heinkel. It was still losing height and the terrain looked impossible for a successful forced landing. *If* they got home they could claim it as damaged. The Merlins were just beginning to overheat, the FW 190s gaining fast, when the first welcome wisps of cloud rushed past the Mosquito's cockpit. Seconds later they were safe in the heart of the cloud.

Michael throttled back. Feeling hunted, he dodged in and out of the cloud banks, flying north, and finally crossing the enemy coast east of Brest. Forty minutes later they sighted the Cornish cliffs.

The camera guns later showed that they had hit the Heinkel's port engine and it was awarded as a 'probable'. They were stood a great many drinks and Michael confessed in his diary: 'I really am enjoying this life'.

Michael and John flew three more Rangers before the end of the detachment, but were frustrated on all three by the weather or mechanical troubles. On the last patrol, Michael was tempted to fly under some high tension cables, but John, suspecting his intentions, yelled an emphatic 'No', and Michael was so surprised at this uncharacteristic attitude from the normally unflappable John, who usually loved low flying, that he pulled away. 'The first of my crazy schemes that he has ever turned down'.

On 3 April the detachment returned to Colerne, Michael relieving his feelings during the flight by diving below an ambling Oxford and zooming vertically in front of its nose at 280 mph. As he switched off his engines at Colerne he sadly reflected that the 'Free Fighting 264' was again no longer free or fighting.

On 23rd April Michael was promoted to wing commander and posted to take command of 604 Squadron at Scorton in Yorkshire. He left 264 Squadron with the rating of 'exceptional' in his log-book, and with nine locomotives, a Heinkel probably destroyed, a Dornier 217 damaged, and the successful attack on the power station at Guerledan to his credit. His posting to 264 Squadron, four short but crowded months earlier, a posting viewed with such dismay, had been the most rewarding and satisfying of his service life to date.

CHAPTER XVII

Victories over the Sea

When Michael had left 604 Squadron in December 1942 he felt that he had finally severed all connection with the squadron, never dreaming he would one day command it. After his departure the tide of events and promotions overtook 604 Squadron, and there were many changes. Early in 1943 the squadron had moved to Ford, staying until 24 April, when it had again been moved, to Scorton in Yorkshire. Just before the move north, Wing Commander Wood had been lost over the Channel, flying an interception of FW 190s, and Squadron Leader Gonsalves had been temporary CO until Michael arrived at Scorton on 24 April, in time to attend a dance given in the squadron's honour.

Michael's DFC was gazetted on 3 May 1943, in recognition of his fine leadership in 264 Squadron and his successes in Intruder operations, and he was determined that his new command regain a little of its former glory. Although a few old friends were still serving with the squadron, many of the original outstanding members had been posted or lost, and with the rapid development in the air war 604 Squadron no longer had anything to teach the other night fighter squadrons. In the hectic pioneering days of trial and error, 604 had taught other squadrons everything it had learned, and these, profiting from this teaching, had attained the same high standard.

Officially, 604 Squadron was at Scorton to rest and re-equip with the new AI Mark VIII radar, but the squadron was part of the defence of the Hull and Middlesborough area, and on 15 May, after only three weeks at its new base, it shot down two raiders, bringing the squadron's total to seventy five enemy aeroplanes shot down at night.

In June, Michael sent John Quinton and Flying Officer Jeremy Howard-Williams to 68 Squadron at Coltishall on a temporary exchange. His reasons were twofold: he and John had been flying together since October 1941 and Michael thought a short change would do them both good, detecting boredom in himself and a blasé attitude in John. Jeremy Howard-Williams and his operator, Tony Nordberg, Michael considered one of his best crews, but he felt they needed stirring up and encouraged to develop a little quicker. Michael had no intention of permanently parting from John, but he knew that a short period with Quinton would be of immense worth to Howard-Williams, and that he could help raise Tony Nordberg's sights a little.

It was during the fortnight that Michael and Nordberg flew together that they flew a patrol with comic, though very nearly tragic results. An American night fighter squadron, equipped with Beaufighters, had been posted to Scorton for training, a posting which put Michael in a quandary. He had been told by the AOC that the training of the Americans was entirely his responsibility, but that he had no jurisdiction over them at all. Matters were further complicated by the attitude of the American crews. Michael was told, in no uncertain terms, that they were trained pursuit pilots, and they needed no help ... thank you very much. It was a situation which called for the exercise of tact and guile, and Michael reacted in a characteristic way. What a pity, he commiserated with the American colonel in charge of the squadron, that his squadron was not yet allowed to fly operationally. Perhaps one of his pilots would like to come along one night as a passenger in a Beaufighter.

The colonel agreed, and on the night of 13 June Michael and Nordberg took off on a practice interception under Goldborough control, with Captain Ehlinger USAAF standing in the escape hatch well behind Michael, holding firmly to the handle grips on the fuselage sides. During the practice there was a raid on Hull, and control vectored Michael on to an enemy aircraft, Tony Nordberg soon picking up the contact on his AI. The American watched with intense interest over Michael's shoulder as Michael followed Nordberg's instructions and suddenly, dead ahead, they saw the dark shape of the enemy bomber. They were in an ideal position and Michael was just about to open fire when Nordberg shouted a warning: 'Look out, there's a Beau behind us!' Michael's reaction was instantaneous. He put the Beaufighter over onto its back, diving away, and the startled American suddenly found himself standing upside down, his surroundings lit up by the flash of the exploding bomber.

Flying Officer Wills, also with an American passenger, was flying the other Beaufighter. Intent on the enemy bomber, he had not even seen his CO's aeroplane. On landing all the much shaken American could say was, 'Well, Goddam. Well, Goddam,' shaking his head in disbelief.

After this the American colonel instructed all his crews to listen to and learn everything they could from 604 Squadron, and teaching them became a rewarding task. Although first class pilots, with plenty of experience, the American pilots had an exaggerated respect for Sir Isaac, and could never quite reconcile this with the carefree way the 604 pilots threw their Beaufighters about the night sky.

Michael was next in action on the night of 25 July. Taking off at 12.15, with Tony Nordberg as his operator, Goldborough control vectored them on to a hostile. Nordberg picked up the bomber on the AI and successfully guided Michael to a visual. As he viewed the vague shape in the darkness ahead, with his recent experience fresh in his mind, Michael was faced with the dilemma of all night fighter pilots. Could it by any chance be a friendly aircraft? He felt sure it was a Dornier, but that small doubt stayed his finger on the trigger. Rory Chisholm had once shot down a Beaufighter, thinking it was a Ju 88 (luckily the crew baled out unhurt); suppose he were to make the same ghastly mistake and send two or more fellow countrymen to their deaths. It was an agonizing decision. The range opened a little and Tony Nordberg turned back to his radar in case they should lose the visual.

'If it is friendly it's acting very strangely.'

'Why?' Michael asked, still watching the dark shape.

'Because it's dropping a mine,' Nordberg replied, distinctly seeing the blip on his screen as the mine parted company with the enemy aircraft.

The uncertainty was resolved. Michael opened fire. He saw some strikes on the enemy bomber, but its mission completed it was now diving away at high speed and the Beaufighter lost contact. On landing, however, Michael was delighted to find that three of his crews had scored positive victories. Flight Lieutenant Wood and his operator, Flying Officer Ellis, had been flying a practice interception with Flying Officers Keele and Cowles, but had been vectored on to a Dornier and shot it down, following this success within minutes by destroying a second. Even this was not the end of the night's successes. William Hoy, the A Flight Commander, found a third Dornier in the darkness for the squadron's third victory that night.

It was not only at night that 604 Squadron sought out the Luftwaffe. Each morning a German weather reconnaissance aircraft flew out over the North Sea, its course bringing it to within a hundred miles of the coast, east of Whitby, and within range of the ground radar. 604 Squadron named these aircraft 'Weather Willies' or 'The Milk Train' and decided to terminate their activities. Two Beaufighters would leave Scorton just before dawn, gain as much height as possible and wait for the enemy at the position in which it usually appeared on the radar. In the event of not getting a visual it was hoped they would be near enough to pick up the German on the Beaufighter's AI.

The first attempt at the interception of the Milk Train was an unqualified success, William Hoy and Le Conte engaging a Ju 88 and shooting it down into the sea. Michael and John tried their hand on 16 August, with Flight Lieutenant John Surman flying a companion Beaufighter, but the cloud was extremely thick and they failed to make contact.

Another attempt a week later met with more joy. Michael and John took off at 5.20 am, the second Beaufighter again flown by John Surman. The Beaufighters reached the usual position half an hour later and circled at 18,000 feet. Another half an hour passed before Goldborough control vectored them twenty miles to the east, positioning them in the eye of the morning sun. The anticipated contact came soon after. Michael was warned that the enemy had appeared, six miles ahead of the Beaufighters. He flew the vectored course and suddenly saw a Ju 88 two miles ahead and a little above the cloud base at 5,000 feet.

The Beaufighters turned, putting themselves between the sun and the enemy, and dived to attack. The German pilot saw them coming and began to climb, but Michael closed onto its tail and opened fire from three hundred yards. Cannon strikes appeared all over the Ju 88 and the port engine burst into flames, the cowling hurtling back towards the Beaufighter. Michael took violent evasive action and saw the Ju 88 dive away into the cloud. Michael followed, John keeping contact with the enemy on his radar, and as they broke cloud the Ju 88 was just below them, the port engine and petrol tank well alight. The German pilot made a valiant effort to ditch, but his aeroplane was all but out of control and it crashed into the sea, disappearing in a quarter of a minute, leaving nothing but a patch of oil on the surface, a hundred and thirty miles north east of Middlesborough.

After landing and making out his combat report, Michael, still in his flying clothes, visited the church of St John of God in Scorton village. As he entered the church the priest came out of the sacristy to say Mass. Michael went up to the altar, told the priest he had just killed four men, and asked if he would say his Mass for them.

A message intercepted during the day revealed that the crew of the Ju 88 had included a senior Luftwaffe meteorological officer. Knowing that rescue aircraft would be sent the squadron mounted a series of patrols in the area. A Ju 88 was seen, and damaged, but it evaded the Beaufighters in the cloud.

No 604 Squadron ended 1943 with thirteen victories scored since its move north, with three DFCs added to the squadron's honours board.

Gerald was still Station Commander at Ford throughout 1943, a distinctive year for the station. In March, 418 City of Edmonton Squadron, RCAF moved to Ford and continued its successful night operations against Nazi occupied Europe. Gerald was full of admiration for the pilots and navigators of the squadron. He told a reporter:

I have never met a squadron with such keenness and determination. A great deal of credit is due to their commanding officer, Wing Commander Davoud (Paul Davoud) DFC, of Kingston, Ontario. They have the finest form of discipline. They never have to be told to do a thing. In the air or on the ground, all personnel seem to have the knack and knowledge to sense what is expected of them and carry out their work with precision and dispatch. They take off in darkness, just two men in a Mosquito. They know they are expected to destroy enemy aircraft, wreck trains, destroy railway junctions and generally play hob with Jerry in the night. They work alone, coming up on their target through expert navigation, then find their way home to land on a field engulfed in darkness.

Ghost raiders, call them what you will, they're the finest pilots and navigators in the world. I'm lost in admiration for their incredible skill, determination and courage. They're a squadron of which the Royal Canadian Air Force and Canada can well be proud.

On 1 April a thanksgiving service for the twenty-fifth anniversary of the RAF was held in Tortington church and Gerald later addressed the station over the Tannoy. May saw the station's sports day. Prince Bernhardt of the Netherlands and the Duchess of Norfolk attended, and a certain Corporal Sidney Wooderson, the world's record holder, not too surprisingly won the mile event with a time of 4 mins. 38.5 secs. – an extremely creditable performance considering the conditions.

While at Ford, Gerald often flew the station's Tiger Moth as his personal aeroplane, using it to visit both Arundel and Alresford. In October, a young night fighter pilot, Jeremy Howard-Williams, who had been away on a short course, was returning to Ford in a Hornet Moth, a light, two seater cabin biplane, similar in size and configuration to a Tiger Moth. Seeing a Tiger Moth below him, and thinking it was a pupil out joyriding, Howard-Williams decided to have a little fun. He dived – gently, so as not to alarm the pupil too much – and pulled out on the Tiger Moth's tail. To his surprise and consternation, however, the Tiger Moth pilot quickly reversed the positions, settling himself comfortably on the tail of the Hornet Moth and remaining there despite all Howard-Williams' efforts to dislodge him. Howard-Williams finally broke off the mock combat and, as he admits in his biography, 'flew home, much chastened'.[1] On landing at Ford he found that the Tiger Moth had also landed, the pilot being Gerald, who had amply demonstrated that hand and eye had not lost their cunning and skill since 1918.

In March 1944, 604 Squadron was re-equipped with Mosquitos and Michael, the only pilot with any experience of the type, had the task of converting his pilots to their new aeroplanes, passing on his knowledge gained in 264 Squadron. Each Mosquito, he told them, had its own particular stall characteristic. Most dropped the starboard wing quite gently, others the port wing, equally gently, but about one in twenty dropped the port wing very hard indeed. The only other problem was that of the aerodrome birds. The plovers and gulls had learnt to avoid the Beaufighters taking off, but were fooled by the faster take-off of the Mosquitos, and until they adjusted their evasive tactics a number of birds were killed.

In early April 'Boom' Trenchard visited Scorton. Now Lord Trenchard, and Marshal of the RAF, Trenchard visited many RAF stations during the war years, keeping in touch with the young flying crews, inspiring them as he had those of a generation before. Michael asked Trenchard if 604 could be sent south. He felt the squadron had been in the north long enough, and that too many enemy aircraft were being destroyed on the ground by the RAF heavy bombers, instead of night fighters. It was also obvious that the invasion of Europe was in the not too distant future, and he asked if 604 could be the first night fighter squadron to return to the continent. Trenchard was amused at Michael's request, protesting that he now had little say in such matters, but at the end of April the squadron was ordered south to RAF Hurn.

1. *Night Intruder* Jeremy Howard-Williams. David and Charles, 1976.

CHAPTER XVIII

Invasion

Michael flew down to Hurn, Hampshire, on 2 May, the majority of the aeroplanes having been flown down over the previous few days. Despite the upheaval of the move, and a certain amount of chaos, the squadron managed to keep up to state and some operational flying was done, the squadron's first success from its new base coming on the night of 14 May, when John Surman and his operator, Flight Sergeant C. Weston, destroyed a Dornier Do 217, and Flying Officer R. M. MacDonald damaged a Ju 88. Having his haircut in Christchurch the next day, Michael was amused by the barber's comments on the last night's raid and very proud of his crews.

That night he and John made their own contribution to the squadron's success. They were scrambled a quarter of an hour before midnight, with Sopley control warning them of trade coming in from the south. Climbing to 10,000 feet, Michael got a visual, which turned out to be a Wellington, but soon afterwards the controller, Squadron Leader Seldon, gave them another contact, John picking it up on his AI and directing Michael to visual. The enemy aeroplane was weaving considerably, but turned west as they saw it and flew straight and level, the black shape gradually resolving itself into a Ju 88. Michael climbed to just below, steadied the Mosquito and closed in. It was the classic Cunningham approach. Michael had so often described this to his pupils – 'seeing it slightly above, going right below to identify and finally a sharp squirt from behind' – and he and John had often laughed about the day they would have a chance to use it. The nose of the Mosquito rose a little; Michael pushed it down gently until his sights were on at a range of a hundred yards. 'I fire. Almost instantly there is a vivid explosion as the whole aircraft blows up.'

A mass of flaming debris came back at the Mosquito. Michael immediately pulled back on the control column, and applied full rudder, the Mosquito rapidly doing three or four flick rolls.

'Contact', said John, as he got another blip. 'Above ... below ... above ... below ... what the hell are you doing?'

'Spinning', said Michael.

'Oh', commented John in his matter of fact way, concentrating again on vectoring Michael on to a fresh contact.

The Mosquito was now in thick cloud and they chased the second bomber, John giving a stream of instructions as the enemy pilot took evasive action. At 2,000 feet the Mosquito broke cloud. Michael could see the coast just ahead and he flew inland. Almost immediately the flak opened up and Michael, deciding he was over Poole, broke off the chase. 'It is silly to fly through balloons and flak, and anyway it's (the bomber) probably a friendly.' He called up base, asking for a course and distance to Hurn.

Sopley's reply was a shock. '360 degrees, 75 miles'. The Mosquito was over Cherbourg, not Poole!

The Ju 88 was Michael's first positive victory at night. As he closed in to fire he wondered what the enemy crew were doing at that moment in the darkened bomber, unaware that they had only a few more seconds of life. As he pressed his triggers he felt no vindictiveness, had no time for sorrow, only a desire to 'break up that big black shape'. After the explosion, watching the remains of the bomber fall in flames was a terrifying sight – even more terrifying to realize that he was the cause – but Michael was unworried, only anxious to find and destroy another. Next evening he and Jack Meadows went for a walk, sitting in the heather overlooking Christchurch, the Isle of Wight plain in the distance. It was a warm, sunny, and above all, peaceful evening. Michael looked out to sea. Over there, a few miles to the south, was the grave of the five men he had killed a few hours before, and he was conscious of the tragedy and sadness he had brought to German homes. His deep religious faith enabled him to rationalize the grim business of war, both the necessity to kill and the probability that he might himself be killed, and he entered his feelings in his diary.

> I more strongly realize how little death matters since it is only a means to Heaven. I feel that I have just been a cog in God's machinery, and that he has collected certain souls at their appointed time.

He confided these thoughts to his companion.

> I tell Jack he must be very brave if he does not believe in Heaven. He must have so much to lose. I know that I can only gain if I am killed, but if I did not believe that, I think I would play it safe and take the easy job if it were possible.

Jack Meadows answered that he was prepared to take risks for the sake of society and his own personal satisfaction. But Michael knew that without his faith the thought of death for himself and others 'would stand over me like a nightmare'.

On 2 June 1944 Michael was summoned to Northolt, flying over in the afternoon. After tea in Hillhouse, those present congregated in a well guarded room at the back of the house. As Michael entered he saw that the room was dominated by a large table. On the table was the plan for the invasion of Nazi Europe. In the briefing which followed, Michael learnt that he had been given command of twenty-six aircraft from several squadrons and was to be responsible for night support of the invasion force from the night of D-Day minus one.

The next day he flew to Colerne to discuss the administrative details, and returning to Hurn he read the whole plan for Overlord, taking what notes he needed. 'I have a wonderful, thrilling three hours – an eventful birthday!'

Looking out of his bedroom window when he woke on 5 June, Michael saw the weather was bad. He dressed leisurely and ate an unhurried breakfast, but an order came for him to report to Tangmere at 11.30. It was a fateful summons. Air Vice Marshal Hugh 'Dingbat' Saunders briefed the squadron and station commanders. D-Day was to be next day. Michael flew back to Hurn and assembled the squadron. When all were present he quietly told them the momentous news. There was a gasp, then a whoop of joy. The long awaited day had come at last.

Michael flew back to Colerne with John and set about organizing his rather motley command. Its task was to provide five patrols during the hours of darkness over the area just ahead of the parachutists' dropping zone. The crews were to fly on a free lance roving commission, seeking out any enemy aircraft attempting to interfere with the land operations. Michael had been forbidden to fly, and standing on the airfield later in the evening he watched the waves of Dakotas, laden with paratroopers, flying overhead on their way to the invasion area. Frustrated at being grounded, pacing the dispersal, Michael was joined by a Roman Catholic padre who had earlier given communion to the crews. The padre looked up at the Dakotas.

'How awful for those poor boys up there,' he said sadly to Michael.

'Better than being on this bloody ground,' Michael exploded, a squadron commander grounded on the most important night of the war. The padre laughed, cheered by Michael's matter of fact attitude.

No 604 Squadron's particular task was initially the protection of

Allied shipping in the Channel, and on the night of 7 June, Michael and John flew a patrol over the British beaches, controlled by a control ship (FDT 217). They saw no action, but Flight Lieutenant John Hooper and Flying Officer S. Hubbard destroyed an Me 410 near St Lo during the second patrol of the night for 604 Squadron's first victory of the invasion.

Despite bad weather, Michael and John flew patrols on the 8th and 11th of the month. They had no luck, but on 12 June, John Hooper and Hubbard gained their second victory, a Ju 188 near Cherbourg, and Flying Officer R. 'Dusty' Miller and Warrant Officer Catchpole destroyed a Heinkel 177. These successes were continued the next night, when Flight Lieutenant Frank Ellis and Flying Officer P. Williams gained their first victory, a Heinkel 177, which exploded so close to their Mosquito that some pieces of clothing were later found in its radiator. 604 was now really getting into its stride and the following night Flying Officer Terence 'Timber' Wood and his operator, Flight Lieutenant S. H. 'Neb' Elliott destroyed one FW 190 and damaged another for probable. This was a popular success. Neb Elliott was admired by all. Thirty-three years of age, he had lost a leg as a boy, but had successfully overcome this disability to become an operator.

On 15 June the weather deteriorated badly during the day and by evening was 'pretty murky'. 11 Group refused to allow anyone to fly, but Michael was only too aware that the bridgehead was still small, that all help possible was needed. In addition, since the nine days from the start of the invasion, 604 had not missed a single night in protection of the ground forces and Michael was determined not to start now. After an hour of hanging about dispersal he told control to inform Group that he was going to fly, whatever the weather. Group agreed but specified that only Michael should fly.

As Michael and John taxied out the rain was teeming down and visability was down to 400 yards. Michael turned on to the runway and opened up the Merlins, racing blind along the runway and into the air. The Mosquito went into cloud at 50 feet and Michael climbed up through it to a more comfortable height. Unlike the majority of pilots, Michael had always enjoyed flying in adverse conditions, and despite the rain beating against the cockpit, and being thrown about by the turbulence, he and John began to enjoy themselves, agreeing it was rather fun. Despite their efforts the patrol brought no reward and they returned after three and a quarter hours.

Michael flew two patrols over the next five days, but luck seemed to be eluding him and he saw no action, although the squadron gained another two victories. These were again first victories for the crews concerned, and Michael was gratified by this, feeling that it showed a far better squadron than one in which all the successes were achieved by a few select crews.

Michael had been keen to go to France for sometime, in order to visit the controllers who had been working so successfully with the night fighters under his command. These mobile radar units had been training with the night fighter squadrons since the early spring of 1944 and had gone to Normandy soon after D-Day. To be fully effective the units – usually in a lorry – needed to work close to the front line fighting and their work was both dangerous and difficult. A great mutual understanding and respect had matured between the crews and their controllers and Michael was anxious to visit the latter and give them a personal 'thank you' in appreciation of their efforts. On 26 June he managed, after a 'lot of wangling', to obtain permission for the trip and he set off during the afternoon in the squadron's Oxford, accompanied by John Quinton and his army liaison captain, Bill Hart. Michael was terrified at the thought of being shot down in the unarmed Oxford, a fear not helped by Flight Lieutenant Maitland Thompson, who paraded the squadron in a mock funeral parade as they left Hurn.

All went well, however, and they landed safely at A1 airfield near Isigny. The countryside looked fairly normal, only the signs, 'Mines ... Minen', and a few shell holes showing evidence of the recent fighting, and they were taken to the Chateau de Toqueville near Barfleur. Michael was told that 'just beyond the wood' a pocket of 2,000 German troops were still active in the peninsular, but was assured that he had no need to worry as some thirty RAF Regiment troops were between them and the enemy. This was scant comfort for, as Michael pointed out, the RAF troops were at lunch at that moment!

While visiting control, Michael found that Wing Commander Guggenheim of the RAF Regiment was planning a patrol in order to ascertain if the high ground to the west of St Pierre Eglise was clear of the enemy and suitable for a control post. Michael asked if he might go; he was given a tin hat and a Khaki battledress and they set off in the evening. The party consisted of an armoured reconnaissance car and a jeep; the car containing the driver, machine gunner, Michael and the Wing Commander; the jeep following with a sergeant and a pilot officer. John Quinton and Bill Hart, to their disgust, were not allowed to go.

The patrol went first to St Pierre Eglise, then further west, soon meeting up with the advance American patrols. They were now in dangerous territory, not knowing the positions of the German forces which were still in the area. Stopping at a crossroads, Guggenheim decided they should leave the jeep and proceed on foot. Apologising to the driver of the jeep for leaving him – 'quite unnecessarily as he was most relieved' – they set off down the road to the village. Guggenheim leading, then Michael, armed with a rifle, which he held like a shotgun, followed by the pilot officer, who was not enjoying himself at all. The armoured car brought up the rear, in reverse for a quick getaway. As they entered the village, known to have still been occupied by the enemy that morning, they expected to be greeted at any moment by a burst of machine gun fire, but all was quiet.

Despite their dangerous position, probably more dangerous than any airfighting, Michael felt an exhilarating sense of excitement as they crept cautiously forward. It suddenly occurred to him that this was exactly what he had trained for in the 4th Camerons, four and a half years before, and he longed to see something to shoot at. Actually he saw no point in ascertaining whether or not the village was in enemy hands, reasoning that even if it was not, they could not be far away, probably just outside, but it amused him to follow the aggressive Guggenheim, whom he thought showed an offensive spirit worthy of 604 Squadron, and he had difficulty in restraining his laughter at the pilot officer's voluble agreement everytime Guggenheim observed that the enemy must be very close.

They carefully explored the houses in the village. All was still, the only sound that of shells bursting in the country beyond. They walked up the main street, step by cautious step, feeling very naked, and expecting machine guns to open up any second, but a peasant suddenly appeared, followed by a number of others, including women and children, and the prosaicness of their appearance shattered the unreal situation. 'I feel like a fool, creeping along and thinking I was a soldier. It is like waking up from a dream in the middle of a big room with lots of people.'

The peasants could give them little information and by the time they had progressed to the other side of the village the ground was shaking with shellfire and aircraft were roaring overhead. Guggenheim decided they had gone far enough – an assessment with which the pilot officer heartily agreed – and they returned in the armoured car to where they had left the jeep, collecting a few stray shots from either side on the way. They passed the halted American patrols, who shouted they were waiting for reinforcements before taking the village. 'It's all right, old boy – we've just done it!' They later learnt that they had been within three hundred yards of a strongpoint of over seven hundred German troops.

After going into Cherbourg, Michael's party then visited the control at GCl 74, finishing an eventful day in Barfleur, where they drank and talked into the early hours. They visited another control the next morning and, finding an abandoned dugout full of brandy, filled their jeep to bursting. On his return to England, on 29 June, Michael presented his SASO, Toby Pearson, with several bottles of the brandy, but he made the mistake of visiting without having had a shave or a rest. His appearance, combined with a natural tiredness after the last exciting but strenuous four days, caused the SASO to ask how long he had been in command of 604. Michael's answer and appearance convinced Pearson that he was in need of a rest.

What was to be the last week of Michael's command of 604 Squadron was marked with a great deal of success, both personal and for the squadron as a whole, and it was appropriate that he should leave his first command at the peak of such success.

On the night of 2/3 July the weather was extremely bad and Group ordered that there was to be no flying. Michael went into the crew room.

'I've been ordered not to fly. Who's coming with me?'

Every single hand in the room immediately shot up. Michael had expected little less. He thanked them all, but chose just Dusty Miller and his operator to accompany him.

Michael and John took off in Mosquito NG-X, climbing away from Hurn at 11.35 pm. They patrolled the beachhead north of Cherbourg and after one and a half hours Michael called up Flight Lieutenant Jerry Nodes at 15082 GCl control, who gave him a vector and told him to hurry. John experienced a quantity of 'window' on his AI, but managed to obtain a contact crossing their nose, three miles ahead. Michael closed in quickly under John's instructions and finally saw a Ju 88 at 2,000 feet.

Michael overshot a little, was directly below the Junkers and a little in front, so he broke away hard to port and then back again to starboard. Unfortunately the German pilot did exactly the same, nearly colliding with the Mosquito, but Michael turned quickly to port and watched as the enemy aircraft dived gently towards the sea. Closing to 250 yards, with a 15 degree deflection, Michael opened fire. There was a huge white explosion, and as they pulled away to starboard Michael and John saw the Ju 88 going down steeply, black smoke pouring from it. Orbiting quickly, they searched for signs of the enemy, but saw only a fire on the sea below. Returning, they were diverted to Ford, and on landing found the Mosquito's windscreen had been damaged by debris from the stricken Ju 88. Neither Michael or John had seen the enemy aircraft actually hit the sea, but they were sure the fire was where it had crashed, and in view of this, and the damage to the windscreen, the award was later raised from a probable to a destroyed.

Dusty Miller and Catchpole had also shot down an enemy – a Ju 88 north west of Le Havre – and the following night another Ju 88 was destroyed by Dennis Furze and Flight Lieutenant Downes in the same area. Two nights later 'Dinty' Moore and Jimmy Hogg, both warrant officers, shot down an Me 410 south west of Caen for 604 Squadron's 99th victory. Michael's crews were doing him proud during the closing stages of his command.

The squadron's new CO arrived on the morning of 8 July. Wing Commander Desmond Hughes, DFC and two bars, had considerable day and night fighting experience, both in the home and Far East theatres, and Michael took him up in NG-X that afternoon.

At 12.30 on the night of 8 July, Michael and John took off for their last operational flight in 604 Squadron. Both were conscious that the squadron's score stood at 99 and were anxious to round off their service with the squadron by getting the century. They patrolled for over an hour before control informed them of trade on its way to bomb the British beaches. The controller brought them south, positioning them in the bomber stream, and before John could pick up a contact, Michael saw a dark shape crossing their front, 2,000 feet above them. He immediately recognised it as a Dornier Do 217 and turned after it, John calling out the range as he closed the distance. Before they could close the range sufficiently, however, the Dornier was fired at by Allied shipping in the darkness below and it immediately dropped two mines and turned north, climbing rapidly away from the flak. Michael narrowed the range to 150 yards, fired a long burst as the bomber entered cloud, and both he and John saw an explosion in its fuselage before the cloud closed around it.

A short time later John picked up another contact, only three miles ahead. Michael closed in quickly, seeing the enemy while it was still a mile distant. He positioned the Mosquito underneath the hostile, a Ju 88, but the enemy pilot had been warned of his presence and began to take violent evasive action. Michael stuck to him, matching his man-oeuvres, and firing long bursts of cannon and machine gun fire. The Ju

88 pilot dived steeply, the Mosquito following at full throttle, Michael firing another long burst from three hundred yards. There was a vast red explosion and the enemy aircraft went down, blazing furiously, to crash between the towns of Tronville and Harfleur. Only two of the crew baled out, and Michael circled the crash for several minutes before returning to base. Landing at five minutes past three, they made out their combat reports, everyone at dispersal congratulating them on scoring the squadron's 100th victory. It was a fitting end to Michael's command of 604 Squadron and a curious parallel to Gerald's achievement in September 1917, when he had shot down 56 Squadron's 200th victory.

Under Michael's command, 604 Squadron had regained some of its former prestige and success, following his guidance and example. The squadron had shot down twenty three enemy aircraft during the fourteen months of his command and Michael had himself destroyed four enemy aircraft, damaged another and was awarded a sixth as a probable. These successes earned him a DSO, and John Quinton's superb operating was rewarded with a well deserved DFC. Michael left 604 Squadron with his logbook endorsed 'Exceptional' by Group Captain Morsby. Under the heading, 'Any Points in flying or Airmanship which should be watched', an unknown hand has added, in pencil, 'Sky Happy!!'

Michael's new posting was to HQ 85 Base Group at Uxbridge, and he began his new duties on 19 July 1944. Fresh from leave, he immersed himself in his new task of co-ordinating fighter tactics, keeping in touch with the squadrons by commuting in a variety of aircraft. These visits enabled him to fly the odd offensive patrol, and although John Quinton was now Navigation Officer at 142 Airfield, Michael usually managed to arrange for them to fly together on these sorties. They flew a night patrol on 23 July, with no sightings, and another on 25 August, when they were the first night fighter of the Group to patrol Paris.

In the middle of September 1944, Michael was posted to the command of Training Wing, 54 OTU at Charter Hall, managing to get John Quinton posted in shortly after arrival. They made several trips to France and Belgium over the next months, but their operational days were over – at least against the Luftwaffe – and the cessation of hostilities in May 1945 found them still at Charter Hall.

CHAPTER XIX

Far East Command

At the end of the war in Europe, Michael turned his sights to the Far East, where Japan was still fighting. Before the end of the war he had already put in several requests for a posting overseas, but had been refused on the grounds that no aircrew who had completed more than one tour in the European theatre could be posted to the Far East. It was time to cut corners and enlist the help of old friends, and Michael visited Air Vice Marshal Hugh Saunders, now Director General of Postings. Saunders gave him a warm welcome and waved him to a chair.

'Well, Michael, what are you doing here. Have you asked Group for permission to see me?'

'No Sir', replied Michael. 'I was afraid they might refuse.'

Saunders laughed. 'Yes. Well, what do you want?'

'I want to go to the Far East, Sir. I'd like a squadron – anything from a Swordfish to a Liberator – and I'm willing to drop a rank to squadron leader to do so.'

'H'mm', mused Saunders. 'Why haven't you applied through the usual channels?'

'I have, sir, but they turned me down. People with more than one tour of ops are not allowed to go out east.'

'I see,' Saunders said. 'I suppose you've done two tours.'

'No, Sir. Actually I've done three.'

This amused the Air Vice Marshal, who promised to have a word with Sir Keith Park, now C in C Far East Air Forces, but he pointed out the difficulties, and promised nothing. Michael thanked him and left. He had been back at Charter Hall only a short while before receiving a priority signal, posting him to HQ Air Command South East Asia at Karachi.

There was no posting for John Quinton, who was miserable at the prospect of being left behind, but with his usual cheerful disregard for small details, Michael told him to pack his bags and come anyway, and on 6 June 1945, the anniversary of D Day, they left Poole Harbour in a Sunderland flying boat of BOAC, flying over the old invasion beaches of Utah and Omaha on the first stage of their three day journey to India.

On arrival at Karachi, Michael found he had been posted to command 84 Squadron at Charra, Bengal, equipped, the P Staff thought, with Liberators. Michael's heart sank. Saunders had called his bluff. On Tuesday, 12 June, Michael and John flew in a C Class Empire flying boat to Calcutta. Charra was 200 miles north west of Calcutta and they made the last stage of the journey by train, arriving at the small station after dark, three miles from the squadron mess. Luckily, the squadron had received a signal about them, and a car arrived to take Michael to his new command. The driver was surprised to find a new CO, having been told it was merely a flight commander he was to collect, and he told them that the squadron had actually moved to St Thomas' Mount, Madras, only the rear party and two aircraft remaining at Charra. This was disconcerting after all their efforts to reach Charra, a long, hot and extremely uncomfortable journey, but Michael and John were delighted with one piece of news – the squadron was equipped with Mosquitos.

Michael toured the aerodrome the next morning and met the NCOs and men. He was impressed by the personnel left at Charra and hoped that the main party would be as good, but he sensed that squadron morale was poor. The squadron had been off operations for eighteen months and had been in both the unsuccessful Greek and Singapore campaigns. There was a general air of feeling 'mucked about' by the numerous changes, not helped by a rather uninspiring CO and uninterested flight commanders. Recently re-equipped with Mosquitos, the squadron had just had two fatal crashes and were far from confident with their new aircraft, chiefly, Michael later found, through lack of adequate training. Michael, with his usual optimism, felt sure that the nucleus of a good squadron was there, but John was dubious, asking Michael to show him one crew that was equal to the below average crew in 604 Squadron. Michael had to admit that John was right. Where 84 stopped, 604 started. But they were judging people as efficient war machines and the 84 crews were at that time badly trained and not adjusted to the realities of war. Michael realized that what they needed was concentrated and intensive training. The air crew were a particularly nice lot of people and he felt they had immense potential. He only wondered whether or not he could instil into them the offensive enthusiasm and competency they would need to match the Japanese in the assault on Malaya and Singapore, which were clearly the next target for our forces.

Although Michael was disappointed by the unpreparedness of 84 Squadron for war, he was most impressed by the spirit of the squadron. It had been at Shaibah for many years and legends and traditions were legion. The troops were wonderful, only equalled by those of 56 Squadron.

As soon as the whole squadron was installed at St Thomas' Mount, Michael set about its training – and it really was a crash course. Within a few weeks, however, the whole squadron was beginning to move in the right direction. What they thought of him he dared not think, but by mid-August he began to feel that he had command of a really great squadron.

Michael's hopes of operations against the Japanese were dashed by the end of the war in the east on 14 August 1945, but 84 Squadron had been picked to play a leading part in the return of the RAF to Singapore, and on 31 August was ordered to move to Baigachi, near Calcutta, as quickly as possible, for the first stage of their journey to the liberated island. By a supreme effort everything was ready by the next day, take-off being set for 3.00 pm, but at noon Michael received an order cancelling the move. Now wise in the ways of HQs, Michael put the order in his pocket and promptly forgot it. The day after the squadron reached Baigachi it received an emergency signal ordering it there.

Michael led 84 Squadron into Kallang aerodrome, Singapore, on 12 September. The aerodrome was being used to evacuate the newly freed prisoners of war from Burma to Australia in Dakotas, and there were many ex-84 Squadron prisoners of war in hospital in Singapore. They were delighted to have a visit from their old squadron, but were in a terrible state, one boy not even able to remember his rank or trade. Twelve members of the squadron had escaped captivity, sailing to Australia in a small boat, which they had named 'The Scorpion' after the squadron crest. They had only an aircraft sextant, a compass and a school atlas, but they reached Australia safely after forty eight days.

The squadron mess was set up in a Japanese 'comfort house' a polite euphemism for a brothel, all the officers having a room each. They were looked after by Chinese house boys, who cooked and cleaned for them, everybody becoming very houseproud, 'liberating' furniture and comforts from all over town. These efforts came to nothing however. Michael felt they were too near HQ, with its attendant red tape, and he had the squadron moved to Seletar on 23 September.

Michael was concerned with the fate of the squadron's groundcrews, still at St Thomas' Mount, and on 27 September he and John set off to visit them. The weather was good until two hundred miles from Rangoon and the Mosquito was diverted to Moulmein in Burma. The Japanese at Moulmein had not yet officially surrendered, but all was well, and with much saluting the Mosquito was marshalled into position by Japanese troops, a Japanese general sending his staff officer to make sure they had everything they needed, including a hot meal. British troops were expected the next day. The weather was clearing; Michael had the Mosquito refuelled and they made the thirty minutes flight to Mingladon, staying the night in an hospitable but crowded Mess. Next day they made two attempts to reach Madras, but weather conditions forced them to spend another night at Mingladon and they finally arrived at St Thomas' Mount next day, beating up the Mess on arrival. The main body of the groundcrews had just left by ship for Singapore, but those remaining were delighted to see them.

This was an interesting trip for Michael, with he and John making sightseeing trips to Poona, Delhi, Colombo and Kandy. Two old friends from 56 Squadron days were at Kandy HQ, Morton Pinfold, now a Wing Commander, and George Smythe, now a Squadron Leader. Both were surprised and pleased to see Michael, and George Smythe gave priority to shipping out the remainder of the squadron's groundcrews.

Michael and John flew back to Seletar via Rangoon on 11 October, to find that the main body of groundcrews had arrived. 'It is a joy to see them.' Over the next few days the squadron flew many of the repatriation officers around the outlying districts and islands, collecting POWs from isolated locations, and later in October, Michael and John flew to Saigon, then capital of French Indo-China. Saigon was still guarded by Japanese troops, with Japanese aircraft flying supplies to their forces in the hills, cut off by the Amanites, and as the Mosquito came in to land they were warned by control. 'There are many Jap aircraft in the circuit, they have no clue at all. Look out.' Many such places were still under Japanese rule, having not yet officially surrendered to the British forces, and isolated RAF crews, landing at such, were accommodated in the Japanese Messes or the best hotels. As Michael commented in a letter home to his mother: 'It is a funny situation.'

At the end of October, Michael and John Ramsden, the squadron engineering officer, flew to Kuantan on the east coast of Malaya to investigate a Mosquito crash. While there they met many army officers from Force 136, who had been working with Chinese guerrillas behind the Japanese lines, including an old friend from Ampleforth, Alan Macdonald, now running the military and civil administration. After interviewing the local fishermen in the vicinity of the crash, and rewarding them for having recovered the bodies from the sea, Michael and Ramsden returned to Kuantan, where Michael borrowed a truck from Lieutenant Colonel Freddie Chapman.

Michael had decided it would be a worthwhile experience to drive across Malaya to Kuala Lumpur, a distance of 250 miles, and he enjoyed enormously the trip through the jungle, 'seeing Malaya in the raw'. Arriving at Kuala Lumpur, they were picked up by Flight Lieutenant Ferguson in a Mosquito and flown back to Seletar, finding on arrival that the air was thick with rumours of trouble brewing in Java. On 31 October the squadron was ordered to Batavia, the Javanese capital.

As with the former French colony of Indo China, the Indonesians in Java were determined to resist the return to power of their former colonial rulers, in this case the Dutch. As in Indo China, the guerrilla forces in Java had harassed the Japanese army throughout the occupation and they considered they had won their right to independence. They had no objection to the British, trusting them, and knowing of the United Kingdom's policy of eventual self government, but national feelings ran high when it became known that the British forces were merely holding the island until the Dutch arrived, to restore the pre-war status quo as laid down by the United Nations.

These feelings were exacerbated by the attitude of the first Dutch troops to arrive, and discontent flared into open rebellion. The British forces were in a delicate position. At the onset their sympathies were with the Indonesians, who they found a charming and friendly people, but the easy arousal of the Indonesians by agitators, and the excesses and atrocities they perpetuated, including the murder of Brigadier Mallaby, quickly lost them this sympathy and, despite having little regard for the attitude of the Dutch, British opinion hardened against the Indonesian cause.

At 2.40 pm on 31 October, Michael and John Quinton, with Leading Aircraftman Shakespeare, landed at Batavia aerodrome to the east of the town. Walking to the control tower, which was bristling with guns, they were met by an unarmed wing commander, who took them to see the Station Commander, Group Captain David Lee, and the AOC, Air Commodore C. E. Stevens. Michael told them that the remainder of the force – eight Mosquitos from 84 Squadron, plus six from 110 Squadron – would be arriving later, but Lee and Stevens were unconcerned. They had not expected the reinforcements quite so soon and the position had calmed down a little since their request. However, although not as serious as it had been, they considered the situation was still explosive and were glad to see the Mosquitos arrive later in the evening, reinforcing the Thunderbolts of Nos 60 and 81 Squadrons already at the base. Each Mosquito had ferried in an airman and these serviced the aeroplanes to meet any eventuality that might arise the following day. The Mosquito crews were given a warm welcome and, although the messes were rather crowded, Michael considered that the excellent local beer more than compensated for any discomfort.

Michael was in command of a composite squadron of 84 and 110 Squadron Mosquitos, but after the excitement of the move the next few days were something of an anti-climax, only local reconnaissance flights being made. Michael flew his first sortie on 9 November, 'reconnaissance before battle commences', but all was quiet, and two days later he was ordered to take a detachment of six Thunderbolts of 60 Squadron and two Mosquitos of his own command to Soerabaja in the east of the island. On the afternoon of their arrival, Michael flew Brigadier Loder Symons of the Royal Artillery to inspect the town. A recent conference with the native leaders had been unproductive and it had been decided to clear the insurgents from the town next morning.

There was little opposition at the start of the operation, but after two and a half hours it hardened considerably and Operation Apple was put into force: five minutes of land and sea bombardment, followed by bombing of the enemy positions by four Thunderbolts and a Mosquito of 84 Squadron, flown by Flying Officer 'Chas' Chesney, and Flight Lieutenant G. E. Pettit. Chesney attacked the main government building, the HQ and strongpoint of the Indonesian forces, and his Mosquito – actually Michael's own PY-X – was hit by small arms fire from the ground.

Michael was exhilarated by being back on operations, however limited, and at the chance to put his squadron through its paces. 'For the next few weeks we have a really wonderful time. The ops are quite exciting and reasonably dangerous. There are a lot of flak guns, Bofors and 3.7 and these are either dead accurate or well off. Those that are hot really make you weave. It is grand practice for the new boys and lots of them really feel that they are now fully operational.'

Two days after the opening of the attack, on 12 November, Michael and John attacked the Hotel Brunette, but the bombs refused to release, and in another attempt, later in the afternoon, they failed to explode. Michael made another attack, two hours later, but although this time one bomb did explode, it overshot its target and Michael had to be content with strafing the hotel with his cannon and machine guns.

Michael's own Mosquito, PY-X, had been sent to Seletar for repair after the damage sustained on 10 November, and flying it after its return, Chesney was again hit by groundfire, this time in the main spar, writing off the Mosquito. Michael and John had flown this Mosquito almost exclusively since joining the squadron and it was hard to lose a favourite aeroplane.

On 21 November, Michael and John flew a tactical reconnaissance to inspect the roads running to the rear of the town, taking Colonel Morris of the Royal Tank Regiment as a passenger. Morris wanted to see if the roads were suitable for the movement of his tanks, but in the event he was forced to rely on Michael's assessment, not being accustomed to reconnoitring positions at the speed of a Mosquito weaving to avoid heavy flak. Michael dived along the roads from 4,000 feet, building up to 380 mph in the dive and climbing steeply away from the groundfire.

Operations were somewhat handicapped by political opinion in England, the support aircraft being allowed to drop only a minimum of bombs, at one stage even being forbidden to shoot up the flak guns firing at them. To many people in England the war had ended with the surrender of the Japanese and there was a reluctance to lose lives in putting down what appeared at the time to be a minor uprising. The army went forward slowly, taking a great deal of trouble to keep casualties to a minimum, but with its effectiveness curtailed by its orders, the RAF could not give their complete support and these tactics cost lives, the town not being taken until after three weeks of fighting. Thunderbolts and Mosquitos flew bombing, groundstrafing and reconnaissance missions, even spotting for ships' guns, and Michael asked for reinforcements from the remainder of the squadron still at Seletar.

Group Captain Lee gave permission for Michael to have two additional Mosquitos, guessing that Michael would take four, but Michael sidestepped this ploy by getting eight. Michael found that the operations in Java gave an accurate assessment of the quality of his crews. He left it a completely voluntary choice which crews came to Soerabaja to fly on operations, he and John amusing themselves by guessing which would be the next to arrive. They were seldom wrong, and the result was that all the keen crews gravitated to Soerabaja, creating a real squadron spirit.

Michael flew back to Seletar in November to visit the groundcrews and explain the situation in Java to them. He visited Batavia at the end of the month, and on returning to Soerabaja he found that 84 had suffered its first fatal casualty of the operation; Squadron Leader John Slip and his operator, Flight Lieutenant Trevor Andrews had been killed when their Mosquito had crashed after a strafing run. John Slip had been chosen as A Flight Commander by Michael in July, soon after taking command of the squadron, and he had been married only a few weeks before his death.

Michael flew to Singapore in early December to arrange for a replacement flight commander in Slip's place, flying on to Kuala Lumpur to visit RAF HQ Malaya. On his return to Soerabaja he found that the centre of operations was now moving towards Batavia, the squadron detachment there gradually taking over more of the operational flying from the Mosquitos at Soerabaja. By the end of December the main task at Soerabaja was completed and the arrival of the whole of 60 Squadron made the Mosquitos' role still less important.

Sir Keith Park inspected Soerabaja on 20 December, complimenting Group Captain David and Michael on the station, a thing, he confided, he rarely did. The next day, Michael flew fighter cover for Sir Keith's Dakota, the C in C insisting on flying low over the flak area. At first the Dakota flew sedately at 4,000 feet – 'à la Transport Command' – but with Sir Keith taking over the controls it dropped down to under a thousand feet – 'à la Fighter Command'. 'I have never seen a Dak being thrown about so much,' Michael recorded later, as Sir Keith, who had flown Bristol Fighters in the First World War and a Hurricane in 1940, weaved amongst the flak. Control then radioed with a request for Michael to attack a train and Sir Keith cut in on the RT with his permission. 'Yes. Carry on, two six.' In the event, two trains were seen and Michael, attacking the second, blew it up in a cloud of smoke and steam. It was quite like old times in France.

Michael flew to Seletar later in the day, visiting Group Captain Pinfold and arranging for John Quinton's promotion to Squadron Leader. 'He is the first squadron leader (flight commander) that the Navigators' Union has produced in any fighter or fighter bomber squadron. He certainly deserves it.' That night they had a celebration, despite beer being 12/- a pint, everyone being delighted at the popular Quinton's promotion.

January 1946 was marked by Michael's flying hours reaching 2,000, entered in his logbook on 2 January. On 5 March, Michael flew John to Kelland in a Dakota. John had been posted home to England for demobilization. Four and a half years of friendship and partnership were coming to an end. Michael sadly entered in his logbook, 'Last trip with Johnnie', noting with a nostalgic amusement that although far from being a Mosquito the Dakota was lettered X, always their favourite aeroplane letter. It was an evocative parting, full of memories of dangers shared. Michael wrote in John's logbook.

As radar operator, navigator and straight navigator over a period of four and a half years which includes three operational tours, and the task of navigator leader over three years – exceptional.

John wrote, in turn:

Best of luck Mike and thanks a lot for four and a half years of really wizard flying.

Life is seldom tidy, however, and on a visit to Singapore at the end of the month Michael found John still waiting for his ship to sail. John went out to the aerodrome to see Michael off, and Michael tentatively suggested that he might like to come back to visit the squadron for a couple of nights. John needed no second invitation. 'He just got in.'

Michael and John flew one last patrol together, a motor convoy protection patrol on 21 March. There was no Nationalist activity, nothing to shoot at, and the patrol was a pleasant trip, flying round the hills, finally ending their partnership on a quiet note.

Michael remained in command of 84 Squadron until the beginning of December 1946, flying sorties against the Nationalist forces, exercises with the Fleet Air Arm, and even a filming session for British Movietone News. Thanks to his leadership and example the squadron was now a highly efficient unit and he had twice saved it from disbandment. He had heard of the first disbandment order just before a visit by Air Chief Marshal A. J. 'Ugly' Barrett, and picking an opportune moment Michael told him the sad news. Barrett was sympathetic. 'Write me a full report on the squadron and let me have it as soon as possible.' Michael smiled and produced a report from his pocket, 'I thought you'd ask for one, sir.' Barrett gave the report to Air

Marshal Hollinghurst. 'Holly' was an old friend of Gerald, having served under him at Ayr as a young fighter pilot in 1918, and he wrote to Michael. 'I was very much amused by your *Cri de Coeur*. Of course we can't disband your glorious squadron.'

A year later 84 was again under threat of disbandment and Michael's appeals to both Group and Command had been unsuccessful. Michael sent an urgent message to Hollinghurst. 'Sir, please remember my last *Cri de Coeur*', sending it in code with a 'Priority – Emergency' classification. The communications officer pointed out that only AOCs were entitled to use such a category as it automatically stopped all other signals. Michael knew that it would never reach Hollinghurst any other way. 'Send it.'

Michael threw a party that evening, everybody down in the dumps at the prospect of disbandment, puzzled at Michael's cheerfulness. A signal came from 'Holly' the next morning. 'Don't worry. It is all right.' Two signals later Michael received an order cancelling the disbandment.

At the end of 1946 Michael was delighted to be given command of 60 Squadron. He had been on flying duties continuously since his first posting to 56 Squadron in 1940, and he had feared that his next posting on leaving 84 Squadron would be a desk job. As one of the last acting wing commanders in the command, Michael was now demoted to squadron leader, but in typical fashion he threw a party to celebrate his demotion ...

60 Squadron had left Java in November 1946, unhappily stripped of its Thunderbolts, and had arrived in Singapore by sea. During the first week in December the squadron took up its quarters at Tengah, where Michael took command on 9 December 1946. 60 Squadron was to be re-equipped with the Spitfire XVIII, but the new aircraft were slow in arriving and it was not until March that the squadron was up to its full peacetime compliment of eight Spitfires, plus one Harvard for training. The pilots were delighted with their new aircraft and before long Michael asked Command for permission to train his pilots in night flying. Command refused, but did give Michael permission to fly at night. Next night Michael took off. Following his usual direct way of solving difficulties, he flew straight to the Command Senior Mess. Twenty minutes of low level aerobatics over the mess, the Spitfire's lights full on, convinced Command that the Spitfire was quite safe to fly at night and 60 Squadron was allowed to begin training.

The squadron also formed its own aerobatic team of four Spitfires, Michael usually flying a solo display at demonstrations. With his malicious sense of humour still operating, Michael had his own technique for enlivening these displays. It was generally accepted that a Spitfire should not be spun close to the ground, and Michael took full advantage of this. He would start his display with all the appearance of a deplorably bad pilot, staggering over in badly executed loops, rolling off the top in as sloppy a fashion as he could manage, gradually building up an impression in the minds of the spectators that here was an unusually inept pilot, who would probably kill himself before he was much older. The climax came directly above the VIP enclosure. Staggering up in a final pathetic attempt at a loop, the Spitfire suddenly flicked over into a spin. To the horrified VIPs a crash seemed inevitable – and what was worse, straight into them. They lost no time in beating a hurried and undignified retreat, scattering in all directions as the Spitfire hurtled down at them. Michael pulled out at nought feet, and continued with a show of immaculate aerobatics, in the opinion of one of his pilots writing home, 'as good a display of individual aerobatics as one could see anywhere in the world. He is an exceptional pilot.'

Another trick was inspired by the Griffon engine of the Spitfire XV 111 making an impressive collection of explosions and smoke if throttled back suddenly. Approaching the VIP stand inverted, Michael would produce the required effects, with the usual gratifying effect on his audience.

In July six Spitfires were flown to Kuala Lumpur to take part in an Army Co-operation exercise lasting several days. At the end of the exercise a flying display was given before 10,000 people at the local airport, one attraction being the appearance of the first jet aeroplanes to be seen in the Far East, two Gloster Meteors at Tengah for tropical trials. At the conclusion of the Meteors' high speed pass over the field, Michael, not to be outdone by the jets, dived his Spitfire from 10,000 feet, flattening out at optimum speed for his own pass over the spectators, matching the speed of the Meteors. His fitter was heard to complain that he was sure he could hear the Spitfire's rivets popping as it hurtled across the field!

Michael's command of 60 Squadron came to an end on 8 December 1947, the new CO, Squadron Leader J. H. S. Broughton AFC, arriving on 20 November. Michael had been hoping to ferry a Dakota home to the UK, not only to have a pleasant and leisurely journey home, but as a convenient transport for the effects he had accumulated during his time in the Far East. But it was necessary to obtain the appropriate pilot's rating for the Dakotas and Michael's insistence on flying it like a Spitfire, influenced his rating to that of co-pilot. He left for home on 13 December 1947, flying in easy stages over the next eight days and arriving on 21 December. Apart from a six week visit during the early summer, he had been away two and a half years.

CHAPTER XX

Peace comes again

At the end of the war in Europe, Gerald went back to the city. He was a member of the Stock Exchange in both London and New York, and although he retired in 1950 he retained many of his business interests, being a director of several companies. Throughout his life Gerald retained a deep affection for his many American friends and their country, and since the days of the Liberty Bond tour of 1919 had frequently visited the USA. With the end of the war he quickly renewed his old acquaintances in the States, and was delighted when his brother in law, William Griffin, was knighted by King George VI for his work in promoting Anglo-American friendship as President of the English Speaking Union and director of Lease-Lend, one of the few Americans to be so honoured.

During the 1950s Gerald became much involved with the Fishmongers, one of the oldest and most influential of the City guilds, and during his time as Prime Warden he invited Prince Philip to speak. Gerald also commissioned the official portrait of the Queen by Annigoni, who later became a personal friend, advising Carrie and Gerald on the design of the Catholic chapel which they created in a wing of Alresford House in memory of their son Billy.

During these later years, as a Knight of Malta and a Papal Chamberlain, Gerald was involved in assisting Pope Pius XII at regular intervals. His Scottish heritage was reflected in belonging to the Royal Company of Archers, the Queen's bodyguard for Scotland, and in this capacity, together with his four brothers, he was in attendance at the coronation of Queen Elizabeth as a Gold Staff Officer. He was always closely interested in local affairs and served as Deputy Lieutenant for Hampshire under the Duke of Wellington.

Gerald's main interest, however, was people. Everyone was of interest to him, and he had the gift of making friends with a great number of people, no matter what their role in life. But above all he was a family man, in his quiet, unhurried manner the pivot of his household. He always had time to discuss problems and interests with Carrie and the children and he liked nothing better than to retire to bed before the 9 o'clock news, where he would be joined by the rest of the family, who would tuck into oranges and apples while relating the gossip of the day. His family meant everything to him and he was never so happy as when they were all gathered together at either Alresford or Farlie, when he was sure to be involved in every game and activity, especially that which he loved best: sitting in the evening at the piano, playing by ear all the popular tunes from the 1920s to the current day. He had never had a lesson, but he had a superb sense of rhythm and a natural ear. Everyone loved these evenings, and there was always singing to his accompaniment.

This talent also carried him through more formal occasions. His youngest son, Peter, remembers that at a party for old age pensioners in the village of Bray, when Gerald was expected to make a speech, he asked those present if they would prefer him to play the piano instead. He then delighted them by accompanying their singing for the rest of the evening. This was typical of Gerald: the feeling of personal communication with any age and on any level. Whether a grandchild of four, an employee, or an airman under his command, all were aware of this complete rapport, of being treated equally. Gerald had that rare gift of putting everyone instantly at their ease. His eldest daughter Anne, once asked him how he had acquired the talent. 'Among the Scottish ghillies, out stalking on the moors during my youth', Gerald told her. 'They're a naturally taciturn and individual race; if you can talk to them you can talk to anyone'. Indicative of Gerald's regard for people was his insistence on his children being polite to everyone, especially to those who had no right of reply. Anne remembered far worse 'rockets' for not saying 'thank you' to a lift-man in a busy shop, than rudeness to any member of the family, who could always retaliate.

If the saying that, 'wit is being able to make jokes; humour is being able to make them about yourself', is true, then Gerald had humour, generating a sense of fun to those around him; and this, together with his deep religious conviction, carried him through many challenging years.

Gerald still kept up his association with 56 Squadron, his interest and affection unalloyed by service with any other squadron, for despite his long service in the RFC and RAF he had served only in 56 Squadron. In addition to his own and Michael's service with the squadron, Gerald's own son, William, later flew with the squadron, making it almost a family affair.

William Michael, Gerald's eldest son – always called Billy – joined the RAFVR in 1944. He remustered for training as a pilot in 1945, was discharged on appointment to a commission in June 1946, and started his flying training at No 19 FTS Cranwell in August. He soloed in DH 82a (N6790) on 22 August, after eight and a quarter hours of instruction, graduating to Harvard 11Bs. He passed out from the FTS after two hundred and six combined hours and was rated as an above average pilot. He was then posted to No 54 OTU at Leeming to fly Mosquito 111s. Passing out from Leeming, he was first posted to 85 Squadron, and then, in November 1949, to 56 Squadron.

On 29 March 1950, while practising formation flying in a Meteor in preparation for the Farnborough Air Show, Billy broke away from the formation after completing a roll, apparently to avoid another Meteor. He was too low to recover and crashed fatally. He was buried at Alresford with full RAF honours. Billy's death was a tragic loss to Carrie and Gerald; a cruel stroke of fate, which had seen his father and uncles come through two wars unscathed, to die in a peacetime flying accident.

In 1953 Gerald organized a 56 Squadron reunion, which was held at Claridges on 4 March. Over sixty officers were present and the guest of honour was Lord Trenchard. Among the guests were Lord Tedder; Air Chief Marshal Sir William Dickson, Chief of Air Staff; Air Vice Marshal the Earl of Bandon; Air Marshal Sir Philip Babington. Many former commanding officers of the squadron were present, including the current CO, Squadron Leader Spooner, and pilots from both wars. These last included Michael, from the squadron's Battle of Britain period; the days of 1916–1918 being well represented by Gerald himself, Wing Commander M. H. Coote, Major E. J. L. W. Gilchrist and Squadron Leader D. Grinnell-Milne.

After Lord Bandon and Squadron Leader Spooner had made their speeches, Gerald gave a short history of the squadron, touching on the greatest period of its history in 1917 and 1918, giving the company his memories of McCudden and Ball. Lord Trenchard then spoke of the value of tradition, and of the days in France in the first war, when the squadron had 'the finest band and the best cook in the RFC'.

In January 1955, 56 Squadron's commanding officer, Squadron Leader 'Twinkle' Storey, wrote to Gerald asking for suggestions as to the most suitable person to present the squadron with its standard. Protocol was such that the squadron was not allowed to ask royalty, although unofficially the Station Commander was trying for Her Majesty the Queen or the Duke of Edinburgh. Nothing came of these plans and Gerald wrote to his cousin, Rachel Davidson, Lady in Waiting to HRH The Duchess of Kent. The Duchess said she would be delighted to present the standard, but would have to be asked officially. Gerald immediately set the wheels in motion, but he had reckoned without the apathy and tedium of red tape. It was not until over a year later – and much work on Gerald's part – that the Duchess was officially invited to present the standard.

Gerald's patience and perseverance had been rewarded, but he was still not finished. He wrote dozens of letters, to everyone he could think of, to ensure that the coming ceremony had the fullest possible coverage in the national press and news media; generally acting as a one man publicity campaign for the squadron and the presentation. He advised Major Kaisin, then commanding 56 Squadron, on many points, and roughed out a programme and guest list. One of Gerald's ideas was to have an SE5 at the ceremony, and on 29 March, together with Major Kaisin and Christopher Coles of the Air Ministry, he travelled down to Vickers Ltd at Weybridge to request the loan of their SE5. It was agreed that the SE should be at Waterbeach for the presentation, standing next to a Hawker Hunter jet fighter, the squadron's contemporary equipment, and Gerald made all arrangements for its transportation and insurance during the journey. He also made sure that the SE received as much publicity as possible, writing personally to *The Aeroplane*, the *Tatler*, *The Times*, the *Daily Express* and *Time Life*, and entertaining to lunch several people whom he thought could possibly help the cause in one way or another.

The members of the old RFC were also remembered. An article in the *Daily Express* – the result of a letter to Max Aitken, himself a pilot in the Hitler war – brought Gerald a letter from his old fitter at Ayr, asking if it would be possible for him to attend the ceremony. Gerald immediately wrote to Kaisin, requesting invitations for the fitter and his wife.

The great day finally arrived. Despite the bitterly cold weather the occasion was a great success, all the arrangements working smoothly. Nobody had done more than Gerald to bring the day to fruition and he must have been very proud as, flanked by his brothers Michael and Andrew, he watched the presentation of the standard. The memories that must have crowded his mind can only be imagined, but as he explained to the Duchess the details of the SE5 he must have relived many memories of 1917–1918.

Gerald was to have one more contact with the SE5. A few years later it was rebuilt by the Aircraft Experimental Establishment at Farnborough, and Gerald wrote to C. E. Berens, congratulating him on a wonderful job and asking if it would be possible to have his photograph taken sitting in the cockpit of the SE5, as a companion to a similar photograph taken in 1917. In August 1959 the rebuilt SE5 was handed over to the Shuttleworth Trust and Gerald gave a talk on the BBC about his experiences while flying the type in the first war. A month later, on September 29, he travelled over to Farnborough to have the photograph taken.

Gerald had several copies of this photograph printed and mounted, and he signed one for his sister in law, Mrs Selina Hulings of Baltimore, USA. 'Forty Years On. So much love. Gerald. Xmas 1959'. But he was never to have the pleasure of giving the photographs. Gerald's heart had been giving concern for sometime, and during a trip to America in the summer he had been examined by Carrie's brother, George Garden, who advised him to see a specialist, on his return to England. On Friday, 11 December, Gerald took a family party to the circus: his own children, grandchildren, and two Iranian boys for whom he was acting as a guardian. During the interval, Gerald's daughter Anne, who had a great weakness for fortune tellers, visited one in a circus booth. The fortune teller summarily dealt with the usual prophecies of her kind, of travel, money, and such, and impressed upon Anne the absolute necessity of having a large family Christmas party. Anne, who had no intention of having a large gathering, thought the woman mad, but she reiterated many times that a large party was essential, insisting it should be held.

After the circus it was decided that, the London flat being too small to sleep everyone comfortably, Gerald, his son, Peter, the two Iranian boys and his daughter Carolyn, should drive down to Alresford. When Gerald failed to come down for breakfast next morning, Carolyn went to his room and found him suffering from a heart attack. Despite all efforts to save him, Gerald had another, fatal attack. It was nine o'clock on 12 December 1959. Somehow it seems so suitable that Gerald should have died so peacefully after this family party, the kind of party he loved so much. He lies today in the churchyard at Old Alresford church, next to his son Billy.[1]

Anne did have a large family party at her Hambledon home that Christmas, of necessity including all those from Alresford, knowing

1. Carolyn (Carrie) Constable Maxwell died on 10 February 1984.

that that was what her father would have wanted.

This is how Anne remembered him:

'He adored the cosiness of family affection, but never usurped it or made one feel guilty if it wasn't always forthcoming due to some personal pressure. You always left him feeling happier and a more reassured person, because he generated such warmth and under-standing, a wonderful sense of fun, and yet was totally undemanding of our time. He just wanted to fit in and enjoy whatever was going on – be it nursery tea with his grandchildren or catching up on news of older members of the family.

'He had an innate sense of wisdom and commonsense, coupled with tremendous compassion and time for everyone, which made him the great leader he undoubtedly was. No matter who you were, or what you did, he cared equally and gave of his best. No problem was too trivial for his concern; often one never learnt of the things he had done for people till years afterwards – but wherever he had served in some capacity he was remembered by all with tremendous affection.

'One thought so often of the many things one could have done for him, but did not do. He gave out so much more than we ever gave to him and yet accepted so eagerly what we did offer and seemed quite unconscious of what we did not. That, I think, was the essence of his greatness and his sanctity.'

CHAPTER XXI

Ampleforth

With his wars finally over, Michael took stock of his plans for the future. His youthful thoughts of the priesthood had remained dormant throughout the war years, but during his last year in the Far East he had again given them serious consideration. The priesthood was not something he particularly wanted, but he felt strongly that it was God's will, and he decided that at the end of his tour in the east he would visit Ampleforth and consult the Abbot. In May 1947 he had attended a conference at the Central Fighter Establishment at West Raynham in Norfolk and while in England he had visited the Abbot, the Right Reverend Herbert Byrne OSB, and it was agreed that he would enter Ampleforth Monastery as a novice when he returned to England.

The Air Ministry, unaware of Michael's personal plans, had informed him that he would go to Staff College at the end of his command of 60 Squadron, and on Michael's applying for a year's absence to enter Ampleforth, the AOC, Air Vice Marshal Sir John Whitworth-Jones, asked him to report at 'gin time' to talk over the situation. As a result of this informal discussion, Whitworth-Jones recommended Michael's application to Sir Hugh Pughe Lloyd, the C in C, who formally requested the Air Ministry's permission, adding that anyone with such firm convictions should be helped in everyway possible, but with the opportunity left open for their eventual return to the RAF if they wished.

With Air Ministry permission granted, the way was open for Michael to enter Ampleforth, but with his firm grasp of realities he realized that to enter a monastery in Yorkshire, straight from the more worldly pleasures of the Far East, would be too violent a transition and he wisely took four months holiday, two of which he spent in the USA, before entering Ampleforth on April 27 1948.

Michael joined the novitiate as Brother Paul, spending his first two years in studying the rule of St Benedict, the theory and practice of prayer, philosophy and allied subjects. He then began the study of theology and taught for short periods in the school. In this aspect of his activities he was given responsibility for the RAF contingent of the school's combined cadet force, commanded by Father Peter Utley, an ex-RAF officer who had entered from Cranwell and spent several years in the service.

On school holidays, Michael took the cadets to visit RAF stations, where he occasionally met old friends. This delighted the cadets, who learnt of past escapades. Billy Drake, for instance, an old friend and veteran of the battles of France and North Africa, where he had won a DSO and DFC, was sure, or pretended to be sure, that Michael must have been court martialled for some particularly heinous crime to have been demoted from Wing Commander to Flying Officer. The boys enjoyed it all enormously.

During Michael's time at Ampleforth he heard the sad news of John Quinton's death. After demobilization, John had married and had a son, but he could not settle in industry and in July 1951 he rejoined the RAF. He was posted to 228 OCU, RAF Leeming for a refresher course and on 13 August took off in a Wellington on a training flight. Included in the crew was a 16 year old ATC cadet, Derek Coates, making his first flight. At 5,000 feet above the Yorkshire village of Hudswell, the Wellington collided with another training aircraft, the fuselage breaking in half. In the rear half were John Quinton and Coates, with only a single parachute in sight. John quickly clipped the parachute on to Coates' harness, held the release handle, and pushed the boy out of the shattered fuselage. Derek Coates landed safely, but John and seven other officers died in the crash. John Quinton was awarded a posthumous George Cross for his courageous and unselfish heroism, and the ATC inaugurated the Quinton Trophy, awarded to the best ex-ATC apprentice at the RAF Apprentice School at RAF Halton.

In tribute to his friend, Michael wrote:

'I found John Quinton the perfect partner. He was a kind person, highly efficient at his job and utterly discreet. He never appeared to show any sort of fear, but he was imaginative, and anyone with imagination must feel fear, even if they do not show it. He had an almost embarrassing faith in my flying, which helped me enormously.

'John was always anxious to engage the enemy and found every opportunity to do so. His "offensive enthusiasm" was possibly less voluble than my own, but it was just as strong. He was wonderful support. In the air he was most efficient. He always had everything he needed, never forgot anything. His last act was typical in that he had his own parachute handy, and equally typical that he would help another person before himself.

'John was a great help in assessing people. One of the tasks of a squadron commander in war is that of assessing those who flew under his command. It was vital that anyone who was getting over-tired should be rested promptly. A few days enforced leave might allow a person to recover, or a period away from operational flying might save his life and allow him to do another tour of operations once refreshed and rested. John was most helpful in judging between the person in need of help and the one who needed encouragment or firm handling.

'We had a very peaceful time flying together – apart from weather and enemy aircraft – because we never quarrelled in the air. We had a rule that either could say anything derogatory to the other, but the one receiving the sharp word was not permitted to reply. But in fact we seemed to work in great harmony with each other.'

As the time drew near at Ampleforth for Michael to either take his Solemn Vows or leave, it seemed that for him departure was the right course. He knew he would always be grateful for his time at Ampleforth, and that it was a wonderful privilege to have been there. He had no doubt that for a person with a full career vocation it is the happiest and most fulfilling life there is, but for others it is not, and Michael realized that he had a short service vocation: that although it had been right for him to enter, it was equally right for him to leave.

Leaving Ampleforth was to start life afresh. Since his majority he had been caught up in events, the duties and demands of war, and the four years at Ampleforth had ended a definitive period of his life; he now had to decide on its future direction. He was offered a job in the family firm of Robert Stuart, but although the offer was attractive, the RAF and flying was still in his blood and he wrote to Sir Leslie Hollinghurst, now Air Member for Personnel, for advice. 'Holly' replied by return post. He had arranged Michael's return with the full and delighted approval of the Chief of Staff. In November 1952, Michael was given the substantive rank of squadron leader and he attended an Officers' Administration course. This was followed by a flying refresher course at No 22 FTS at Syerston in January 1953, where he flew Harvards for a month, getting his green instrument rating. At the end of March 1953 he was posted to No 209 Advanced Flying School at Weston Zoyland to fly Gloster Meteors, completing the course in mid-July. His next posting was to 228 OCU at Leeming, where he flew Meteor NF X1s. Michael had first been at this OTU as a flight lieutenant, in the days when it had been No 54 OTU. He had returned twice more: as Chief Flying Instructor, with the rank of squadron leader, and as Wing Commander OC Training. It was his first time as a pupil!

On 12 November Michael was posted to No 23 Squadron at Colti-shall to fly De Havilland Vampires. He was back in the atmosphere he loved, that of an RAF fighter squadron, and when Squadron Leader Jacomb Hood was killed in a flying accident in January 1954, Michael was given command. The previous month he had flown the first Venom to arrive at the squadron, and as re-equipment with the type continued through the January and February of 1954, Michael was again cast in the role of instructor to his junior pilots. Michael had always enjoyed instructing, having the facility of instilling confidence in those he taught, demonstrating the limitations of the aeroplane and showing by example how each problem which arose could be resolved. One such was in diving a Venom steeply. As Mach 1 approached the aeroplane became difficult to control, even with two hands holding the control column. Talking quietly as the Venom went out of control, Michael would explain to the pupil the correct recovery procedure. 'We will now regain control', he would say casually, as he throttled back and waited for the denser air to slow the aeroplane until it was again controllable. By Michael making what was easy, demonstrably so, the pupil lost all fear of the situation, and was confident he could deal with it if it arose in the future.

In April, Michael was made OC Flying at Coltishall, and as OC of an 'all weather wing', would fly in appalling weather, improving his knowledge of flying in adverse conditions. He would go into the crew room on these occasions and ask for a navigator to come with him – whereupon all the navigators would quietly disappear. He was still the 'Mad Monk' or 'Slappie Maxie' to most of them, his stance when giving his briefings, hands clasped in front of him, completing the impression of a parson delivering his sermon.

Michael remained at Coltishall until January 1956. He was then posted to the Central Flying School at South Cerney for a refresher course in instructing. At South Cerney he flew Provosts, his total hours topping the 3,000 mark.

In April 1956, Michael was given command of the Oxford Univer-sity Air Squadron. He could have asked for no more evocative posting. He had come full circle in exactly twenty years.

Michael was happy to be back with the OUAS, flying and instructing on the de Havilland Chipmunk, but twice during his time as CO it was rumoured that the squadron was to be disbanded, and he fought as hard to save it as he had when 84 Squadron had been similarly threatened. Ignoring the correct channels of Group and Command, Michael went to the Air Ministry to see Christopher Soames, then Secretary of State for Air, and a personal friend. As Michael was filling in an entrance form, Soames happened to come into the building, and greeting Michael asked what he was doing at the Ministry. Michael explained, and although Soames was already late for an important meeting, he agreed to listen to Michael's case as they walked to his office. Soames went through the rear of his own office and out into his PA's outer office, where a number of very senior RAF officers, several of whom Michael knew, were waiting to see him.

'To think we have all been kept waiting for you', said an air commodore on seeing Michael.

'I knew you wouldn't mind, Sir,' Michael replied with a smile.

A year later there was another rumour that the OUAS was to be disbanded. Michael had a long talk with Duncan Sandys, then Minister of Defence, pleading his case over lunch. Sandys was sympathetic, and Michael found him an impressive and helpful person. The Oxford University Air Squadron is still flying.

Michael remained in command of the OUAS until April 1958, when he went to the Central Fighter Establishment at West Raynham, flying Meteor, Hunter and Javelin aircraft. While at West Raynham he was Wing Commander Tactics, helping to plan for an air war in the 1970s.

In March 1960, Michael was made commanding officer at RAF Gan in the Indian Ocean. He spent a very pleasant six months at Gan, living in his own bungalow and entertaining various high ranking officers who visited the island. After giving his guests a tour of his little domain, finishing up at his bungalow, Michael would ply them with a cocktail of his own mixing, gin and King coconut juice, before 'pouring' them back into their refuelled aeroplanes. With gin at eight shillings a bottle he could afford to be generous with his measures.

Returning to England in 1960 he went to Western Command as the Air Liaison Officer to the GOC at Chester and while there, on 20 July 1961, was invited by a brother officer to his wedding. Michael was not keen, but finally went, sitting at the rear of the congregation and looking for a possible dinner date. His attention was caught by a small family group of father, mother and daughter. The girl was dark, lovely, and Michael was impressed by how happy they all looked.

Later, at the reception, he introduced himself to the family, found them drinks, and invited the girl – who on closer acquaintance he found charming – to dinner that evening. Her name was Susan Davies and the dinner date was quickly followed by several more meetings. Two months later they became engaged and were married on 20 January 1962. They had two sons, Hugh and Thomas.

When Michael asked his AOC for permission to marry, he also requested that he be allowed to study military problems in Africa. His AOC endorsed the request, which was then passed to Air Marshal Hector MacGregor, C in C Fighter Command, for his approval. MacGregor took the view that any officer in his command who could be that impertinent should be given every encouragement, and Sue and Michael spent a very pleasant three months' honeymoon touring Africa.

On their return to England in April, Michael was posted to HQ Scottish Command, remaining there until he retired from the service in June 1964 with the rank of wing commander.

Michael had spent the greater part of his adult life in the RAF, almost twenty-five exciting and rewarding years. During his service he had flown nearly fifty different and widely varying types of aeroplanes in both peace and war, from the Avro Tutor of 1936 to the 0.93 Mach Hawker Hunter. But the qualities he had brought to the RAF cannot be measured simply in terms of hours and aeroplanes flown. As Gerald had before him, Michael left a lasting impression on those with whom he had served and commanded. In the words of one of his friends of Battle of Britain days. 'My memories of Michael Constable Maxwell are of a most likeable, untidy, quietly gregarious young gentleman, simply yet wholeheartedly devoted to defeating his country's enemies, and a member of a very honourable and patriotic family. I hope all goes well with him.'

Michael Hugh Constable Maxwell DSO DFC died on 15 August 2000.

APPENDIXES

Appendix I

Aerial Victories of Gerald J. C. Maxwell as Recorded in the 56 Squadron Victory Lists

Date	Type	Classification	Location	Remarks
24/4/17	Albatros D	O.O.C.	Hamel	Green in colour. Shared with Lt. Knight
4/5/17	Albatros D	O.O.C.	Sauchy Lestrée	
11/5/17	Albatros D	O.O.C.	Pont-à-Vendin	Red in colour.
12/5/17	Albatros D	O.O.C.	E. of Lens	Green in colour. Shared with Captain Broadberry
15/6/17	Two seater	Destroyed	Fort Carnot	Shared with Captain Prothero
20/7/17	Albatros D	O.O.C.	Poelcapelle	Black and white in colour
20/7/17	Albatros D	O.O.C.	Poelcapelle	
26/7/17	Two seater	O.O.C.	N.E. of Ypres	
14/8/17	Two seater	O.O.C.	E. Westroosebeke	Shared with Lt. Sloley
18/7/17	Albatros D	O.O.C.	Menin	Black and white in colour
18/8/17	Albatros D	O.O.C.	Menin	A Flight victory
21/8/17	Albatros D	Destroyed	N. of Thourout	Black and white in colour, with V markings round fuselage
22/8/17	Albatros D	Destroyed	E. of Houthulst Forest	
22/8/17	Albatros D	O.O.C.	E. of Houthulst Forest	
11/9/17	Two seater	O.O.C.	E. of Houthulst Forest	
16/9/17	Two seater	O.O.C.	Hooglede	
20/9/17	Two seater	O.O.C.	E. of Lines. E. of Ypres	
21/9/17	Two seater	Destroyed	Verlinghem	

29/9/17	Albatros D	Destroyed	Staden	
29/9/17	Albatros D	O.O.C.	Staden	Shared with Flight
30/9/17	Albatros D	O.O.C.	Comines	56 Squadron's 200th victory
16/6/18	Two seater	Destroyed	Nr. Hamlin-court	
16/6/18	Two seater	Destroyed	Nr. Wancourt	
27/6/18	Fokker Dr.I	O.O.C.	Peronne	Black and white check around fuselage
28/6/18	Fokker D.VII	Destroyed	Nr. Dompierre	
1/7/18	Fokker Dr.I	Destroyed	N.E. of Albert	Bright red in colour. Shared with Captain Crowe
5/7/18	Fokker D.VII	Destroyed	Nr. Dompierre	

Appendix II

SE5s and SE5as flown by G. J. C. Maxwell during his service with 56 Squadron

Gerald flew a total of 17 SE5s and SE5as during his first tour of duty with 56 Squadron. The majority of these were flown in tests, deliveries, or one or two isolated patrols. The SEs mainly used were:

A4863   One of the thirteen original SE5s of the first production batch, issued to 56 Squadron while it was still at London Colney. Gerald flew this aeroplane to France on 7 April 1917, and flew it in combat until his forced landing on 28 April, when it was completely wrecked and written off squadron strength.

A8902   Gerald flew this SE5 of the second production batch until he went on leave on 19 May 1917. Lieutenant Toogood then flew A8902 until he was shot down on the evening of 26 May by Vizefeldwebel Deiss and Unteroffizier Woidt of Schutzstaffel 19.

A8921   On his return from leave in June 1917, Gerald flew this SE on daily patrols, flying it to England on 21 June 1917, when 56 Squadron was recalled to combat the Gothas.

B502   This SE5a was collected from the depot by Cecil Lewis on 13 July and Gerald first flew it three days later. He used B502 almost exclusively for the rest of his service in 56 Squadron in 1917. On Gerald's return to England in October 1917, B502 was allocated to Captain L. W. Jarvis, who flew it regularly. It was subsequently flown by a number of pilots until wrecked in a crash on 18 November 1917, killing the pilot, Lieutenant J. P. Waters.

On Gerald's return to 56 Squadron in June 1918 he flew eleven different SEs, but using mainly B8402, D6068, D6216, and D6218 on patrols.

D6216   Gerald shot down a Fokker Dr1 on 1 July 1918 while flying this SE and four days later destroyed a Fokker DV11.

D6218   Flying this SE, Gerald shot down a Pfalz D111 over Douai on the evening of 19 June 1918.

Types of Aeroplanes Flown

Gerald loved to fly. During his service in both wars he avidly flew as many types of aeroplanes as he possibly could, and during his period of command at Ford in WW II he was renowned for flying, if at all possible, every type of aeroplane that landed at or visited the station. His WW I logbook carries a total of thirty seven types flown between 1916 and 1918. He flew the Maurice Farman, both Longhorn and Shorthorn; BE2c, d, e and g; BE12 and 12a; Avro 504 of various types; Armstrong Whitworth FK3 and FK8; Martinsyde G100; RE8; Sopwith 1½ Strutter; Bristol Scout; SE5 and 5a; Sopwith Camel; Spad V11; Bristol M1c; Sopwith Dolphin; Bristol Fighter; DH9; DH4; DH6; Curtiss JN4; Sopwith Pup. Enemy aeroplanes he flew were: Albatros D11; D111; Fokker DV11; and Hannover CL111. Between the wars Gerald flew his own Hornet Moth.

No record is available of the aeroplanes Gerald flew in the second war, but he is known to have flown a Tiger Moth, Hornet Moth, and a Hurricane and many other types while at Ford. He entered the jet age by flying a Gloster Meteor, thereby bridging the generations of aeroplanes from the Maurice Farman Longhorn of 1916 to the Meteor of 1944; from the Longhorn, which would almost hover if flown into a stiff breeze, to the 400 mph plus of the Meteor. Gerald's final total of aeroplanes flown is reputed to have been 168 types.

INDEX